T0304351

The
DE PALMA DECADE

REDEFINING CINEMA
with Doubles, Voyeurs, and Psychic Teens

LAURENT BOUZEREAU

RUNNING PRESS
PHILADELPHIA

Running Press
Hachette Book Group
1290 Avenue of the Americas, New York, NY 10104
www.runningpress.com
@Running_Press

First Edition: September 2024

Published by Running Press, an imprint of Hachette Book Group, Inc.
The Running Press name and logo are trademarks of Hachette Book Group, Inc.

The Hachette Speakers Bureau provides a wide range of authors for speaking
events. To find out more, go to www.hachettespeakersbureau.com or email
HachetteSpeakers@hbgusa.com.

Running Press books may be purchased in bulk for business, educational, or
promotional use. For more information, please contact your local bookseller or the
Hachette Book Group Special Markets Department at Special.Markets@hbgusa.com.

The publisher is not responsible for websites (or their content) that are not
owned by the publisher.

Print book cover and interior design by Amanda Richmond.
Image credits: All photography courtesy of the author.

Library of Congress Cataloging-in-Publication Data
Names: Bouzereau, Laurent, author.
Title: The De Palma decade : redefining cinema with doubles, voyeurs,
  and psychic teens / Laurent Bouzereau.
Description: First edition. | Philadelphia : Running Press, 2024. |
  Includes index. | Summary: "An in-depth look at acclaimed filmmaker
  Brian De Palma's unrivaled creative output from 1972 to 1981, featuring
  brand-new interviews with the filmmakers along with cast and crew"
  —Provided by publisher.
Identifiers: LCCN 2023050314 (print) | LCCN 2023050315 (ebook)
ISBN 9780762485574 (hardcover) | ISBN 9780762485581 (ebook)
Subjects: LCSH: De Palma, Brian—Criticism and interpretation.
Motion picture producers and directors—United States—Interviews.
Motion picture actors and actresses—United States—Interviews.
Classification: LCC PN1998.3.D4 B683 2024 (print) | LCC PN1998.3.D4
  (ebook) | DDC 791.4302/33092—dc23/eng/20240213
LC record available at https://lccn.loc.gov/2023050314
LC ebook record available at https://lccn.loc.gov/2023050315

ISBNs: 978-0-7624-8557-4 (hardcover), 978-0-7624-8558-1 (ebook)

Printed in the United States of America

LSC-C

Printing 1, 2024

TO MARKUS

Brian De Palma on set of The Fury *and ready to roll.*

CONTENTS

INTRODUCTION

My obsession with Brian De Palma's cinema began, appropriately, with his film *Obsession*. Seduced by his unique visual style, I connected with a cinematic language and grammar that came to define a certain type of 1970s American film. Although at times unfairly dismissed as an Alfred Hitchcock imitator, De Palma emerged as an auteur and is widely celebrated around the world today, where even his least successful films are now recognized as cinematic benchmarks and cult classics.

Starting with *Sisters* in 1972 and concluding with *Blow Out* in 1981, De Palma produced an unrivaled, decade-long run of thrillers and horror films in which he seamlessly intertwined recurring themes with filmmaking techniques. (This volume purposely excludes the outlier *Home Movies*, as a satirical semi-autobiographical drama De Palma directed in 1979.) Voyeurs, doubles, and outsiders were brought to life through his use of split screens, split diopters, slow motion, and other flourishes for which De Palma became known. Purposely presented out of what would have been a predictable chronology, I have regrouped the films thematically to best illustrate the director's artistry.

There's also a clear pattern through these movies, as they seem to belong within the same universe. And although there's the undeniable De Palma–Hitchcock connection—with echoes from *Rear Window* (1954), *Vertigo* (1958), and *Psycho* (1960)—is it fair to label De Palma a copycat? Isn't he, rather, the legitimate heir to the Hitchcock kingdom?

The critics—and the division amongst them—add to the complexity of De Palma. At one point in *The Fury*, one of the characters says, "what a culture can't assimilate, it destroys" when speaking of the story's psychic twins. Was De Palma talking about himself? Ultimately, what is the verdict? Is De Palma a misunderstood victim? What's undeniable is that he was part of a movement in filmmaking aiming to remain independent within studio culture alongside his friends Steven Spielberg, Francis Ford Coppola, John Milius, Martin Scorsese, and George Lucas. He remains one of the most controversial and influential figures of seventies cinema, worthy of a contemporary reexamination through interviews I have conducted with Brian, his casts, and his colleagues over the years, as well as my own recent reflections on his films.

De Palma is also, without a doubt, a provocateur—he likes to shock, get reactions, but this may reflect a profound view on human nature, through characters who are flawed, at times in the most disturbing way. There was no intention here to make a social treaty or statement or defend the controversial aspects of De Palma's work—for which there are some—but, rather, to focus on his intention to tell a story in visual terms. I sympathized with and loved De Palma's films immediately. That discovery coincided with my personal journey—on one hand, as a movie lover, and on the other, as I learned to navigate through life. The horror made me feel safer in a world that scared me; it made me compassionate with the so-called monsters—the freaks—because, being the victim of intense bullying at a very young age, I perceived myself as such. Experiencing the extreme of what Carrie went through was reassuring; it never got that bad in real life. And when I started "cruising," experiencing casual encounters, I always thought of Kate Miller in *Dressed to Kill*, and how her sad, yet ominous, situation depicted a predilection that sex could be deadly.

In 1966, Brian De Palma directed a short documentary called *The Responsive Eye* for a Museum of Modern Art exhibit. The exhibit aimed at establishing "a totally new relationship between the observer and a work of art." While entirely real to the eye, it was expected that each observer would "respond to them differently." The response to the exhibit as De Palma presents it in his film, shows both admiration and rejection alike. The reception to most of De Palma's films is reflected in that theory, as is my approach as I looked back at the titles featured in this book. My interpretations are based on the actual finished art, on what we see, even if such implied result was never intended by the filmmaker. It's my own "Responsive Eye" to De Palma's cinema.

De Palma's style overrides logic and social statements; there's so much to see in his films that it's impossible not to recognize the genius behind each frame and his long, dramatic shots. All is carefully planned, framed, and the result is undeniable. Saying that there's a complete connection between De Palma's recurring themes with the filmmaking itself is understanding that there's a world—a dimension—that belongs solely to him and his cinema.

THE
SPLIT

De Palma in one word? How about "split"? It applies on several levels. Here, through the split personalities of his characters in *Sisters* and *Dressed to Kill*. But split, as in one of De Palma's signature lenses—the split diopter—as well as his use of split screens. Split is also reflected by the mixed reviews and perceptions over his films. "Split" echoes throughout De Palma's oeuvre—it divides and connects us to his universe. And thus, it begins...

Margot Kidder has a split personality and deadly intentions in Sisters.

SISTERS

—— 1972 ——

*I got the idea for Sisters from a Life
magazine article about the [conjoined] twins
Masha and Dasha. I was also inspired by the
photograph of them, sitting on a couch together—
it's an image I reproduced in the movie, with
Dominique and Danielle sitting by a pool.*

—BRIAN DE PALMA
(DIRECTOR / CO-WRITER / STORY BY)

THE STORY: Danielle Breton (Margot Kidder), a young, seductive model, meets Phillip Woode (Lisle Wilson), a handsome business-man, on a television game show called *Peeping Toms*. They decide to spend the evening together, but in the middle of their dinner, they are interrupted by Emil Breton (William Finley), Danielle's ex-husband and also her doctor. Later, once they've gotten rid of the obnoxious man, they become intimate, but Phillip pays little attention to the large scar on Danielle's right hip. The next morning, he is awakened by the sound of Danielle arguing with Dominique, her twin sister; today is their birthday, and Dominique is jealous of the presence of a stranger in the living room. Suddenly, Danielle doesn't feel well and she asks Phillip to go to the drugstore to get her medication. On his way back, he buys a birthday cake, but when he presents it to Dan-ielle, asleep on the couch, it's, in fact, Dominique, who grabs a knife and stabs him to death.

Grace Collier (Jennifer Salt), a reporter, witnesses the murder from her window. She immediately calls the police, who seem reluctant to believe her; Grace is the author of a column on police brutality and racism entitled "Why We Call Them Pigs!" Grace's argument with the detective (Dolph Sweet) of the local precinct leaves enough time for Emil and Danielle to clean the apartment and hide the victim's body in a folding couch. Ultimately, the police find no evidence of the crime, but Grace will not let it go, and her editor forces her to inves-tigate further with a goofy private detective named Larch (Charles Durning). The investigation reveals that Danielle and Dominique were conjoined twins. Grace follows Emil and Danielle to an asylum, where Emil hypnotizes Grace to erase Phillip's murder from her memory. We learn Emil had gotten Danielle pregnant, prompting Dominique to try to kill her sister. Emil had to perform an emergency separa-tion, though Dominique didn't survive the surgery. Every time a man seduces Danielle, Dominique's vengeful personality takes over. Dan-ielle becomes Dominique one last time and murders Emil. By killing him, she is, at last, liberated from her sister's personality. Grace is safe but, because of the hypnosis, she cannot remember ever witnessing Phillip's murder. However, Larch has followed the couch with the body to a train station in Canada and is waiting for someone to arrive and pick it up!

As I watched *Sisters* again, I immediately recalled the terror of discovering it for the first time. Of all De Palma's horror/thriller films of that specific era, it remains the one I find most disturbing. Perhaps that feeling is due to the frightening yet memorable score by Bernard Herrmann that opens the film, with images of twins forming from embryo to babies. Or it could be the overall production values—clearly low budget but still very affecting, with bare sets and limited locations enhancing the dread of near-empty spaces, reminiscent of old hospital rooms. There's also the choice to make William Finley appear creepy, complete with a hunchback, thick glasses, and a gigantic bruise on his forehead (caused by a fall after he cleaned blood off the floor of his ex-wife's apartment). All these elements are complemented by a gruesome and graphic murder, a nightmare sequence, and De Palma's most significant staple—the split screen. To this day, *Sisters* defines De Palma's nightmares and style.

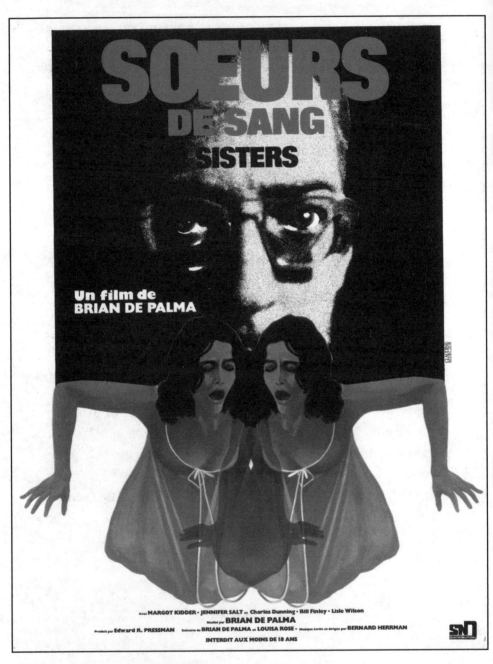

A French theatrical poster for Sisters.

ALL EYES ON THE SCREEN

The original script was written by De Palma and Louisa Rose. It started like the movie, with a television game show called *Peeping Toms*, in which the host explains the setup to two contestants who must predict what an unsuspecting man will do in a real-life, candid situation—in this case, when he sees a blind woman (a decoy) who starts undressing in the wrong locker room. This sequence remarkably sets up the key theme of the film: voyeurism—the watcher and the watched. Though Danielle is posing as an innocent victim and Phillip as the peeper, the sequence telegraphs what's to come, with Phillip both the victim of the show's prank and of Danielle's alternate personality.

During the game show, the television camera pans across the audience. Emil, Danielle's ex-husband, is present, looking up suspiciously, as if annoyed for being "watched." Later, during final applause, his seat is empty, and immediately our attention is drawn to the absence of a character we have yet to meet more formally. The interesting and bizarre choice to have Emil appear as grotesque and as weird as possible connects back to Dominique and Danielle. As conjoined twins, they invoke the concept of "freaks"; possibly Emil feels like one as well. Though seemingly a strange choice to not have the doctor/ex-husband be more of a romantic lead, Emil's appearance is part of the tapestry that De Palma slowly constructs, here specifically revealing that Emil/Dominique/Danielle are part of the same world.

BRIAN DE PALMA: I went to graduate school with Louisa at Sarah Lawrence. I really love her; I'd directed one of her plays. I wrote a couple of drafts of the script. And I remember going to her apartment and thinking, well, maybe Louisa can have some input into this story, since it was about women. I said, "Louisa, take a whack at it. See how it goes."

De Palma in discussion with Kidder, and actor William Finley listening in the background.

REMEMBERING MARGOT

Margot Kidder was coming off the feature film *Quackser Fortune Has a Cousin in the Bronx* (1970) when she landed the lead role in *Sisters*. Her performance is particularly impressive, as she displays "the other" and the repressed side of her split personality, convincingly looking completely different. The role and the way she inhabited it foretold the promising career she'd have over the ensuing decades.

JENNIFER SALT ("GRACE COLLIER"): I met Margot when we were both doing screen tests for the movie *Fat City* [1972]. And there were three actresses testing: Candy Clark, who got the part, Margot, and me. She came into the trailer to give me the dress that she'd been wearing in the screen test. We just began jabbering and we became friends; we went out to dinner, and we decided to look for a house together at the beach. And that's what we did. Brian claims that he came out to visit and he never left.

BRIAN DE PALMA: I don't think I had any specific actor in mind for the female leads when I originally wrote it. When I got out to Trancas Beach, where Jennifer Salt and Margot Kidder had a house, that's when I got the idea of using them both.

JENNIFER SALT: During the holidays, we had a big Christmas tree. We would all sit around, give each other presents. And one Christmas, Brian gave both Margot and me the same present, which turned out to be the script of *Sisters*.

FIRST SLICE

Sisters marks De Palma's first killing during this specific decade. The victim is Phillip Woode, who pays a high price for casual sex, just like Kate Miller (Angie Dickinson) would a few years later in *Dressed to Kill*.

As Phillip brings a cake to Danielle in celebration of her birthday, she—as Dominique—grabs the knife from the cutlery set she won on the show. (In the referenced script, the victim is also stabbed with a knife, but one he bought with the cake; Danielle won a wardrobe of multicolored pantyhose in that draft.) Danielle stabs her lover right below the groin, in the mouth, and then repeatedly in the back; Phillip—and the masculinity he symbolizes—is murdered by the "double," as we believe at that point that Dominique, the deranged twin sister, is the killer.

BRIAN DE PALMA: Talking about designing the murder scene, obviously she goes for the groin immediately. But then I thought, well have I ever seen somebody stabbed in the mouth? So, I said, "Let's do that." I filmed it in shadow—and the same

Not such a happy birthday—Kidder strikes and kills in one of De Palma's most disturbing scenes.

with Margot stabbing him in the back. In suspense or horror movies you always got to figure out, how am I going to kill them? Am I going to use a knife? Am I going to use a straight razor? Am I going to shoot them? It's always a problem in terms of trying to do something original.

PAUL HIRSCH (EDITOR): The blood hitting the wall. The first take you saw a few drops, barely visible on film. Then, we had the take that we used in the film. And then the third take looked like somebody had taken a bucket of paint and thrown it against the wall. But what I remember of that scene is a segment where the victim drags himself across the floor to the window; I felt it went on too long, but once we put in Bernard Hermann's music, it didn't seem lengthy anymore.

In a last effort to survive, Phillip drags himself to the window. Once the "peeper" of the game show, he strives to be the peeped, hoping that someone looking in from the building across the way will catch his last word, "help," written in blood on the window, before he collapses for good. The window itself represents the shape of a television screen, furthering the connection to Phillip's introduction via the game show. Accompanying this moment is Bernard Herrmann's macabre score, which begins as a childlike musical phrase underlining the birthday and abruptly turns violent for the murder—for which the composer used a Moog synthesizer, with sounds suggesting human screams. It's highly effective, disturbing, and contributes to the mayhem and sudden shift in tone of the film; from that point forward, *Sisters* sinks into horror and madness.

FINDING GRACE UNDER THE MACABRE

Grace Collier, the local reporter who catches the murder from across the way, is described in the script as the "Gloria Steinem of Staten Island." She is a resourceful single woman, fighting the system and risking her life to solve a crime, while the cops are presented as ineffective and, clearly, like everyone else in the film, undermining her. As portrayed by Jennifer Salt, Grace is powerful and no-nonsense, with an activist mind and determination. Unlike Danielle, she is not particularly feminine or seductive. But she is a significant addition and standout to other women in films of the time, which included Ali MacGraw in *The Getaway* and Liza Minnelli in her defining role in *Cabaret*, both released in 1972. A new kind of heroine, she also serves as the model for characters in other De Palma films, such as Liz Blake from *Dressed to Kill*.

JENNIFER SALT: Brian informed my sense of being an artist. His freedom as a director was so natural. He's a Virgo. He's very precise, and details are everything to him. You could say that

Jennifer Salt as Grace Collier is trying to solve a murder she witnessed while looking out her window.

he's the opposite of the way John Cassavetes made films, for instance. His gift is rooted in a very intellectual process. Like the split screens. I remember the difficulty of getting action to happen at the same time; it was tricky.

De Palma ingeniously introduces Grace while taking advantage of a split screen narrative device in the murder scene. Grace's reactions and Phillip's death play out side by side in real time.

BRIAN DE PALMA: I went to see Bill Finley in the play *Dionysus in 69* and I said, my God, this is unbelievable. That's when I filmed the play of *Dionysus in 69*. My idea for *Dionysus in 69* was, I was going to shoot the narrative of the play, and Bob Fiore was going to shoot how the performers interacted with the audience. And we did it, obviously, simultaneously trying to avoid each other as we were shooting, and we presented it using split

One of De Palma's trademarks, the split screen displays a perfect match to the duality of Kidder's character, here with co-stars Salt and Dolph Sweet.

screens, from beginning to end. It was basically experimental; we were discovering stuff as we were putting it together. And I used split screens in *Sisters*—it had to be filmed with two cameras shooting simultaneously. It was not that complicated because I'd had the experience with *Dionysus in 69*.

PAUL HIRSCH: In my mind, up to that point, split screens were used for "telephone calls" like in the Rock Hudson–Doris Day film *Pillow Talk* [1959], or *Airport* [1970]. It was also used in a very stylish way, with multiple screens, in *The Thomas Crown Affair* [1968], for instance. It was that time for innovation, invention, and experimentation in cinema.

A NEW VICTIM

Sisters first screens the same year as Hitchcock's *Frenzy*, which very much holds on to the tradition of women as victims seen in films like *Psycho*, *Rosemary's Baby* (1968), or any Dracula movie of the time. With the murder of Phillip Woode, De Palma is swimming upstream, surprising the audience with the unexpected murder of a man.

Lisle Wilson, as Phillip Woode, is one of De Palma's few male murder victims.

Phillip Woode is also a Black man, an intention in the script. The specific aspect of the casting is underlined by the fact that when the camera reveals the audience at the TV game show, only two Black men can be spotted amongst mostly white women. Additionally, Phillip is awarded a gift certificate for a night of "dining and dancing" at a Manhattan restaurant named the African Room, which clearly makes Woode uncomfortable. After the show, out on the street, Phillip looks at the gift certificate, shaking his head with a knowing smile.

Later, when Grace calls the police about the murder she witnessed, she specifically describes the victim as Black. In addition to recognizing Grace as a reporter critical of the police, they appear uninterested in investigating the crime. As Grace tells her editor later, "A white woman kills her Black lover, and those racist cops couldn't care less. I saw it happen and they won't investigate." The color of Phillip's skin hinders any sense of justice, adding a new layer to the horror.

Racism also came into play in the script, with a different lead-up to the murder, in which Danielle gets sick and Phillip takes her to the doctor. On the drive back, Phillip is rear-ended, leading to an altercation with the other car's driver, who liberally uses the N-word. This encounter very much emphasizes the fact that, initially, the script was more socially motivated, and Phillip exists in an unsafe world even before his murder.

HITCHCOCKIAN HUMOR

Sisters is very much in the tradition of the kind of humor seen in Hitchcock's *North by Northwest* (1959), for instance, where Cary Grant's nagging mother nearly gets him killed, with the macabre edge of *Rear Window*, where a man murders his wife and cuts her up into pieces. That humor is present with Grace's tactless mother (Mary Davenport) "harassing" her daughter about her "little job" writing for a newspaper, hinting at her status as an unmarried woman (in the script, her parents try to set her up with a "balding, bespectacled suitor"), and referring to the failed relationship she had with her editor. But the mother also delivers important information on a local asylum and their approach to therapy, letting the inmates roam around freely—it's where the climax of the film will eventually take place.

BRIAN DE PALMA: One idea led into another, even casting Jennifer's own mother, Mary Davenport, as her mother in the movie. I used her in a couple of other films, *Home Movies* and *Dressed to Kill*. I loved Jennifer's mother. She had a great sense of humor, she was really a good actress, and I just hit it off with her.

JENNIFER SALT: [My mother] had been an actress and gave it all up. But Brian had gotten to know her and called her Mommy. He just told her, "You should play Mom," and she did. It was fun to act with her. It was very real. We didn't plan any of that out. She wasn't at all like the character she played, but she had her own little snobbisms and passive aggressive ways. [*Laughs*]

There's the fun dynamic between Grace and the private investigator Joseph Larch, played by Charles Durning, with whom she teams up to solve the murder. Durning portrays Larch as skillful and knowledgeable. He strong-arms Grace into following his intuition. He is bold in his approach, but also played up as a bit of a bumbling private detective. His pushback to Grace challenging him sparks some deadpan humor. And while she investigates Danielle, Larch follows a couch that Emil had removed from the apartment, knowing it contains Phillip's body. (In the script, Emil led Grace and Larch to believe the victim was in the couch, but had, in fact, chopped him up and carried out the pieces in two suitcases.)

BRIAN DE PALMA: Humor, of course, relieves the tension in the audience. And that's my personality. I see the humor in practically everything. I don't take this stuff too seriously. And many actors will tell you, they always want to try to make me laugh. I remember John Lithgow, when I first saw him in a play with Bill Finley in Princeton when I was in college, all he remembered was me laughing in the front row. Jennifer always said she wanted to find a way to make me laugh. And that's just who I am.

As for the couch...

BRIAN DE PALMA: The body in the couch has an interesting backstory. Originally, I tried to have Filmways finance the film. They had made *Hi, Mom!* [1970] and distributed *Greetings*

[1968]. But Marty Ransohoff, who had run Filmways and considered producing the film, never believed I could put a corpse in a couch. He said it can't be done. I replied, "Yes, it can be done." He remained convinced that nobody would ever believe this was possible. So, I made it a big item in the movie. And it's really the actor we put in the couch; I did it in one shot.

DOCUMENTING NIGHTMARES

At some point during her investigation, Grace meets with a *Life* magazine journalist who did a piece on Dominique and Danielle. He shows Grace a short documentary film (assembled by future film critic and screenwriter Jay Cocks) that retraces a brief history of conjoined twins and highlights the case of the surgery that separated Dominique and Danielle. In the documentary, Dr. Pierre Milius—probably named after John Milius, the filmmaker of *Big Wednesday* (1978) and *Conan the Barbarian* (1982)—explores the conflicting personalities of the two young women; although Dominique is the disturbed one, and Danielle, in appearance, the "normal one," Milius says, "Danielle can only be so because of her sister."

Later, Grace is drugged, hypnotized, and induced into believing she is Dominique. She, literally, experiences being a conjoined twin to Danielle. This segment is simply pure cinematic genius. Like the documentary film, it is in black and white, with distorted echoey voices, Herrmann's upsetting score, and a cast of disturbing characters straight out of Tod Browning's *Freaks* (1932).

BRIAN DE PALMA: We got these circus people for the dream sequence, including Eddie the Giant. We had dancing triplets . . . They were all very nice, but Margot and Jennifer were completely freaked out. One of the funny things is that one of my assistants, Amy Robinson, who went on to be a producer,

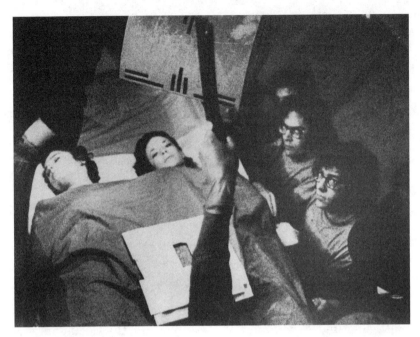

The filming of the separation surgery was carefully designed for the actor not to miss the mark with a meat cleaver!

had to bring Eddie the Giant home, in her tiny Volkswagen. It was a very crazy day.

JENNIFER SALT: The horror is fun, it's playtime, it's dress-up. It's nothing like what he will turn it into. There's no music, there's no atmosphere; it's just like, "Scream, Jennifer." I did a lot of screaming. I was a big screamer.

Furthermore, De Palma sets the action in, what appear to be, abandoned spaces rather than the expected aseptic white rooms. It all seems decrepit and unsanitary. In this segment, everything comes into focus—how Emil fell in love with Danielle, got her pregnant, how Dominique tried to "kill the baby" with the gardener's sheers, and how it precipitated their physical separation. The surgery is highly stylized, taking place in the middle of a pool, and is rife with startling and bizarre imagery:

The meat clever used to separate the twins is found inside the cutlery set that Danielle won in the TV game show; the private detective Larch, in a surprising appearance, grabs the cleaver and passes it around, while the *Life* magazine reporter—surrounded by other twins, nuns, and priests—takes notes.

As Emil raises and brings down the cleaver, Grace wakes up from her trance, screaming. The drama then plays out for real, revealing the true tragedy of *Sisters*. Emil and Danielle could never be together because Dominique—alive or dead—was always there, awakening each time a man got between their bound flesh. Emil tries to exorcise Danielle of Dominique, but the evil twin has awakened, and she slashes the architect of their separation. In the most grotesque dance, Danielle walks to the bed where Grace is lying, semiconscious, dragging Emil, who is bleeding to death, as if attached to her. They both fall over Grace and, for a moment, they look like they're all conjoined, triplets, bound by blood. The sequence concludes with Grace's scream merging with the sound of an ambulance's siren, rushing to the scene.

PAUL HIRSCH: There were three parts to the dream, three separate sections. In each of them, we zoom into Jennifer's eye, beyond anything that had ever been technically done before. I think it was shot in 16mm. But the first part of the dream was a handheld shot walking through an asylum of some kind, with all these various patients. The Canadian doctor was in a priest's costume. The second part of the dream is seen through a two-way mirror, and it's a single shot of Emil seducing Danielle with Grace as Dominique. There's no cut in it at all. In the last section of the dream, the cinematographer overexposed the film. Brian was very upset—it had all those extras from the circus, holding candles, and they had been sent back home; so, Brian came up with a different concept for the scene, and included Charles Durning and the reporter from *Life* magazine. There's this one flaw in the scene; when Bill Finley raises his arm to bring down the cleaver, the speed wasn't right, and I slowed it down in one angle. It doesn't really work and always bothers me when I watch the film.

Sisters has three endings. The first one depicts Danielle at peace with the death of her sister; in a moving statement, she finally admits, "My sister died last spring." The second shows Grace, back at her parents' home, in her childhood bedroom, surrounded by toys; the detective questions her about the murder she witnessed, but, having been brainwashed to forget all of it, she repeats, "It was all a ridiculous mistake. There was no body. There was no body because there was no murder." The third ending is all about macabre humor, depicting Larch, still waiting for someone to come pick up the couch at a deserted train station in Canada. Herrmann's (deadly) "birthday cake" musical cue reminds us of the dead body buried inside it.

De Palma's films are so memorable for their opening sequences, but with *Sisters*, he also sets a trend for himself with equally powerful endings, whether it be nightmares in *Carrie* and *Dressed to Kill*, the exploding body of the bad guy in *The Fury*, a dizzying reunion between father and daughter in *Obsession*, the tragedy of the *Phantom of the Paradise*, or a scream in *Blow Out*. *Sisters* lays the groundwork for these memorable conclusions.

THE CUT MAN

Sisters is the second collaboration between De Palma and editor Paul Hirsch. Hirsch's connection with De Palma's visual style was already apparent in their first film together, *Hi, Mom!* But with *Sisters*, you can tell the sophisticated approach of split screens, as well as sequences like the brainwashing nightmare segment, are paced economically and with great power. Each cut has a significance; in fact, you think you see more than you do, as in the killing of Phillip Woode, which is done in shadows. Hirsch, who has become a friend through my many interviews with him, shares not only a similar sense of humor, but a true understanding and appreciation of cinema with De Palma. Their love of Hitchcock, for instance, led Hirsch to suggest composer Bernard Herrmann, a choice that would virtually change the entire spirit of *Sisters*, elevating it to an A+ status.

PAUL HIRSCH: Brian had planned to edit the film himself and he hired an assistant editor to organize the material. Apparently, after the first few days, dailies were a complete disaster. Brian was very unhappy with the way the material was presented. Simultaneously, production got word that there was another movie about twins being made by Robert Mulligan, *The Other* [1972]. Ed Pressman, our producer, was very concerned about getting *Sisters* out before *The Other*. He spoke to Brian, said he had to get an editor working on this right away. And that's when I got the call. I was very excited to get the job. I hadn't worked on a feature in three years. I'd been cutting trailers and low-end commercials to survive. I was on staff at a company called Calliope Films and I didn't want to give up my job because freelance life at that time, I was in my early twenties, could be challenging. I was able to bring the job to the company, and I stayed on staff while I cut the picture for Brian.

Some of the film was shot in 16mm, some in 35—we were constantly converting the editing machine from 35 to 16mm and back to 35. I have these memories of my assistant and me constantly switching format, lifting the heavy picture head off, and then putting another one on.

HERRMANN'S MOODS

The first time I identified composer Bernard Herrmann was François Truffaut's *Fahrenheit 451* (1966). That film's score is lush, romantic, and as far away from what one would have imagined the music needed to be. Similarly, the score to *Sisters* brings a whole new dimension to the film.

PAUL HIRSCH: Bernard Herrmann did a brilliant score. I remember reading a review that said Bernard Herrmann's music would make "blank" film compelling, which was something we agreed with, although we thought our film was a little better than just "blank" film.

BRIAN DE PALMA: I knew of Bernard Herrmann because of Hitchcock. Paul had put music from *Psycho, Marnie* [1964], and *Vertigo* as temp track; we looked at each other and asked ourselves, is this guy still around? Why don't we get him to do the score? We found out he lived in England. And that's how we got in touch with him.

PAUL HIRSCH: Ed Pressman, the producer, was looking to raise more money while we were shooting. It was an independent production, and he needed more financing. Brian said to me, I'd like to show a scene from the movie to some potential investors, and I thought we'd show them the murder scene. I said okay, and I knew from my experience as a trailer editor that presentation is very important, and I knew I couldn't pre-sent this without music. By coincidence, I had just seen *Psycho* on TV, where it was driven home to me how important the music is in a film. I was determined to use the music from *Psycho* by Bernard Herrmann to track under the murder scene. I showed it to Brian, and he was electrified. He had seen the scene before without music, but suddenly, with Benny's score from *Psycho* underneath, it became something completely different. He decided that, in his enthusiasm, we should put music throughout the film. At the same time, they pursued Benny and sent him a copy of the script in London. He had left Hollywood after Hitchcock threw out his score for *Torn Curtain* [1966]—he was so wounded by this that he'd moved to London and was doing small films there. To everyone's surprise, he said sure, I'm interested. We arranged a screening in New York, and he flew in from London—we screened the film on the west side of Manhattan. We start the picture, and as soon as one note of Benny's music comes in, he starts yelling, "Stop, stop. This is all wrong. Stop." Brian and I were terrified, and he says, "This is all wrong. Take it out, take out all the music." I turned the knob all the way down so you wouldn't hear the music and got to the end of the film.

Sisters opens with the images of embryos forming into twin babies. Herrmann's opening cue for this sequence simply assaults the viewer in a way that contrasts the beauty of creation inside a woman's womb, and twists it all through music, setting up the horror to come. Without the opening music cue, we could be witness to the beginning of a drama, perhaps even a love triangle that includes a tenacious ex-husband. The music does the heavy lifting of giving a voice to the genre. Using Moog synthesizers mixed with conventional instruments, the score conveys the tragedy of Danielle and the screaming terror within her. Also in the opening cue, a bell-like clarion announces the stronger, more lethal, aspect of the twins—almost a call to death—while the sound of tiny bells, as evoked by the glockenspiel, evokes the innocent, childlike presence of Dominique.

BRIAN DE PALMA: [Herrmann] said, "It's too slow in the beginning. Nothing happens. And you're not Hitchcock. They're not going to wait around, because nothing happens until the murder." So, he offered the opening credit cue, and we came up with that montage of the twins developing inside a womb to go over this terrifying music.

There's another musical layer in the film that has rarely been acknowledged. When Grace goes to the Time & Life Building to meet with the reporter who has researched the history of conjoined twins, he shows her a documentary film. The short subject mixes real-life footage and photographs with scenes involving Dominique and Danielle. Herrmann scored this "documentary" as well. And though it has a similar somber tone, it lives completely outside the rest of the movie as its own little film within the film. It's truly a hidden musical gem inside an already very rich score.

BRIAN DE PALMA: Herrmann was such a commanding presence, you let him take the lead. I liked him enormously, immediately. But he's legendary for being a cranky genius with a volcanic temper. Everybody who's ever known him always does Bernard Herrmann imitations because he was so distinctive and such an eccentric. I consider myself one of the most romantic directors because I'm very concerned with the emotions that are so well illustrated with the music. And I've used every great composer of my generation and I started off with the greatest—Bernard Herrmann. I worked with Ryuichi Sakamoto who recently died, Ennio Morricone, Pino Donaggio, and John Williams. Looking back over my films, I feel that you must get engaged emotionally. You must feel something, and I'm very emotional, especially with music. I can't really listen to music because it's very touching to me.

DIVIDED SISTERS, DIVIDED REACTIONS

GEORGE LITTO (AGENT): At that time, I was an agent, and I received a call from Ed Pressman who had produced a film called *Sisters*. He was having difficulty getting a US distribution deal and he asked if he could show me the film. I happened to be in New York, and I went to the Rizzoli Screening Room to watch [it]. When the lights came up, I said, "I like this film and I can get distribution for it. But I particularly like this director. He's almost as good as Hitchcock." The person standing next to me was the editor, but I didn't know that—Paul Hirsch; he told Brian that I liked the film. I represented a lot of people Brian admired, like Waldo Salt [coincidentally, Jennifer Salt's father], Dalton Trumbo, Robert Altman, Joseph Losey. And so, Brian came to see me; and I made the deal for AIP [American International Pictures] to distribute *Sisters*.

BRIAN DE PALMA: AIP wasn't excited about the film because the first test screening was in tandem with a comedy, and it didn't go well at all. But what changed was when the film was shown at FilmEx, a festival in Los Angeles [in 1972]. We showed it at midnight at the Grauman's Chinese Theatre and the audience went nuts. That's what got AIP excited about releasing it [in 1973] and when everybody started to talk about *Sisters*.

Sisters was well received; of note, Roger Ebert wrote in the *Chicago Sun-Times*: "Brian De Palma's *Sisters* was made more or less consciously as an homage to Alfred Hitchcock, but it has a life of its own and it's a neat little mystery picture." He particularly highlighted Jennifer Salt as a "women's lib Lois Lane" and how Grace is a tribute to the classic Hitchcockian character—possibly recalling Lisa (Grace Kelly) from *Rear Window*, Lila Crane (Vera Miles) in *Psycho*, or even Eve (Jane Wyman) in

Under hypnosis from Finley's character, Emil Breton, Grace is conditioned to experience herself as Danielle's twin, Dominique.

the underrated *Stage Fright* (1950), characters who will stop at nothing to solve a crime. Richard Schickel, in *Time* magazine, also praised *Sisters*, but deplored that the film's distributor positioned it as a "routine shocker." What's interesting in comparing Ebert to Schickel is that the first one does his best not to reveal the plot twist while the other flat out spells out the plot and concludes, "*Sisters* provides moviegoers with the special satisfaction of finding a real treasure while prowling cinema's bargain basement." Kevin Thomas, in the *Los Angeles Times*, hailed the film as a "triumph in style, a tour de force of storytelling" and praised the camera work as well as the score by Bernard Herrmann. Amazingly and on the opposite side of the spectrum, Jerry Oster of the New York *Daily News* viewed the film as "too reminiscent" of Hitchcock, and Pauline Kael, in

The New Yorker, later to become De Palma's greatest defender, described the film as "cheap," disappointingly, and completely missing the point of the director's intentions.

The advertising campaign highlighted other reviews:

Literally scared the shit out of me. —Village Voice

An intelligent horror film is rare these days. It is just the thing to see on one of those nights when you want to go to the movies for the fun of it. —New York Times

The most skillful, entertaining, and imaginative horror film since Psycho. —Rex Reed (who would later completely trash other De Palma films, accusing him of being a Hitchcock copycat).

PAUL HIRSCH: I was very proud of the movie. It was my idea to use Bernard Herrmann and when we had a midnight screening at the Chinese Theatre in Hollywood, the place was filled with film fans, and they cheered when Benny's name came on screen. But it felt like a new experience, seeing this film that I had lived with for months. I worked two stretches of thirty-five days in a row without a break. I had one day off and then worked another thirty-five days. So, I had lived so intensely with this film and every splice was one that I had made. And here it was being projected on the big screen. *Sisters* was definitely a big step up for Brian. A change in importance of the production and also in direction toward the horror and thriller genre.

The importance of *Sisters* cannot be minimized as it launches De Palma in a new genre, one that would label him for better or for worse, as a Hitchcockian director. Despite the acclaim, De Palma did not see an overnight change in his career.

BRIAN DE PALMA: *Sisters* was successful compared to what it cost to make, but I don't remember getting too many offers after it. Most of my subsequent films were all independently financed.

ONLY THE BEGINNING

All of De Palma's films that followed during this period would reference *Sisters*, both cinematically and thematically–later, critic and cinema professor Robin Wood wrote a profound feminist essay and theory on the film, citing it as De Palma's finest achievement prior to *Blow Out*, and as one of the great American films of the seventies. In his essay, Wood explains that Grace is dominated by the cop, the private detective, her newspaper editor, her mother pushing her to marriage, and, ultimately, by Emil when she is brainwashed. Wood writes that, at the end of the film, Grace "is reduced to the role of a child, tended to by

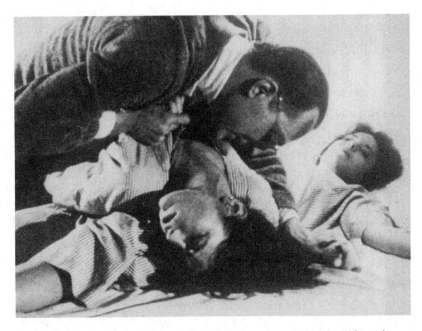

In the bloody conclusion, Emil, Danielle, and Grace appear to be almost bound together.

her mother, surrounded by toys, and denying the truth of which she once alone had possession." Going any deeper would simply be paraphrasing Wood's brilliant analysis, but *Sisters* continues to stimulate discussion. Most recently, Quentin Tarantino published his own thesis on the film (and on De Palma himself) in his compelling book, *Cinema Speculation*. There's so much in *Sisters* that announces all that De Palma stands for that it remains the appetizer, rather than the film's deadly birthday cake, of things to come.

I didn't see *Sisters* on the big screen until I first came to New York in 1982. In fact, on my second day there, I read in the newspaper that *Sisters* was playing in Times Square, as a double feature with *Dressed to Kill*, and braved the streets of Manhattan for the first time simply to see those two films. But I had seen *Sisters* many times on videocassette in France. I forced my younger sister to watch it, and it freaked her out so much that I would play pranks on her, imitating Emil, saying, "Dominique is dead . . ." *Sisters* for sure has impressed and haunted me.

Angie Dickinson in one of her most defining roles, as Kate Miller, a woman trapped by her own fantasies.

DRESSED TO KILL

—— 1980 ——

Directors are observers.
We're peering through a camera
looking at people doing things.

—BRIAN DE PALMA
(WRITER / DIRECTOR)

THE STORY: Kate Miller (Angie Dickinson) is pleasuring herself in the shower as her husband shaves. Suddenly, a man appears from behind and assaults her. She screams, and we realize this was a nightmare. We find Kate in bed, having unsatisfying sex with her husband. The repressed, middle-aged housewife complains to her psychiatrist, Dr. Robert Elliott (Michael Caine) about her husband's pathetic performance and tests her sexual worth by trying to seduce him, unsuccessfully. Kate then picks up a handsome stranger in a museum—before she leaves his apartment, she discovers he has a sexually transmitted disease. In a panic, she rushes out, but must return after she realizes she forgot her wedding ring. When the elevator door opens, she is attacked by a blond woman, wearing sunglasses, brandishing a straight razor. Prostitute Liz Blake (Nancy Allen) is witness to the crime and becomes—at once—the star suspect as well as the killer's next prey. The killer, a transgender patient of Dr. Elliott's named Bobbi, wants to have gender affirmation surgery, but Dr. Elliott won't approve it. Bobbi threatens Elliott on his answering machine and confesses to stealing his razor and murdering Kate. After an attempted attack in the subway, Liz is saved by Kate's son, Peter (Keith Gordon), who, out of guilt for not spending the day with her, is determined to solve and avenge his mother's murder.

At the police precinct, Detective Marino (Dennis Franz) puts pressure on Liz to break into Elliott's office after Peter captured—on a hidden camera—images of Bobbi coming out of the shrink's front door. In order to gather proof, Liz pretends to seduce Elliott and, in the process, discovers that Bobbi IS Elliott. As Bobbi tries to attack Liz, she is saved by a female detective who was tailing her all along (someone the audience thought was the killer). Elliott suffered a split personality disorder; each time the Elliott personality got turned on, Bobbi took over and killed the subject of Elliott's arousal. Elliott is put away but continues to haunt Liz's dreams.

*Brian De Palma, Master of the Macabre, Invites you
to a Showing of the Latest Fashion... in Murder.*
—From the original ad campaign for *Dressed to Kill*

During the summer of 1980—I was taking an English course at McGill University in Montreal, Canada. I had seen the enigmatic, sepia-toned, one-sheet poster of *Dressed to Kill*, featuring a woman in high-heel shoes, sitting on the edge of a tub as she adjusts a stocking, and a bizarre male figure looking in, as well as a photo of Angie Dickinson in the shower scene, in *Time* magazine with a review entitled "Knife of Brian." I knew nothing else of *Dressed to Kill* except that I had loved the director's film *Obsession*, and I knew he had done *Carrie*—which I had yet to see due to its "no one under eighteen admitted" rating in France.

After class one day, my friend Jean and I decided to see *Dressed to Kill*, an experience causing in me an absolute "coup de foudre," a shocking event, a cinematic discovery of the highest degree, one that would allow a deep fascination with Brian De Palma to take root.

"It was almost as interesting watching you react to the movie as watching the film itself," my friend told me as we left the theater.

At the time, I was blown away by the language of images and the cinematic values, as well as the Hitchcockian elements. It was particularly tender as Hitchcock had passed away in April 1980, a few months before *Dressed to Kill*, clearly De Palma's homage to *Psycho*, came out. I had discovered Hitchcock in my early teens in Paris, where the films of the "Master of Suspense" consistently played, and *Dressed to Kill* felt like it was part of an evolution in cinema on the most primal level, "a next-generation Hitchcock." And while it clearly was influenced by *Psycho*, *Dressed to Kill* had its own language, grammar, and universe.

STARTING WITH *CRUISING*

The history of Brian De Palma's script for *Dressed to Kill* goes back to the 1970 novel *Cruising*, written by Gerald Walker, magazine editor for the *New York Times Magazine*. The book would eventually become a film directed by William Friedkin and released the same year as *Dressed to Kill*. Although hailed by Gore Vidal as "a brilliant and, sadly, unforgettable study of one of America's most persistent sexual nightmares," and by best-selling author Ross Macdonald who wrote, "I recommend it to readers who have passed the Céline test and are prepared to imagine that the secret life of our cities can be internally terrible," the novel *Cruising* is a hateful, unpleasant book.

The novel goes between three points of view. It's the story of a psychotic serial killer, a student named Stuart Richards, who hates being a gay male and murders men of a certain physical type. But it's also told from the perspective of John Lynch, a racist, homophobic, antisemitic cop, who is selected by his boss, Captain Edelson, to infiltrate the underground gay community because he resembles the victims. Edelson decides he doesn't want Lynch to know this fact, as expressed in Edelson's journal.

As the story evolves, we find out that the killer, Stuart Richards, loves movies like *Laura*, (1944) and *The Third Man* (1949), has a bad relationship with his parents, and was dating a married woman who became pregnant; she later returned to her husband, and they gave up the child for adoption.

As Richards kills again, Lynch grows on edge with his assignment. He fatally stabs a guy he mistakenly suspects to be the psycho, but who turns out to be another undercover cop. Richards reads about the crime and goes on a violent rampage in a bath house, stabbing six men until an attendant stops and kills him. It appears the case is closed, and Lynch gets a promotion. Soon thereafter, Edelson discovers that Lynch's next-door neighbor, a young, gay playwright, was brutally murdered, and he starts to ponder whether Richards was, indeed, guilty of the crimes. Lynch, meanwhile, has been consumed by his inability to accept his own attraction to men and has become a killer.

The film version of *Cruising* (1980) was ultimately made amidst protests of its depiction of homosexuals at a time when the community was struggling for recognition and inclusion. Director William Friedkin followed the book but decided to create a much more ambiguous universe. The killer is played by different actors (including one of the victims), with the voice of the murderer dubbed by the actor portraying Richards's father. Although embraced to a degree today, even by some members of the LGBTQ+ community—now that more positive portrayals of the community exist—the film was vilified when it was released and still is in some circles.

De Palma's version, written in 1974, however, would have been different. He was more intrigued by the killer's amorality than being a repressed homosexual. The script introduces a man named Quentin Lee, who has interviewed convicts on death row, including an unrepentant murderer who suggests, "If you want to know about killing, do it!" With that in mind, Lee plots to commit (and film) the perfect crime—one without any motive. He "rolls the dice" with his TV remote control and selects a handful of potential celebrity victims. He ends up killing a famous talk show host. To our surprise, Lee then removes a latex mask (something De Palma would later utilize in *Mission: Impossible*, 1996) and reveals himself to be a man named Linley—an actor in fact, a modern Lon Chaney. We've been watching "a movie within the movie." Linley, clearly a psychopath, reveals that the film was cancelled right in the middle of shooting due to lack of funds. "It doesn't matter now," Linley says, "Quentin Lee gave me the theme for my own movie. A sort of real-life diary." Linley intends to film himself carrying out senseless crimes—he murders a gay couple but drops the camera as he goes after one of the victims and fails to capture the killings. He turns the camera on himself and says, "I killed them. Both of them. Right in the shower. Just like in *Psycho*. Better than *Psycho*." After this murder, the police assume that the psychopath is gay and send John Lynch, a cop who fits the physical traits of the victims, undercover in the gay community as bait. When the press links the killer's sexuality to the victims', Linley's perfect, senseless, and motiveless crime is tarnished, and he decides to prove everyone wrong with a new victim. He randomly selects Kate, an insecure housewife who picked up a stranger in a museum and caught a sexually transmitted disease. Posing as a repairman, Linley stabs Kate to death in the elevator of the building where she had her one-afternoon stand and captures it all on the security video camera.

As in *Dressed to Kill*, Kate is introduced through a wild erotic fantasy. Instead of a shower, she's at a football game, having sex with a stranger while everyone—including her husband, Mike—cheers, "Close to touchdown!" Mike wakes her, and they have sex with Kate faking an orgasm. Later, Kate picks up the stranger at the museum before her fatal encounter with Linley.

Like the novel *Cruising*, De Palma's script has Captain Edelson assign John Lynch, a homophobic cop, to go undercover, and Lynch winds up mistakenly murdering another undercover cop. But the "straight" killing of Kate has broken the pattern, and Lynch is, ultimately, released from the case and promoted. In a bizarre denouement, Linley decides to top Kate's murder by killing a famous guru at a convention, with hopes he will be shot down by security, who will then discover a suitcase containing footage of his crimes. By sheer coincidence, Lynch is on duty at the event and catches Linley holding a gun. They have a confrontation and Lynch realizes Linley is the killer. In the confrontation, Lynch shoots two bystanders, but lays the blame on Linley, who he also kills. He is hailed a hero for averting the murder of the guru and receives a medal from the mayor. The script concludes on a police report of the murder of Lynch's next-door neighbor, a gay man. Evidence suggests the crime differed from Linley's methods, and with Lynch signing off on the trouble, we're left to question if Lynch himself has become a murderer.

It's fascinating to see how De Palma brought Kate along from her origin in the *Cruising* script to her appearance in *Dressed to Kill*. In a strange twist of fate, *Dressed to Kill*, with its handling of split personalities, itself had different identities over time, starting with its *Cruising* beginnings. It changed and evolved from script to film (including scenes that didn't make the final cut) to the theatrically released version that was recut to avoid the film getting an X rating (which would have prevented the distributor from properly promoting the film and would have reduced the scope of the potential audience).

Both the storyline and the filmmaking echo one another thematically in a way that reflects the complexity of the characters and the movie's own specificities.

GEORGE LITTO (PRODUCER): I read the script and I thought everyone else would like it. But it pushed the envelope [and] had very controversial elements for American major studios. Ray Stark [of Rastar / Columbia Pictures] was initially interested, but Brian [felt] he'd have to compromise over his creative vision if he went with Ray . . . Having exhausted every possibility, I went to Sam Arkoff with whom I'd done a lot of business over the years and [who] was a big admirer of Brian's. I called Sam, said I would get him the script at 9 a.m. the next day, and that if he called by noon, we could close the deal over lunch. Sam put up six million dollars—and we made the film that Brian wanted to make.

Dressed to Kill succeeds in luring the viewer into its world from the very beginning. You get seduced into the film immediately with the sultry, sensuous music by Italian composer Pino Donaggio playing over the opening credits—title cards against a black background, with an appropriately sharp and thin font for the title and the names. The theme carries us into the film, shot in the widescreen format.

Differing from the film, an earlier version of the script, starts with Kate brushing her teeth and stepping into the shower, reveals that the shower scene is a fantasy dream as Mike wakes his wife saying, "What's the matter, honey? You were moaning and tossing." He then proceeds, as in the film, to have pathetic morning sex with her to the sound of the clock radio. Once satisfied and unaware of his wife's faked orgasm, Mike gently taps her on the cheek and exits to the bathroom, while we stay on Kate, clearly unimpressed by her husband's performance.

But in the film, the camera travels through a bedroom toward a bathroom with De Palma immediately putting the viewer in a voyeuristic position, and revealing a man, Mike, stripped to the waist, shaving with a prophetic straight razor while his wife, Kate, pleasures herself in the shower as she stares provocatively at her oblivious husband. Suddenly, a male figure appears (played by Robbie L. McDermott) and grabs her from behind. Kate manages to remove the hand covering her mouth and screams as she is engulfed in the haze of the steamy hot water of the shower.

ANGIE DICKINSON ("KATE MILLER"): Kate was very sensual, and she very much needed to have her feelings satisfied. And if you're not getting that at home, well, soon you've got to go somewhere else. That's why she was so vulnerable. It was fairly clear-cut. I certainly knew about passion. I knew about frustrated passion.

The shower scene was shot on a soundstage. It was hell. It was difficult being naked, worrying about your hair and your makeup, and still perform. It was quite elaborate and precise. Brian knew exactly what he wanted. I just remember it as being very, very tedious, and specific, and difficult. But [Robbie] was very kind, polite, respectful. I also remember being quite physically thrown about—I tripped and hit the steam pipe with my foot. But that only helped the scene, of course. We rehearsed it without the steam, without the shower on, and all along, you're aware of the crew, the camera, the lights, the microphone, and then you have to forget it all. That's what acting is all about. It was well rehearsed, well directed, well acted, and we got it done.

Yet, in the original script, De Palma envisioned another opening entirely, with an unexpected, true-to-life inspiration.

BRIAN DE PALMA: The whole beginning was originally different. Once in college, I started to shave my face and then I started to shave my neck, and I thought, what would happen if I shaved off my chest hair? What happens if I shave off all the hair on my body? What happens if I shave off my pubic hair? So, the film opened with a guy who's got a straight razor in a scary space. He's taking all his hair off, all done in very tight close-ups. And then he gets to his penis and blood streams down his leg.

The scene involving Elliott shaving his body was filmed with Robbie L. McDermott serving as another body double. Later, in the script but not in the film, when Elliott visits Bobbi's new therapist, Dr. Levy, he learns that "she tried to hack off her genitals. She passed out before she succeeded. A judge made her come to me."

FINDING HIS MARION CRANE

One of the great inspired choices was the casting of Angie Dickinson as Kate Miller (originally Kate Myers, whose name had to be changed because a real Kate Myers was living in Queens, New York, at the time). Within the first few scenes of the film, from the shower to her motherly interaction with her son, Peter, and to the session with her psychiatrist, Dickinson delivers a powerful and moving performance, full of pathos and contradiction that slowly reveals her as a tragic figure. Although Liv Ullmann, Ingmar Bergman's favorite actress, and Jill Clayburgh were considered for the part, Angie Dickinson is perfect in the role. She echoes Hitchcock's choice of Janet Leigh for Marion Crane in *Psycho*. In both cases, it's meant to shock the viewer when the presumed leading lady gets killed early on (within roughly the first thirty-five minutes of the film for Kate and fifty minutes for Marion).

BRIAN DE PALMA: I met Angie the first time I went to the Montreal Film Festival in the late seventies . . . and we hit it off from the get-go. She's a great woman and so funny. I'd always been a big fan of hers from *Rio Bravo* [1959] to *Point Blank* [1967]. All great performances, always tremendously sexy, and I thought of her for the part.

As far as the character of Kate, I never thought about it as a social comment on the bored housewife of the late seventies.

To me, she was a Hitchcockian figure; the beautiful cool blonde, with a little of *Marnie* in her because she's troubled. She's more complicated than you think.

ANGIE DICKINSON: My initial reaction, when I read it was, "Oh, my God, I can't do this, I'm *Police Woman*." I was a great public, popular heroine. I said, "I can't get in the back seat and have sex in a taxi with a stranger." I told Brian I can't do that. And he said, "Read it again." I did, and then he called and said, "This is your director speaking." I reminded him I hadn't said yes yet, but we talked about it. He asked if it would help if I got a double. I thought that was a great idea. It was, "Well, then let's go to work."

What attracted me to the project was the script itself. When I read it, I saw the movie. I thought it was exciting even though I was not particularly a fan of thrillers. The fact that Kate gets killed early didn't bother me. As a matter of fact, when Brian was pleading his case he said, "I need a recognizable person who's willing to die in the movie in the first half hour. I need somebody relatively famous, and I need somebody that the audience will like immediately because I don't have time to set her up. You've got to bring that with you, because the audience must not resent a married woman having a fling." He felt I was the right age and not many other actresses at the time would have fit what the role required, including getting killed off early. It was just a wonderful role. And, that first half hour is all me. [*Laughs*]

THE DIFFERENT FACES OF KATE

Kate's introduction establishes her duality, not only as a character conflicted with her sexuality—the housewife/mother craving sexual adventure—but also through the technical aspect of how that scene was achieved. She's, literally, two women when in the scene itself—Angie Dickinson and a body double (Victoria Lynn Johnson, model and 1977 Penthouse Pet of the Year).

Later, when Kate is picked up by a stranger at the museum, a body double is used at times when the couple is having sex in the cab. And both Kate's orgasm in the cab and some of her screams as she's later killed were dubbed by actress Rutanya Alda—who appeared in several De Palma films, including *Greetings*, *Hi, Mom!*, and *The Fury*. (Alda is also the voice of Dr. Elliott's answering service.) In the end, four different actors play Kate, and each reflects an aspect of her journey, from sex to death.

Clearly influenced by his use of a model for the intimate close-up of Angie Dickinson in the shower and in the cab scenes, he wrote a treatment entitled *Body Double* as he completed *Dressed to Kill*. It became a film in 1984 and, initially, was meant to challenge the rating system that had plagued the release of *Dressed to Kill* and then *Scarface* (1983).

MAKING IT PERSONAL

An essential aspect of the film—not to be overlooked—is how autobiographical *Dressed to Kill* is. Kate's son, Peter, a mirror of the director himself is seen using a camera to spy on Elliott and is, at heart, a science nerd. The personal nature of De Palma's films is something that's rarely, if ever, acknowledged because it's not expected of the thriller genre. De Palma cast Keith Gordon—over Matt Dillon and his nephew Cameron De Palma, who had appeared in *Carrie*—to, essentially, play himself for the second time. He had a very similar role in De Palma's *Home Movies*, a film directed as a training exercise with students at De Palma's alma mater, Sarah Lawrence College, with Kirk Douglas, Nancy Allen, Gerrit Graham, Mary Davenport, and Vincent Gardenia. In that film, Keith Gordon played a kid

who films events surrounding his dysfunctional family, including his father's affair. Gordon is introduced as Peter Miller in
Dressed to Kill while working on a computerized contraption.
Kate berates him for working all night and for not wanting
to join her at the museum, a decision that directly impacts
her fate.

BRIAN DE PALMA: Peter, the science fair winner, inadvertently gets his mother killed and tries to solve the crime by
using his inventions. That computer in the film purposely
looks like one I built; I had the art director make it look exactly
like one of my own contraptions.

KEITH GORDON ("PETER MILLER"): I had a great time with
Brian on *Home Movies* . . . and I knew he had started *Dressed*

*De Palma gives new dimension to voyeurism as Peter Miller (Keith Gordon) "peeps"
on a discussion inside the office of Detective Marino (Dennis Franz).*

to Kill. For the part of Peter, he was mostly seeing very young actors and he was having a hard time finding anyone for the role.

One day, I got this call from Brian saying, "Listen, I'm thinking about going older, would you just come over and maybe we should read through a couple of scenes together?"

[I felt] the script didn't read as strong as his previous films, but I had confidence in Brian—and when I saw the final film, I realized how wrong I was.

ANGIE DICKINSON: Keith Gordon was so loving without being loving. Kate and Peter felt like they were mother and son because they were not overly comfortable with each other. There was Peter, so proud of his contraption. I'm so embarrassed to admit that I was as ignorant as the character I played—and had to ask Brian, "What are binary numbers?" He explained it to me, and I still don't know. So, that suited the dynamic with Keith. But it was a tricky little scene. A lot had to be conveyed all at once.

KEITH GORDON: I was aware that Peter was a lot like Brian—but he never said to me to be, or act, like him. Yet, Ann Roth who did the costumes, got me a kind of safari jacket that was like what Brian wore on set.

Working with Brian as an actor was always fun, he's a great actor's director. He would do a lot of takes, even for simple shots, and would encourage the actors to try something different each time. He'd encourage a certain amount of experimentation, without being directorial. There was tremendous freedom and safety to know there would be another take. Brian was great at walking that fine line where we had freedom, but he always got what he wanted.

ANGIE DICKINSON: Brian wouldn't talk. He's not a man of casual words. He doesn't say, "Isn't it a nice day?" He's either quiet or profound. I ran into him a couple of years after the movie and told him, "God, you were a pain in the ass on the set." And he replied, "I know I was. [*Laughs*] I hate shooting. I love preparation, writing the script, planning the movie." Because he does elaborate long scenes, he just hates it and he's bored. He loves post-production, and to get in and edit the film.

KEITH GORDON: But that first scene between Peter and his mom was the one time I ever had an argument with Brian. Looking back, I had a lot of hutzpah for an eighteen-year-old! His initial concept of the scene was that Peter was very hyper and running around the room. I said, "You know, Brian, Peter's been up all night, he shouldn't have that kind of energy." And he got frustrated with me and walked away. I remember he wasn't around for ten minutes. I thought, I've really blown it. But he came back and said, "You're right, let's do it your way." I was scared I had alienated him but it's actually a great example of how cool he is with actors.

BRIAN DE PALMA: I remember Keith playing it lethargic. [It was] much like a scene with my mother, berating me for being up all night working on computers. To this day, I'm still up all night. I was up all night on the computer last night, sending pictures of locations for my new film to my brother. It's basically something I've done my whole life.

Both *Dressed to Kill* and *Home Movies* feature Keith Gordon, in a semi-autobiographical role. *Home Movies* is the story of young Denis Byrd (Keith Gordon), who is coached by his mentor, The Maestro (Kirk Douglas), to be the star of his own life after a lifetime of being dominated by his older brother, James (Gerrit Graham). Part of the story includes filming his father cheating on his neurotic mom, and falling in love with Kristina (Nancy Allen), his brother's fiancée.

BRIAN DE PALMA: *Home Movies* is very much my family situation. Very close-to-the-heart stories about growing up can be very serious and melodramatic. But I took a comic attitude about it because I thought that was the best way to deal with the material, even though it was quite stressful at the time.

My mother found out that my father was sleeping with his suture nurse; she locked herself in her bedroom and took an overdose of Seconal. I must have been sixteen or seventeen. I had to, somehow, climb through a window to get into the room to see what was going on. I could see that she was hardly conscious. I called my father, and we took her to the accident ward where they pumped out her stomach.

I learned that the only way to make a divorce work in Pennsylvania was to have some photographic evidence of adultery. So, I proceeded to tape my father's phone calls and follow him at night and take pictures.

I took my camera and a knife and went down to [my father's] office. Even though I had a key to open the office, it didn't work. So, I had to use my fist to break through these double glass doors. I ran upstairs, waving a knife in front of my father saying, "Where is she?" And he looked at me like I was crazy. I probably looked crazy, and I was all covered with my own blood [from the broken glass window]. It was an embarrassing situation because the woman wasn't there. I proceeded to run through the office, which had three or four floors, searching for her. And I finally found her in a closet on the third floor, wearing only a slip. And I said, "Wow." I told my father, "We'll see you in divorce court." That, in fact, created the final separation of my parents. And, ironically of course, my father wound up marrying the suture nurse. My mother found a really nice guy who was a dentist, and they all lived happily ever after. It was a happy ending.

REFLECTIONS ON SCREEN

One of my most recent discoveries, after seeing the film, literally, hundreds of times, happened when Kate arrives and buzzes the entry door of Dr. Elliott's office. De Palma begins planting red herrings and establishes the duality of the characters within the filmmaking itself with Kate crossing paths with another patient who is leaving, a blonde in a long, dark coat who, in retrospect—and before we know Elliott is the killer—could be Bobbi. I had never noticed that the blonde was, in fact, played by Susanna Clemm who also plays Bobbi throughout the film (except during the last scene when Bobbi threatens Liz and is shot by the undercover cop, Detective Luce, also played by Clemm!).

BRIAN DE PALMA: For Bobbi, I got Susanna Clemm, who was the same size as Michael Caine, and we worked out a pair of glasses that had a nose on it that matched Michael's, and she played the role all through the movie except in the last scene where we finally got Michael Caine in costume.

But that early sighting was clearly intentional as the script underlined "A blonde PATIENT leaves." These clues are essentially planted ahead of the viewers even encountering the character of Bobbi in the story. This layer is almost exclusively designed

In an earlier split-diopter moment, Kate tries to seduce her psychiatrist, Dr. Elliott (Michael Caine), unaware of the duality that torments him.

by and for the director, as part of the universe of the film, with different actors performing the characters of Kate and Elliott.

The dialogue between Kate and Elliott is very banal at the outset, with Kate complaining about her mother coming in from Florida to "surprise" her for her birthday, and—at first—lying about things being "fine" with her husband. Without evoking her fantasy, she discusses Mike's poor performance in bed.

As they talk, De Palma makes use of his signature split diopter lens—allowing Angie Dickinson and Michael Caine to both be in focus.

JERRY GREENBERG (EDITOR): Brian tends to use the grammar of the camera, and one of the things he used in that film, and it was the first time that I became aware of it, was the split diopter. A split diopter is a single lens, shooting a single scene, and [it] makes the foreground and background both in equal focus. It was the first time that I was working with an "imagist."

In this exchange, De Palma also makes use of the mirror image, which will be repeated throughout the film. As Kate comes on to Dr. Elliott and asks him why he won't sleep with her, Elliott's reply is filmed as he looks at himself in a mirror, avoiding eye contact with his patient. This mirror image is the trigger that eventually causes Kate's death.

The mirror image returns later in the film, as Elliott learns of Kate's death from Detective Marino's phone message, he retreats against his armoire, bumps against the full-length mirror, and jumps at his own reflection. And shortly after, there's a brief exchange between Peter and Elliott at the police station, shot with a split diopter, nearly identical to the way De Palma framed Kate and Elliott during the therapy session (except Peter is on the right side of the screen; his mother was on the left). When Peter asks Elliott, "Do you know who killed her?" the shrink is shown in a close-up replying, "No," with the same air of suspicion we felt toward him when Kate asked him if he was attracted to her. Mother and son echo one another. By framing them the same way during their encounters with Elliott, De Palma hands off to Peter the responsibility to avenge his mom. And, by coincidence (or not), *Mirror Image* is the title of Nancy Hunt's 1978 autobiography, a transgender woman whose appearance on *The Phil Donahue Show* inspired the trans element of *Dressed to Kill*.

CRUISING THE MUSEUM

BRIAN DE PALMA: We scouted the sequence in the Metropolitan Museum of Art, but they didn't like the script. They thought it was in bad taste. And because I grew up in Philadelphia, we were able to move the interior to the Philadelphia Museum of Art. It was one of those scenes that I had up in my room all storyboarded, hopelessly preconceived—I would move index cards around, look at them, move them around again. I visited the location, took photos. By the time I shot the movie, I had lived this sequence a thousand times. I'd seen every visual possibility. In those days, I, literally, went to all the locations. I took pictures. I remember in *Murder à la Mod* [1968], my second feature, I first took photos of every shot in the movie, using stand-ins for actors. The way these sequences work is they have to have a visual idea. So, with Angie, we worked through the whole emotional line of the scene. And I, basically, shot all her coverage first; then I had to deal with everything she saw. What makes the sequence great is the combination of her face and what she sees.

JERRY GREENBERG: I must tell you I was not a big Brian De Palma fan at the time. I am now! I read the script and it seemed like just another one of his movies that I didn't like. And I turned him down. But he wouldn't take no for an answer. He

In one of the film's benchmark sequences—paced to an impressive score and fluid camera moves—Kate plays cat and mouse with a handsome stranger (Ken Baker) in a museum.

said, wait until I send you a revised draft. And I couldn't tell him that it had nothing to do with revisions, but that the kind of films he made were not films I would ordinarily go to. Although I must say that I had very much enjoyed *Carrie*, I thought that was wonderful. He insisted that I come down to his office. He was hard at work in this very small dining room, surrounded by mirrors; he had placed these three-by-five file cards and Scotch-taped them onto the mirrors—and on them, he had storyboarded with stick figures, all the shots of the movie. I was impressed that he had thought out the visuals in this very organized and structural way. Other editors might have thought this method would limit their ability to edit, but it endeared Brian to me forever; I knew that somehow working for this man would give me an opportunity to go to a place where I had never gone before. I enjoyed it very much. I wasn't disappointed. And for the first time, I didn't think of the script as the movie. I thought of it as a construct that I could have free rein in, to a certain extent.

Following her visit with Dr. Elliott, Kate ends up going to the art museum on her own, before going to have lunch with her husband and his mother. It is perhaps one of the film's most iconic sequences, a cinematic and visual tour de force, with Kate playing a game of cat and mouse with a handsome man within the galleries of the museum. De Palma originally intended to have a voice-over—basically Kate talking to herself—as the script detailed:

KATE (TO HERSELF): *He's got a lot of nerve trying to pick up such a respectably dressed married woman in the middle of the morning—for God sakes; this is a public museum. I have as much right to sit on this bench as he does.*

55

ANGIE DICKINSON: A few months after the movie was finished, Brian called to say it's looking good and I asked, "When do we do the narration?" And he said we don't need it. I was thrilled, because that had been the plan all along—not to use narration unless he needed it. Now, of course, it helped me act the scene, knowing what was going through Kate's mind.

The "cruising" between Kate and a stranger is paced to a six-minute and sixteen-second musical symphony by the film's composer, Pino Donaggio. The sequence is simply mesmerizing and bewitching as we follow Kate, first as the pursued and then as the pursuer of a handsome stranger. It showcases the film's pure cinematic alchemy, combining Angie Dickinson's pitch-perfect performance, De Palma's unique vision, Jerry Greenberg's editorial expertise, director of photography Ralf Bode's visual brilliance, and the score that tied it all together.

BRIAN DE PALMA: Music is very important in my work for the simple reason that I have long, purely visual sequences. Music supplies a kind of emotional line for them. It sort of directs the audience emotionally, because it's usually a character going through a space and experiencing something. You can read their expressions and music colors them. And Pino did a fantastic score for the museum sequence; it's a great piece of music that "fits like a glove." And that will always be one of the sequences people remember from *Dressed to Kill*, because just everything works within it.

The sequence is designed as its own story, in three suspenseful acts. It starts with Kate, established sitting on a bench, in one of the galleries—she looks at the painting of a woman—*West Interior* by artist Alex Katz—who seems to be staring back at her contemplatively and, perhaps, disapprovingly. With her dark hair, the woman in the painting is Kate's opposite and contrasting image.

Kate's attention then turns to the painting next to it: *Reclining Nude* by Tom Palmore depicting a gorilla on a carpet. Her slightly shocked reaction to it brings almost a smile and some humor to the otherwise tense sequence.

Kate also notices a young couple, with the horny boyfriend grabbing his blonde girlfriend's behind and kissing her while she is begging him, "Come on, look at the pictures!" There's another blonde woman being picked up by a man—she ignores him at first, but we later see them chatting. Kate is surrounded by sex, and by the possibility of it. Those vignettes invoke Hitchcock's *Rear Window*, where Jimmy Stewart plays a man resisting marriage and the charms of (another blonde) Grace Kelly. His view of the adjacent buildings reveals various aspects of relationships being played out, from sad loneliness to rushed marriage and, eventually, murder. Here, the art and the people around Kate seem to be tempting her; while observing the world around her, Kate is also writing in her agenda book to "pick up turkey!" a fact that establishes the story only slightly ahead of the familial Thanksgiving holiday, an even more tragic detail given the circumstances of Kate's untimely death.

But it's innocence—symbolized by a child—that leads to the next act of the museum story. Kate is observing a little girl who, unbeknownst to them, walks away from her parents. We see her running in front of Kate and, in the same moment, a man comes and sits next to Kate—the music, at this point, begins. We've entered a game of seduction.

The man is wearing sunglasses, a clear indication he is not there to appreciate art. But this detail also foreshadows Bobbi, who hides her identity behind dark sunglasses, day and night.

De Palma directs Dickinson, whose character has to decide whether to seduce or be seduced by the museum stranger.

Through this association of two characters with "no eyes," the stranger is the dark angel, the one who delivers Kate to Bobbi, her killer. This approach of connecting worlds is also present in a similar fashion in *Psycho*; Marion has fallen asleep on the side of the road and is awakened by a policeman, who is wearing dark sunglasses. He never takes them off; we never see his eyes. This very much presages the other character with no eyes, Norman Bates's dead, mummified mother in the cellar. When she is revealed—as a lightbulb swings back and forth above her face—we see dark holes instead of eyes, just like the cop who wouldn't take off his sunglasses.

Following the face-forward shots that have so far framed Kate, the camera moves to profile in a three-dimensional effect, with the man in the foreground, then Kate, and—way in the back—a painting that spells it all out, showing two nude women (by artist Philip Pearlstein), reflecting the sensuality and, ultimately, vulnerability of the moment.

De Palma utilizes some clever (and slightly amusing) visual storytelling. There's Kate smiling at the man who, in turn, ignores her. Then, she removes her gloves revealing her wedding ring, scaring him off. Kate goes after the man (without noticing that she dropped her glove). She loses sight of him, but as she gives up, she realizes he is right there, behind her. She plays hard to get and walks off; he follows her. She senses him, he turns into another gallery, and she looks back to an empty room. Disappointed, Kate walks away, past her glove on the floor and, unbeknownst to her, the man picks it up.

ANGIE DICKINSON: As serious as the scene is, it is also humorous, because it gets desperate. At first, she is intrigued. And then she finds him rude. Now, she's going to confront him but can't find him. And technically, it was so complicated, and complex to do—in fact, I was [at times] holding a rope attached to the camera, so I would stay in focus as I walked.

Then comes the first cut in the continuity—so far, we have traveled in this sequence following Kate with no interruption of time. But we cut to her, now standing in front of the statue of a naked woman, and the man, who has slipped on her glove, surprises her. She jumps and walks away, annoyed, eventually realizing she is missing the glove. In the script, the man was saying, "Excuse me . . ." while approaching Kate to give her back the glove.

Kate returns to the bench and—through a split screen—we see a flashback of the man wearing the glove surprising her, and Kate understanding the man was attempting to return it. Now, she desperately goes after the man, trying to get her glove back, but he is fast—avoiding her—and she loses him. The sequence ends with Kate—and the viewers—literally dizzy and defeated, having lost the first of three objects, taking her closer to death: the glove that covered the hand with her wedding ring. This loss marks the end of Act Two of the sequence.

Continuing the split theme of the filmmaking world of *Dressed to Kill*, although the interiors of the museum were shot in Philadelphia, the exteriors were filmed on the steps of The Metropolitan Museum of Art in New York. Kate comes out and throws her remaining glove to the ground as the camera pans to a waiting cab, with the stranger teasing her with the missing glove. We have not met the character of Bobbi yet, but as the camera travels down to the cab's window, she is seen clearly standing there (played by Susanna Clemm), turning her head from Kate to the vehicle, in dark glasses and coat.

JERRY GREENBERG: I never realized that Bobbi was standing there, outside the museum. When it was mentioned to me, I said, what is the point of it if you don't register the character's presence? But the camera saw her—and that was enough to justify it.

As Kate walks toward the cab, we see Bobbi sneaking by behind her. There's a close-up on Bobbi picking up the glove Kate threw to the ground. Perhaps an interesting continuity error, the action is then repeated from a different point of view, but this time, the camera is inside the cab, facing out toward Kate. The man pulls Kate inside the cab, building to a literal climax with Kate and the stranger having sex while on their way to the man's apartment. He lives downtown, at 160 Front Street, near the Twin Towers, which stood erect, dominating the man's building. All of it was strategically framed and designed to underline

Before the character is introduced to the story, Bobbi (here, played by Susanna Clemm) is seen in a panning shot, outside the museum.

the intensity of Kate's sexual experience, concluding the three acts of the cruising sequence.

ANGIE DICKINSON: The specificity of Brian De Palma was most evident to me outside the museum, because he had an enormous shot with a crane, which is critical because everything's moving. I had to do it many, many times. I was not getting it right and it got to be very frustrating. But it was the right approach to do it all in one shot.

Filming the scene in the cab . . . I don't recommend it! [*Laughs*] Buses were driving by and could see me lying down, having one good time in the back of the taxi in the middle of New York . . . Oh, God. And we went around, and around. It was real, no police cut off or anything, just going around, and around, having orgasms all afternoon.

BRIAN DE PALMA: This was a very complicated scene to do because we used a body double for the legs; we shot that later. But I remember being in a cab, with Angie and the actor playing the stranger, driving down Fifth Avenue, building to an orgasmic moment, echoing what happened in the dream of the opening shower scene, and arriving at the man's place where her final screams are going to be heard.

Though the front of the building was on location, the interiors were shot in an apartment on Fifth Avenue—in the very building in which De Palma lived. The floor plans of both his apartment and the one above, where the scene was filmed, were identical, adding to the personal aspect of *Dressed to Kill*. Rarely has a director, literally, brought his characters within his own environment, in this case, in the intimacy of his bedroom.

KATE'S LAST ACT

As Kate wakes up in the stranger's bed, De Palma delivers another three-act sequence that plays like its own film. Act One shows Kate waking up with her wedding ring very much visible on the modern bedside clock, indicating her husband was still on her mind while she cheated on him. As she dresses, the camera retreats alongside the corridor, away from the bedroom, eventually settling on the phone on a desk. Kate looks back toward it and decides to call her husband but hangs up on him after he picks up.

Act Two takes Kate on a search for her panties, the second object she has lost (with a split-screen flashback reminding her of the moment the stranger slipped them off her in the cab). Kate smiles at the memory and puts on her bracelet—for a short second, the camera focuses on her wedding ring sitting on the clock to the left of the screen. It's so short, you barely notice it. It's almost subliminal but, if you see it, it contributes to the mounting suspense. The ring is the third object she'll soon lose (or forget). The scene is underlined by Donaggio's beautiful score—a variation on the theme we first heard in the shower, when Kate tried to seduce Dr. Elliott, and in the cab.

In Act Three, Kate returns to the desk and opens a drawer, which reveals a gym card and the name of the stranger: Warren Lockman. She writes him a note: "I loved the afternoon. Maybe we'll meet again." But she scratches that, pushes the note aside, and writes another, "I loved our afternoon." It is filmed from her point of view, with close-ups on Kate, as well as a wide shot showing her at the desk. (In the wide shot, you will notice a continuity error where the first note is no longer on the desk—but it is there when filmed from Kate's point of view, an interesting detail that unintentionally helps the scene gather a near surreal feeling, the notion that something is wrong and off.) Kate also discovers paperwork indicating that Warren Lockman has contracted a sexually transmitted disease, something that would become very much part of America's growing concerns with the AIDS epidemic a year after the release of the film. In a 1989 issue of *Rolling Stone*, Peter Travers listed the film as number five on his list of top ten best films of the decade, calling it, "a chilling presentiment of the AIDS era." Kate's panic at the discovery and abrupt exit from the apartment mark the end of the sequence, leading directly to the film's most shocking and stylized twist yet.

The big difference between the murder of Marion Crane in the shower in *Psycho* and Kate Miller in *Dressed to Kill* is that Hitchcock operates on shock—Marion steps into the shower and, suddenly, a shadow appears, pulls aside the curtain, and stabs Marion. De Palma approaches the scene in another three acts through suspense and relying exclusively on his cinematic eye rather than logic or realism.

Act One begins with Kate, having discovered Lockman's medical records, in complete distress and waiting for the elevator—the camera moves toward a shadowy figure, hidden behind the fire exit door. Seemingly, Kate escapes the killer when she enters the elevator, unaware she is being stalked. Almost immediately, Kate realizes she has forgotten her wedding ring in the stranger's bedroom (presented in a third split screen/flashback). Kate tries to go back up to the apartment, but her ride is interrupted by a mother and her young daughter entering the elevator. The little girl stares at Kate, almost accusatorially, and her mom whispers to her, "It's not polite to stare." Kate has one last look into innocence (harkening back to the little girl running from her parents in the museum), and as the mom and her daughter reach the ground floor and exit, Kate goes back up to the symbolic seventh floor, invoking the seven deadly sins. In Kate's case, the seventh floor of the building where she had her affair and where she is about to be attacked, couldn't be more literal at the conclusion of Act One of the sequences, with the elevator opening on Bobbi, the killer.

ANGIE DICKINSON: I love the touch of the little girl [staring at Kate in the elevator] because as Brian said to me, "You know how when you're guilty, and somebody looks at you, they're seeing it all?"

Andrew Sarris questioned in his negative review in *The Village Voice*, "How does the murderer know that Kate will be coming back up on the elevator?" A fair question that's, in fact, not particularly relevant to the world De Palma creates; this is a macabre fairy tale, and it doesn't operate on logic or realism. Instead, it's quite the opposite—heightened reality.

Even Hitchcock would push the envelope of logic to fit his storytelling needs—for example, a scene in *Psycho* has Marion's sister finding a tiny piece of paper with Marion's handwriting on it in the toilet bowl of the cabin in which Marion was murdered. We don't question it because it belongs within the provocative world of the film itself, with *Psycho* being the first American movie to showcase an actual toilet. Hitchcock is making a joke by planting evidence in the toilet bowl—and in De Palma's warped world, he freely implies a near-supernatural psychic connection to Kate's killing, which fits in with themes borrowed from his own films, *Carrie* and *The Fury*.

The script describes the sequence with:

The door opens and standing before Kate is the blonde with a straight razor raised high in the air. As Kate covers her face, the blonde slashes the palm of her hand. Instinctively reacting, Kate brings her bleeding hand down to look at it. The blonde slashes Kate's cheek. Kate reaches out for the closing door. The blonde slashes Kate's hand. The door closes as the blonde continues slashing.

The initial attack on Kate is edited in a way to emulate shock and numbing violence. The assault is shown from different angles in a total of twenty-five seconds and eighteen shots, paced to a brilliant *Psycho*-like score. The attack ends with a wide shot revealing a mirror inside the elevator, setting up the geography of the moment yet to come—where Liz Blake (Nancy Allen) spots the killer. The door closes on another violent slash of the razor and Kate's scream. In De Palma's original concept for the scene, he had planned—and even storyboarded—having the razor slicing off one of Kate's fingers, with a close-up of the severed finger hitting the ground. That may have been too complicated to

Kate's tragic and graphic murder, carefully designed and choreographed by De Palma, was "slashed" by the censors prior to the release of the film.

realize, and happily so, as the grotesque beauty of Kate raising her hand and the razor slicing her palm is enough to convey the brutality of the killing. As mentioned with the orgasm in the cab— and continuing his theme of duality— some of Angie Dickinson's screams are dubbed by actress Rutanya Alda. (Fittingly, in De Palma's *Blow Out*, John Travolta plays a soundman in search of the perfect scream for an actress about to be stabbed in a shower for a B-horror film.)

If Act One began with Kate entering the elevator and ended with the attack, Act Two introduces Liz Blake calling the elevator from another floor, standing with a "client," and discussing the stock market. We then go back to the killer slashing Kate in several quick shots, another beat with Liz and her client, and back to the murder in several more shots as the elevator door opens.

The third act begins with the elevator door opening for Liz and her client (who immediately runs away) and amounts to nearly three dozen perfectly choreographed shots, framing the tragic figure of Kate on the floor, desperately reaching out to Liz, with Bobbi hiding on the side, holding the razor. In slow motion (another De Palma trademark) Liz attempts to stop the door from closing. The killer drops the weapon, which Liz grabs as the door closes.

The murder sequence, which totals about five minutes and forty-five seconds, concludes with Liz trying to get help from a screaming housekeeper—who slams the door in her face—followed by her taking the stairs to the ground floor, yelling to call the police. As Liz rushes into the lobby, the camera pans and we end on the elevator door bumping against Kate's bloodied arm and hand, bookending this operatic *danse* that began with the slashing of her hand.

BRIAN DE PALMA: The whole hallway and the elevator were built on a sound stage. It was all storyboarded and very carefully choreographed, with multiple points of view. Filming it was very mechanical because we had very short shots, inserts really. There are a lot of prosthetics, and everybody has to be very patient with a process that's very labor-intensive. We had very small pieces that fit into this very elaborate mosaic that becomes the sequence. But making it is more like gymnastics, with everything having to be precise, and for the actors, it's like an athletic exercise, rather than an emotional thing.

ANGIE DICKINSON: It was quite frightening. Even though we're acting, you really do displace yourself, and you're almost there. You do get so concentrated. It's an ominous thing to look up and see anybody who's about to attack you. The prosthetics were designed by Michael Westmore way before filming—the palm, the throat, I was pretty patched up. I had died in movies but never that way. They would pack a bag full of fake blood on my neck and it would pour out when the razor sliced. It was fascinating.

NANCY ALLEN ("LIZ BLAKE"): There was only one shot where Angie and I are together. The rest of the time, I had to keep that visual in my mind to react for the close-ups. It was also all very technical, which can really wear you down! But one of the things I love about the film is that this entire scene has no dialogue—and that's something Brian did throughout the film. The museum scene, the asylum, and the nightmare at the end don't have dialogue either. It's all guided by visuals and music.

ANGIE DICKINSON: [When Kate reaches out to Liz] she certainly knows she's dying. I imagine death to be that way, you just reach out for anything, anybody, in disbelief that you're dying. I don't remember specifically wrapping and being finished on the movie. I always say that when you're living history, you don't notice it's history. And, so, you just go on about your day, but I thought it was excellent. There's no question about it.

BRIAN DE PALMA: As far as violence, I've always said I've got a high tolerance for blood, but I've also had a very clinical approach to it as doctors do, because my father was a surgeon and I saw things you can't imagine. It was all carpentry as far as my father was concerned. When I was growing up in Philadelphia, my father was a professor of orthopedics at Jefferson Medical College. And during the summers, and even during the year, I used to work at the hospital and follow the residents around doing various jobs, including in the lab, where my father was performing all kinds of surgeries and experiments. I would go on all the different residencies, psychiatric, cancer . . . You name it, I saw it. Also, I used to go in and out of the operating rooms. It was an invaluable education process in terms of watching the way a hospital worked and the kind of people the doctors were, the physicality of surgery, and the precision of it, the strength you need to have. When I worked at the accident ward in Philadelphia at a very young age—sixteen, seventeen—I saw all kinds of people coming in with all kinds of grotesque cuts, gunshots, slashings. It's something I grew up with, basically.

LIFE AFTER KATE

While the first part of the film is almost exclusively a one-woman show with Angie Dickinson as Kate, the second is much more of an ensemble. The humorous rants between Detective Marino and Liz, in contrast with the coolness of Dr. Elliott and Kate's grief-stricken son, Peter, take the film in a different, but equally pleasing, direction. Kate's muted scenes are now replaced with snappy, fun, typical New York dialogue. And you can tell the actors are connecting with one another and having a great time with it. They all bring a different style of acting due to their experience at the time, but each are daring and memorable. There's the courageous acting, particularly by Nancy Allen—not just because of the nudity, but because she elevates the character she plays through the performance. Michael Caine is predictably amazing and daring, as he would be soon thereafter as Christopher Reeve's lover in *Deathtrap* (1982). Dennis Franz completely embraces playing the rude and unsympathetic cop, while Keith Gordon stands out as the intellectual type, very brooding, keeping it all inside. It's an incredible troupe that matches the De Palma tradition of pitch-perfect casting choices.

BRIAN DE PALMA: How I got to Michael Caine was through Sue Mengers, who was my agent at that time. That's how we were able to get big names, and Michael came in, Angie came in, and unlike the way it usually goes, everything worked out.

Michael is the consummate professional, and he enjoyed the concept of the script. He had, at that time, been making a very difficult action picture [*The Island*, 1980] and he thought of our film as a drawing room play—you have a chance to sit down and act in nice clothes. You don't have to do anything too energetic. But he's just a great actor who really appreciates the success he's had, and he loves acting. He works hard. He's great to have on a set because he's so bright and so amusing. He is very grateful to be making movies, which is exactly how all of us should feel. We could be doing a lot of more unpleasant things.

NANCY ALLEN: I was so excited about working with Michael Caine. I just loved him as an actor, and I was so nervous. I remember going the first day of rehearsal. I went out for a walk, I was just trying to get rid of that anxious energy and I finally braved it, went into rehearsal, and he was there, he was very sweet and very charming—we immediately launched into a scene. He realized I was nervous—and after we read the scene, he said, this was amazing! He had a way of saying it [that gave me confidence]. He had a great sense of humor, he put me at ease right away and I felt comfortable. He was very generous with me on the set—he insisted on staying there when the camera was on me and there was barely any room for him to be. And it did make a difference; I could feel his presence.

DENNIS FRANZ ("DETECTIVE MARINO"): I always welcomed working with Brian, and when he told me the cast in *Dressed to Kill*, I just thought, wow, what a great opportunity, and the chance at having some scenes with Michael Caine. In fact, I recall very clearly the first scene I shot with him; I was so mesmerized by him, I was so in awe, I started falling into his rhythm [which was supposed to be serious since he played a psychiatrist]. Brian started snoring and yelled, "Come on, you're putting me to sleep!" Michael laughed and said, "I believe you've fallen into my form of delivery." I was able to find Detective Marino after that!

BRIAN DE PALMA: I had spent a lot of time with New York cops when I was developing *Prince of the City* [Sidney Lumet ended up making the film, with Treat Williams, in 1981]. I knew how cops talked. And Dennis Franz, who had already played a cop for me in *The Fury*, is a great actor. When you have actors like him, you're always trying to find a role for them. But I applied all that I had learned from working on *Prince of the City* and created a character for Dennis to play.

DENNIS FRANZ: I began researching police officers in general when I was doing theater work in Chicago. The first time I played a policeman was on stage with Joe Mantegna in a play called *Cops*—it's about two off-duty detectives in Chicago who get involved in a hostage situation. In researching these characters, we became friends with Chicago's finest. And we would frequent the restaurants they ate at, some of the bars they hung out at. I just observed them all the time. And I picked up certain mannerisms they had, wearing leather jackets, the gold chains, which at that time was standard. For detectives, having that attire was not too far off base. I chose to chew gum; when you chew gum it gives you a different attitude. It helped me create an attitude that I wanted to have with this Marino character. I picked that up from most detectives, that they seemed to be one step ahead of the people they're dealing with. They're very insightful, they're always reading people, and I tried to apply some of that in Marino. Behind the façade, most people in law enforcement are very vulnerable and they're usually very considerate. So, Marino was the beginning of an evolution of that type of character I played, like Andy Sipowicz on *NYPD Blue* or Norman Buntz on *Hill Street Blues*.

Brian really likes it when accidents happen when you start filming a scene. He comes up with ideas, throws them at you, changes the dialogue. At times it does call for improvisation. And he likes that, he encourages that. An example of that was when Marino paraphrases something Dr. Elliott said, basically making fun of it. This was something that Brian added, right there on the spot.

BRIAN DE PALMA: I created the role of Liz especially for Nancy, and her character, the so-called Wall Street hooker, is very much based in truth. In fact, the exterior of the building where Angie ends up with the guy from the museum was a place where Wall Street guys met with hookers. I stumbled across it when I was scouting locations and it gave me the idea for Nancy's character. There was a need for me to base all the characters in a certain reality I had either experienced or witnessed, and then bring a fantasy element to them.

NANCY ALLEN: At the time of *Dressed to Kill*, I was newly married to Brian De Palma, and he was beginning to write the script. I was working on *1941* [1979] with Steven Spielberg, and Brian's routine was, he'd wake up very early, like three, four in the morning; he'd write for a few hours, and he'd read me these scenes that he'd written. Every day was like the next installment. It was such a fabulous script; you could see the movie.

The film takes a new turn, as Liz Blake (Nancy Allen), the witness to Kate's murder, is interrogated by a sarcastic Detective Marino (Dennis Franz).

When he read me the last scene, I said, "Oh, it's going to be such a great movie," and he asked, "You really like it?" I said it was great, and he replied, "Fantastic, because I wrote Liz for you." I had no clue before that. Of course, I was very happy about it because it was a great part. But it didn't happen all that easily because, initially, the movie was going to be done at a different studio, and they had other ideas for that role.

The character of Liz Blake is a high-class call girl. I certainly had no experience at that, and one of the things that Brian suggested was Xaviera Hollander's *The Happy Hooker* [1971]. I also read Nancy Friday's book about women's sexual fantasies, and they were all about a dark stranger. Then there was Ann Roth, the costume designer who had worked with Jane Fonda on *Klute* [1971]. She had met a few call girls through that film and offered to introduce me to that world. She was very instrumental in helping me with all of that.

The humor of the character was important to me. A lot of it is Brian's sense of humor but some of it he picked up from my personality. He always had a twinkle in his eyes about things!

DENNIS FRANZ: Working with Nancy Allen was a particular treat. It was funny to see Brian and her together, as husband and wife and as director and actor. Nancy seemed to be able to tap into Brian's psyche; she would do certain things I knew were bringing a smile to Brian's face. In the scene where I'm interrogating her, it was great to be able to say "fuck," rather than finding a fancy way of saying the same thing. That was one of the first times I got to say that on film!

A TROUBLING TRANS NARRATIVE

A key and controversial aspect of *Dressed to Kill* is De Palma's depiction of a transgender character. (In the film, Bobbi is referred to as transsexual, a complicated term within the LGBTQ+ community. Transgender is now accepted as a more inclusive and affirming term.)

By using Elliott's reveal as Bobbi as a crucial twist to shock the audience, De Palma conflates transness with mental illness and homicidal behavior. The shock isn't merely that Elliott is the killer, but that Elliott is trans. Without a balance of positive trans narratives—made by members of the trans community— something we still do not have enough of today, De Palma's "twist," remains problematic.

But coming off his attempt to make *Cruising*, De Palma found inspiration in an unlikely source.

BRIAN DE PALMA: In my adaptation of *Cruising*, I had several storylines colliding with each other, and intended to film them in different styles. Those ideas were sort of mulling around in my head. The thing that sort of jelled it for me was a talk show where a transgender woman was interviewed by Phil Donahue.

On *The Phil Donahue Show,* Nancy Hunt (1927–1999), author of *Mirror Image: The Odyssey of a Male-to-Female Transsexual,* discusses her background and her life both before and after she transitioned. Not just taking inspiration from Hunt, De Palma weaves the interview into the film itself, with both Elliott and Liz watching the show. The real-life interview brings a documentary flavor to the film (perhaps naively to include positive transgender representation in the film), but also speaks to the criticism of *Dressed to Kill.* In an interview for the blog *Curtsies and Hand Grenades* in 2018, film critic Caden Gardner speaks to the problem of weaving Nancy Hunt's actual story into the film's narrative:

De Palma's knowledge of transness is off as he only sees the surface, but he made a deliberate choice to insert Nancy Hunt's image in his movie. He uses clips, but if you look up Nancy Hunt, you will also know that she similarly rejects trans as trauma and trans as pathology, viewing the mental health community as hostile toward trans people rather than helpful to her and many people in her position. Hunt lives forever in certain transgender archives but she is used ghoulishly in a film where the director laughs and chuckles like the Keith Gordon character about the idea of a trans woman.

Over time, *Dressed to Kill* has been embraced by some members of the LGBTQ+ community, just as other films with troubling trans depictions have. In his 2015 *Out* magazine piece, "The Fine Art of Cruising," film critic Armond White offers that De Palma creates a "timeless path to empathy" for women—both cisgender and trangender—as well as anyone who practices sexual independence. The debate over the film continues to provoke complicated dialogue. Speaking to the dualities explored through the film, it's equally important to give space to voices that are troubled by the film in addition to those who embrace it.

THE NIGHTMARE

Next to the opening in the shower and the museum scene, the nightmare that concludes the film is, possibly, one of the most cinematic aspects of *Dressed to Kill*, one that caught me completely by surprise when I first saw it, and a sequence that confirms the horror and baroque aspects of the film. Playing on the adage "just when you thought you were safe," De Palma takes us to an asylum (shot at 52 Chambers Street, the same location as the police station), where we follow an overly made-up and sexy nurse, played by model/actress Anneka Di Lorenzo. Pretending to be asleep, Elliott lunges at the nurse and strangles her. As Elliott undresses the nurse, the camera rises, revealing inmates going crazy.

BRIAN DE PALMA: The nightmare with the nurse started with a series of images I had of the white shoes. From all my years in hospitals, nurses with white shoes have obviously stuck in my subconscious quite strongly.

The scene, with its strange, operatic setup and stylized lighting, indicates a dreamlike quality. It is followed by the suspense of Elliott—now fully Bobbi—breaking into Peter's home and standing outside the bathroom door, holding a razor, waiting to strike Liz, who is taking a shower. The entire sequence echoes the opening with Kate's attack in the shower and is another moment that relies purely on images, performance, and music. Most shocking is Liz getting out of the shower and, having spotted the shoes of the killer by the door, walks toward the cabinet where there's a straight razor. As she opens the cabinet, De

One last jump—Bobbi continues to haunt Liz's dreams, and perhaps ours as well.

Palma cuts to the shoes—empty—and reveals Bobbi (Susanna Clemm reprising her dual role) in the reflection of the mirror, the razor strikes, slashing Liz's throat!

In the script, the nightmare was slightly different and, potentially, would not have been as effective:

> *Now, at the bottom edge of the door, WE SEE the tip of a white nurse's shoe. Liz frantically grabs the medicine cabinet mirror and slides it open. But there's no shelves, just a rectangular hole in the wall with a disembodied arm wielding a straight razor that is slashing down across Liz's face.*

In the film, Liz screams and wakes up in the same bed where we saw Kate having sex with her husband at the beginning of the film. Only this time, the camera pulls back from a close-up on Liz, with Peter, rushing in to comfort her. She pushes him, not realizing yet she woke up from a dream—and as the camera pulls up, going the opposite way from our introduction to Kate and her husband, one might think that, this time, perhaps, Kate is watching over Peter and Liz as they embrace in a comforting hug, saying, "It's all going to be alright."

NANCY ALLEN: For some reason, it was easier to be naked in the shower than the seduction scene, with Michael Caine wearing lingerie!! But I can tell you that the water [in the shower] was never warm enough! It was cold on the soundstage. It was horrible. Again, it was very complex to film—a lot of different setups, and the prosthetic makeup on my throat. It felt very mechanical but, at the same time, you have to put all that out of your mind and find the emotion of the scene. I remember that the slashing of my throat was very upsetting. It's a very disturbing image. In the original script, I woke up from the nightmare in bed with a client in a hotel room. [As written in the script: *Liz screaming. A john jumps out of a hotel bed: "What's the matter—you must have dozed off for a second." Liz pushes him away and keeps screaming. "You're nuts. You need a psychiatrist." Liz keeps screaming and the john puts on his clothes and races out of the room.*] And it was switched to me staying with Keith's character—it felt like a more positive ending especially after this traumatic experience. The other ending would have gotten a laugh—it was the right decision.

SLASHING *DRESSED TO KILL*

De Palma submitted his completed film to the Motion Picture Association of America (MPAA) and was informed it was likely to receive an X rating—no patron under the age of seventeen would be admitted to see the picture. In 1968, De Palma's second feature film *Greetings*, starring Robert De Niro, was the first American film to receive an X rating under the new rating's classification code. But *Greetings* being an art film, the rating and its limitation didn't hurt the box office—one could even argue it helped the film's success.

With *Dressed to Kill*, the situation was different; the film had a high budget, major stars, and an X rating would mean no proper advertising campaign and a restricted audience. At the time, Richard Heffner of the Classification and Rating Administration (CARA) referred to *Dressed to Kill* as a "masterwork" but nevertheless declared it X rated. To receive an R, De Palma had to make some strategic cuts in the opening shower scene, in Kate's murder in the elevator, and in Liz's nightmare at the end. He also had to replace some of the dialogue in the scene during which Liz tries to seduce Dr. Elliott. The following line was deleted for the R-rated version:

LIZ *[referring to the nightmare she had about a man raping her]: All the time he's talking I can see the bulge in his pants.*

Also, in the X-rated version, Liz said, "He drops his pants, spreads my legs, kneels down behind me." When Liz strips to her sexy lingerie in front of Elliott, he says to her, "Now, why would you want to do a thing like that?" In the X-rated version, Liz replies, "Well, because of the size of that cock in your pants." In the R-rated version, the word "cock" has been replaced with "bulge."

In the shower scene, two explicit close-ups of Kate's caressing her pubic hair had to be removed—the first close-up was swapped for Kate caressing her belly and the second one was substituted by her caressing her breast. Two more shots were cut out entirely: we see Kate and the man moving more suggestively, and a shot of the man's hand covering Kate's pubic area.

But it wasn't only the film's sexual content that needed to be edited. The elevator scene was also "slashed," with major shots removed. Close-ups of slashing Kate on the left cheek and then gashing her neck were cut and substituted by long shots of the killer assaulting Kate and by quick, almost subliminal, close-ups on her, immediately followed by another long shot. And in the last scene, when Liz's throat is slashed, a close-up showing the bleeding, gaping wound was removed.

De Palma finally got the R rating after submitting the film three times.

BRIAN DE PALMA: *Dressed to Kill* was my first real battle with the MPAA and Richard Heffner. My film *Greetings* got an X rating, but it didn't make a difference. *Dressed to Kill* was, I thought, a beautifully made movie and Heffner, basically, was disturbed by the violence in the elevator and the shower sequence, and we were forced to cut out stuff to get an R rating. I was enraged by it, and I felt I was being penalized by being effective, not because I showed too much but because it was so scary and so violent. I thought I'd done very elegant sequences; they obviously were scary and bloody, but well within the range of what was out there at the time. I went to the press and vented my unhappiness with what I was forced to do. And fortunately, we kept all the cuts in the European version. So, at least a version exists with everything in it.

ANGIE DICKINSON: If I were the director, I would want my images up there, right or wrong. That's probably how Brian feels, you know, screw 'em. This is my piece of art. And I can understand that.

In 1981, NBC paid $6.5 million for three telecasts and "NBC–TV censors sharpen their knives for *Dressed to Kill*" headlined the *Los Angeles Herald Examiner*. Indeed, twenty minutes were hacked from the film, frames were blown up to avoid showing nudity, the murder (what's left of it) was colored completely in red, and dialogue was changed. For instance, Kate's line: "He gave me one of his wham-bam specials this morning" became, "He made love to me in his usual selfish way this morning."

A NOVEL APPROACH

As the film was coming out, a novelization credited to both Brian De Palma and author Campbell Black was released. It's a revealing text to read, as it introduces other aspects of the characters as well as storylines absent from the film, serving as an unusual companion to De Palma's script. The novelization presents a different version of what the film might have been and most certainly gives a literary point of view versus the cinematic approach. For those reasons, it's a worthy exercise to share some of the most interesting changes written for the book.

The novel opens with an introduction to Bobbi in a bar, with a guy unsuccessfully trying to pick her up, followed by Kate's shower scene. There're more details about Kate's first husband, Thomas, who was killed in Vietnam, and about a very antagonistic relationship with her mother-in-law. We also get more background information on Liz—she's from Chicago and her father died from cancer. She was a remedial reading teacher who moved to New York and became a high-priced prostitute, which she hides from her mother. Similar information was in a deleted scene from the film, when Liz goes to a client, referred to as "Cleveland Sam" in the end credits, who is too shy to engage in sex immediately. He says he is a married salesman (visiting New York on business) and asks about Liz, who, in turn, reveals her past including a secretarial job with a boss who sexually harassed her, teaching, and, eventually, turning to escort.

Norma, who runs the escort service and never appears in the film, is a sympathetic character in the novelization. After Liz witnesses Kate's murder, Norma comes to stay with her. She rides the elevator up with Bobbi (who, for once, is not wearing her signature sunglasses and is stalking Liz).

We get to share in the personal life of Dr. Elliott and his wife, Anne, who never appears in the film—she's an alcoholic, they're getting divorced, and she taunts him with her new conquest. There's an added segment with Bobbi/Elliott in a mental hospital, thinking of Anne calling Elliott sick for wearing women's clothing, as well as memories of Elliott's sister, Cecelia.

Mike, Kate's second husband, is a lot more grief-stricken after the murder of his wife than he appears in the film. Peter is fifteen—younger than his portrayal by Keith Gordon.

As in the movie, Elliott visits Bobbi's new therapist, Dr. Levy. But in the novelization, Levy plays Elliott a recording of their session, where Bobbi talks of going to boarding school, how the others knew she was different, and being caught wearing her sister's clothes.

Liz seduces Elliott to find information on Bobbi as she does in the film. However, the fantasy she tells to arouse Elliott is different from the movie, offering an erotic dinner-table encounter.

The ending is different from the film—Elliott/Bobbi escapes, dressed as a nurse, and goes to Liz's apartment, pretending to be collecting for a cause. While Liz goes to her purse, she sees a shaved-head Elliott/Bobbi coming toward her. "Any moment now, she would open her eyes and the dream would be over. But it hadn't yet begun."

THE VOLATILE RELEASE

Dressed to Kill generated quite a lot of heat when released—reviews were "split."

The New Yorker's Pauline Kael, who described *Dressed to Kill* as a "suspense comedy" about sex and fear, was the film's (and De Palma's) greatest defender: "[De Palma] has become a true visual storyteller. He knows where to put the camera and how to make every move count, and his timing is so great that when he wants you to feel something, he gets you every time."

On the other hand, the *Philadelphia Inquirer's* Desmond Ryan declared, "What is missing in *Dressed to Kill* is any sense that its director, who also wrote the screenplay, cares about the characters he has created." *Newsweek* called the film "artificial," while Kathleen Carroll headlined her New York *Daily News* review: "*Dressed to Kill*: Mostly mannequins." The division between critics was brought to a boiling point and a war of words by Andrew Sarris in his article "Dreck to Kill," for *The Village Voice*, where he compared the film to a "McDonald's hamburger (complete with chopped meat and ketchup!)" and took on David Denby of *New York* magazine, who wrote as part of his review, "If the anti-porn feminists, the pressure groups, and the more earnest writers at *The Village Voice* get hold of [De Palma] they'll tear him limb for limb," as well as Jim Hoberman (also in *The Village Voice*), who raved about the film's "near-perfect mechanism." Critic Molly Haskell in her seminal book *From Reverence to Rape: The Treatment of Women in the Movies* wrote "*Dressed to Kill* turned Angie Dickinson into a neurotic, sexually insatiable 'older woman' and then pummeled and bloodied her for her desires."

But that was just the beginning.

Liz Blake (Nancy Allen) discovers the aftermath of Bobbi's attack on Kate.

THE DISTORTED IMAGE OF A PSYCHOTIC MALE TRANSVESTITE
MAKES ALL SEXUAL MINORITIES APPEAR SICK AND
DANGEROUS. DRESSED TO KILL FOLLOWS A NEW TREND IN
FILMS: WITNESS THE GAY MALE KILLER OF CRUISING, THE
LESBIAN RAPIST OF WINDOWS [1980], AND NOW THE KILLER
TRANSVESTITE OF DRESSED TO KILL.

THOUGH KATE MILLER DIES AND LIZ BLAKE BLEEDS TIME AND
AGAIN, THREE SCENES—THE RAPE, THE NECROPHILIA, AND A
SLASHING SCENE—WERE TO HAVE HAPPENED IN WOMEN'S
MINDS. AS IF THE EROTICIZATION OF VIOLENCE WERE NOT
ENOUGH, DRESSED TO KILL ASSERTS THAT WOMEN CRAVE
PHYSICAL ABUSE; THAT HUMILIATION, PAIN, AND BRUTALITY
ARE ESSENTIAL TO OUR SEXUALITY.

IF THIS FILM SUCCEEDS, KILLING WOMEN MAY BECOME THE
GREATEST TURN-ON OF THE EIGHTIES:

JOIN OUR PROTEST! MARCH WITH US ON AUGUST 28!

—Women Against Violence and Pornography in Media, San Francisco.

Another group, Women Against Violence Against Women (WAVAW) was created in 1976 in response to a film called *Snuff* (1975), which depicted real deaths and mutilations. At the time *Dressed to Kill* came out, the group had about one thousand members nationally. Approximately fifty of its members turned out to protest *Dressed to Kill* in front of the Hollywood Pacific Theatre in Los Angeles upon release. "A movie like *Dressed to Kill* encourages and perpetuates violence," Stephanie Rones of WAVAW told the *Los Angeles Times*, "and pairs it with sexuality by showing vicious acts instead of loving and caring. Film critics have enormous responsibilities and often write about what they see in a very narrow sense, reviewing only the artistic relevance and ignoring the social relevance. Is a woman being slashed in an elevator funny or erotic or entertaining? Critics should also look at films on a broader level." *San Francisco Chronicle* reviewer Judith Stone countered WAVAW's comments and its attack on movie critics: "Filmmakers have a right to do an honest representation of violence and not clean it up. Real violence is bloody, shocking, and disturbing. I don't think much of what this WAVAW group has to say. They know nothing about criminal behavior. And women do indeed have fantasies; women are being killed. Art has a duty to show it."

WAVAW went as far as writing a letter to *Los Angeles Times* critic Sheila Benson: "We are shocked and greatly dismayed that anyone would find *Dressed to Kill* elegant, sensual, and erotic, a directorial tour de force. We are especially disturbed that a woman would enjoy this film . . . to glamorize [violence] on the big screen is deplorable. And to praise such film as brilliant is totally irresponsible." Benson, who had marched in demonstrations against William Friedkin's *Cruising* (the film was released in February 1980, *Dressed to Kill* in July) was shocked by the accusation: "I don't think *Dressed to Kill* tried to depict murder either as attractive or anything to emulate."

WAVAW's Stephanie Rones, who at the time worked with victims of domestic violence, said the film preyed on the fear of women who go out at night. "The title of the movie itself suggests women bring on rape by how they dress, that women can be dressed to be killed." According to Rones, another objectionable scene showed Liz Blake being harassed by a group of Black men on the subway. A Black woman, Rones believed this problematic scene perpetuated the myth that Black men want to rape white women. She continued, "and Angie Dickinson [fantasizes] about being raped. That women subconsciously want to be raped is a myth also. With rising rape statistics, there are still these kinds of movies. Another point. Most violent crimes are committed by heterosexual men; this one shows a transsexual man. It's only for prurience's sake. The movie represents aggressive and vicious models to mean that women are to be used violently."

While encouraging a boycott of the film, Rones said that the organization was not advocating censorship and that there were men in the group, all coming to the defense of women being the target of violence in film. Angie Dickinson defended the film by saying that denying such facts as violence against women was more damaging than showing it on screen. As for the notion that the film might influence individuals to commit violence against women, Dickinson claimed at the time that "if you have violence in your soul, you'll get it out one way or another. Seeing a movie won't make a difference."

BRIAN DE PALMA: It was terrible, because you get attacked as a misogynist and, you get into these horrendous round tables at press junkets where interviewers come after you. You come off as a woman-hater, which is never how I felt about the way I made these movies. I always said endlessly that women protagonists in suspense movies work for me better because I like to photograph women more than men, and a woman in peril is, to me, more emotionally effective than Rambo in peril. That's just a simple convention of the genre. Violence is just an aesthetic tool, but it made no difference.

ANGIE DICKINSON: I got questioned about it, they said don't you think you were exploited, and I said, "Use another word. Don't use the word exploited." "What do you mean by exploited?" I said, "It's a story of a woman who is vulnerable, and aroused, went off with somebody, and got killed."

NANCY ALLEN: Liz Blake, in comparison to Kate, is a very liberated woman. She's her own person. She had a plan and was a modern woman. Obviously, she probably had some intimacy issues . . . Why doesn't she have a relationship with a man? You don't really know that about her, but again, I thought she was a very strong, great character. The film was attacked by women's groups before it even opened and before many saw it. Some of it was rumors, which in turn helped the movie; it brought a lot of interest and a lot of press that maybe the film wouldn't have gotten if not for the controversy over it. And then, some critics called Brian a "Hitchcock rip-off."

Most reviews attacked De Palma for being a Hitchcock copycat, a "scavenger" of his vaults; Rex Reed in the *New York Observer* wrote that "De Palma has obviously been so influenced by Hitchcock that his work is impotent." Vincent Canby, however, declared in the *New York Times* that what De Palma pulled off was no imitation—it's a film "made by someone who has studied the master and learned, in addition to style, something far more important, that is, a consistent point of view. Among other things, the De Palma camera appears to have an intelligence of its own." And Kael also came to De Palma's defense: "If he has learned a great deal from Hitchcock (and Welles and Godard and Polanski and Scorsese and many others), he has altered its nature with a funky sensuousness that is all his own."

MAD magazine homed in on the parallels with their spoof *Undressed to Kill*—with the reveal that the killer is, in fact, Anthony Perkins, who killed because of the similarities between the film and his own, *Psycho*. And De Palma (renamed Brian De Trauma) receives a Hitchcockian cameo appearance as the man in the shower assaulting Kate.

BRIAN DE PALMA: I was always very open about my use of Hitchcock's language when I made movies because it's the best that exists. If you're working in this genre, Hitchcock's done it all. So, you're inevitably going to use some of his ideas, but you can build upon them, using your own way of telling stories, and your own characters. Once I got labeled as the Hitchcock imitator, people would automatically make comparisons—even when there was no relation, and when it came up in interviews, saying that the shower scene in *Carrie* was inspired by *Psycho*, for instance . . . I have a great respect for Hitchcock, and I also always felt he was being represented inaccurately for most of his career as a sort of glib British entertainer until the French started to take him seriously in the sixties. But it was a very difficult time for me because, when you're put in a defensive position, you never come off particularly well.

NANCY ALLEN: *Dressed to Kill* propelled me into stardom. I didn't necessarily feel it at the time, but it felt great to be part of another wonderful movie.

ANGIE DICKINSON: When I saw the movie at a screening, I just could not believe how good the movie was. That still doesn't ever mean it's going to be a success critically or box office–wise. But I thought it was a marvel, way beyond any expectations. We really felt we had a good movie. I loved Ralf Bode's photography. He had done *Saturday Night Fever* [1977] and I thought he did a brilliant job on this. I knew it looked great, but it took a while to feel that it was a classic.

There's no doubt that Kate Miller is the best work I've ever done. She was not like me at all and that's why I particularly love it. It's not Angie having a good old time, it's Angie acting. And I'm proud of it and I had no idea while Brian was directing, that he was doing so wonderfully by me. I don't know if he knew I had it in me. I really didn't know I would be that good, playing someone so different from me. I could not have done it without Brian's insistent direction every step of the way. I kept the gloves that Kate Miller wore for no reason other than it was a wonderful memory.

A COMPLICATED LEGACY

There can be no final words on *Dressed to Kill*–the fascinating aspect of the movie is that it continues to divide scholars, critics, and people at large. Rarely does a film get such opposite reactions, even as recently as the past ten years with some, on one hand, calling it a masterpiece and on the other, complete trash ... It is, at once, embraced and rejected almost equally.

I am not trying to influence or change anyone's mind, to judge specific views, or to win an argument because there can be none, particularly when it comes to gender identity—I aimed, however, to highlight what I believe are unique and remarkable artistic and cinematic values, outside any sociological commentary. In her essay "The Unintentional Empathy of Brian De Palma's *Dressed to Kill*," Jessica Crets captured this sentiment well while acknowledging the troubling aspect of the film when she said, "It's hard to watch a movie that represents people like you as mentally ill serial killers taking revenge on women for something they had nothing to do with. But there's a compelling metaphor about denying people from being who they are buried under this stylish thriller."

In that respect and insofar as it continues to provoke discussion, *Dressed to Kill* has continued to evolve. For instance, and thankfully, there are more positive portrayals of transgender people in films and television series now, though we still have far to go; back in 1980, there were none.

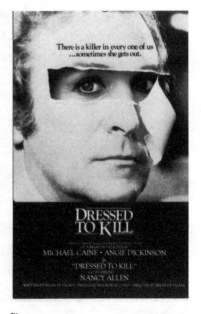

Alternate one-sheet posters designed for the film.

I came out as a gay man around *Dressed to Kill*—I didn't understand why and how the film instilled confidence in me. Regardless of the outcome of Kate's picking up a stranger in a museum, the act felt familiar and relatable . . . and, yes, thrilling, and sexy. Yet, what happens to Kate was a warning, and I never forgot her—she may even have saved my life. I also loved Liz Blake's honesty, humor, and sexual freedom. And I found myself having empathy for Bobbi/Elliott, lying on the ground, wounded, and crying after being shot. I equated Elliott's struggle to my own, and my inability to come out and fully embrace who I was at the time.

Dressed to Kill was part of an awakening, not only in identification but also in the artistry involved with the design and making of the film because the difference I felt is present in every single character in *Dressed to Kill*. All of them are outcasts, victims of society. It's about all of us.

THE
POWER

De Palma's films are powerful. His casts deliver powerful performances, and he had power at the box office. Yes, *Carrie* and *The Fury* are about psychic powers, but they are also about human powers, which people may wield to destroy or control.

Sissy Spacek is Carrie in De Palma's iconic adaptation of the novel by Stephen King.

CARRIE

—— **1976** ——

It's that experience in high school of being the alien; everybody feels they are an outsider. It's the adolescent experience: I'm Carrie, everybody hates me. I'm awkward, I'm slow, I'm stupid, I can't do things in sports. And then, of course, it had the telekinetic element.

—BRIAN DE PALMA
(DIRECTOR)

THE STORY: Carrie White (Sissy Spacek) is a total stranger to life. An outcast in her small-town high school, she lives with an oppressive and fanatical evangelist mother Margaret White (Piper Laurie). But we learn Carrie has telekinetic powers after she gets her period in front of her classmates in the locker room showers. She is frightened by the sight of the blood running between her legs, and all the other girls proceed to humiliate her. Sue Snell (Amy Irving), one of Carrie's classmates, feels guilty for laughing at the poor girl, and asks her boyfriend, Tommy Ross (William Katt), to take Carrie to the prom. Chris Hargensen (Nancy Allen), on the other hand, becomes Carrie's worst enemy after the incident causes her to be barred from the prom ticket by gym teacher Miss Collins (Betty Buckley). With the complicity of her dumb boyfriend, Billy Nolan (John Travolta), Chris plans to rig the election and to pour a bucket of pig's blood over Carrie when she and Tommy are on stage. Despite her mother's protests, Carrie goes to the prom, where she has a sweet and dreamlike time with Tommy—until Chris unleashes the blood. The bucket hits Tommy, killing him instantly. With her powers, Carrie transforms the prom into a circus of death, slaughtering everyone, including Miss Collins. Chris and Billy escape, but Carrie causes their car to flip over and burst into flames. Back home, she is confronted by her mother who believes she must kill her sinful daughter; she stabs her but Carrie responds with the force of her powers and impales the mad woman with kitchen utensils. Ultimately, the house collapses, and both Carrie and her mom are swallowed into the ground. Having survived the slaughter, Sue visits the pit where Carrie's home used to be. As she lays down a bouquet of flowers, Carrie's bloody hand bursts through stones, grabbing Sue, who wakes up in her bed. It was just a nightmare, but as she is consoled by her mother, Sue knows Carrie will never leave her.

Stephen King began writing his first published novel, *Carrie*, while teaching high school English and living with his family in a trailer park in Maine. A few pages in, he tossed them into the trash. Later, his wife, Tabitha King, found and read the pages and told him it was a promising start. The resulting novel launched both the author's literary and cinematic careers. Along with the subsequent film adaptation version directed by Brian De Palma, Stephen King officially became a brand name. *Carrie* is forever part of our culture. It has been quoted, parodied, and copied in films and TV shows. It became more than a horror classic, and the book was adapted several times, including as a musical, on and off Broadway. Few stories can claim so many lives.

In his introduction to the 1999 paperback edition, Stephen King recounted his road to the writing of *Carrie*. He had wanted to explore a story about a girl with telekinetic powers ever since high school, when he read a *Life* magazine article about a presumably haunted suburban home. Initially, poltergeists were suspected but, after examination, the occurrences were linked to something far more unexpected: a teenage girl. When she lived in the house, objects—particularly religious ones—were known to fly around. The article suggested puberty triggered the troubled girl's abilities.

As King began writing in the laundry corner of his family's trailer, he also recalled two girls he had known in school. Tina White (an alias King used to hide her real identity) went to Durham Elementary School with the author. In King's own words, she was the type of kid who had a KICK ME HARD sign on her back. She had black hair with a red hairband and wore the same clothes every day—a white sleeveless blouse and a black skirt that fell "gracelessly" to the lower part of her shins. One year, after Christmas, Tina showed up with an entirely new look; everyone—except King—teased her. Later in life, Tina hanged herself in her cellar. (In another account, King claims Tina shot herself after the birth of her second child.)

The other girl, Sandra Irving (also an alias), occasionally suffered from epileptic seizures and, like Tina, wore modest old-fashioned clothes. She lived about a mile and a half from the little house in which King grew up, with no father in the picture—only a mother and a large German shepherd named Cheddar Cheese. King did some work at their house when he was sixteen and was struck by the sight of a gigantic crucifix on the living room wall, suggesting the family was fervently religious. Sandy died as an adult from an epileptic seizure. (King also once met an intensely religious woman in a Laundromat and wondered, at the time, what her children would be like.) These encounters fueled King's imagination, resulting in the novel.

After the book was finished, it sat for about a month. King still thought it was not good. But then he mailed it to his friend Bill Thompson, an editor at Doubleday. Three weeks later, he received a letter from Thompson saying *Carrie* might work, but the last fifty pages needed to be rewritten (they had been rushed). King rewrote according to suggestions and, soon thereafter, he was officially a first-time novelist. He was paid $2,500—a moderately high amount at the time—for the hardcover, which sold thirteen thousand copies. The paperback, for which King received a life-changing $200,000, climbed the bestseller list with a million copies in its first run, and another four million after the film's release in 1976. The movie tie-in edition proclaimed, "If *The Exorcist* (1973) made you shudder, *Carrie* will make you scream."

In her introduction to the 1991 edition of *Carrie*, Tabitha King dug deeper into the meaning of her husband's novel from a profound—and at times humorous—woman's perspective.

She highlights that Steve had taken some criticism in university writing seminars and workshops over his female characters. With *Carrie*, he was trying to write about women, even though, Tabitha King wrote, he "was almost certainly unprepared to discover, upon marrying me, that once a month, 'wifey' turned into a were-mommy." She wrote that the success of the novel changed their lives forever, "and who'd ever have guessed so much could come out of some girl having trouble with her period."

The power and timeless nature of *Carrie* lie in two themes that resonate both in the novel and the film: being different and bullying.

But above all, *Carrie* is a devastating tale about adolescent terror, the discovery of sexuality, and a modern twist on the Cinderella story. Carrie White is a martyr, cursed in blood from beginning to end. She is "stoned" by tampons when she has her first period in front of her classmates and ends up drenched in pig's blood at "the ball." *Carrie* is the first of a cycle of King's characters, both blessed and cursed by powers that ultimately destroy them—think Johnny Smith in *The Dead Zone* (1983), who wakes up from a coma with a newfound power of precognitive visions by touching people, or teenage Arnie in *Christine* (1983), the male version of *Carrie*, who becomes possessed by the spirit of his car's previous dead owner and takes revenge on the school bullies and others.

FROM THE NOVEL TO SCRIPT

Another important aspect of *Carrie* is the adaptation of the now-classic novel by Stephen King to a script by Lawrence D. Cohen. In the early seventies, Cohen held several jobs, including as a theater and film critic for the *Hollywood Reporter* and an assistant to famed Broadway choreographer/director Michael

THE DE PALMA DECADE

Bennett. Needing money, Cohen went to work for legendary television talk show host and producer David Susskind as a reader. The first week on the job, Cohen found an original script by a high school teacher from the Midwest called *Alice Doesn't Live Here Anymore* (1974); Martin Scorsese eventually made the project. Cohen also discovered the manuscript for *Carrie*. He loved the material but could never convince David Susskind to make the film.

Cohen eventually moved to California, and through a friend, interviewed for a job with the producer Paul Monash, who had a deal at 20th Century Fox.

LAWRENCE D. COHEN (SCREENWRITER): The last thing I wanted to do was work for another producer, but I took the meeting. Just as I was heading down the hall, he called out to say he'd forgotten to mention that he'd just optioned a new, as yet unpublished novel called—wait for it—*Carrie*. A believer in destiny and feeling like I'd been hit by a lightning bolt, I turned around and immediately accepted the job.

When the first script Monash had commissioned was delivered, he didn't think it was good and was certain to be rejected by the studio. Cohen volunteered to write a new draft from scratch. Asked by Monash if he knew how to write a screenplay, Cohen confidently replied "yes," and went home to start writing.

LAWRENCE D. COHEN: When I finished my script, Monash gave me his enthusiastic approval and turned it in to the Fox brass. [After reading it] the studio wasn't interested in developing it any further; what's more, they'd immediately put it into turnaround. We were done at Fox. Luckily, Marcia Nasatir, the West Coast book agent who had optioned the film rights to Monash, had just been hired by United Artists and named the first woman vice president at a major film studio. She immediately offered us a home there.

For several reasons, when Brian came in, we went leaner and meaner in terms of what would ultimately emerge on the screen. But it was important to me that [Stephen] like it . . . That's just something that's a tenet of mine as a screenwriter when I do adaptations. I'm hopeful that the novelist will both give me latitude to change things yet be happy with the end result.

The novel—which described Carrie White as a solid, beefy girl with a pudding face and a body covered with pimples—was genre-bending, not a straight-on narrative. It reads almost like nonfiction, complete with newspaper articles, book excerpts (including a memoir written by the sole survivor, Sue Snell), interview transcripts, and testimonies. King uses these accounts to further build out the world of his novel. For instance, we learn from a newspaper clipping of a rain of stones at the White house when Carrie was three. Or a fictitious book, *The Shadow Exploded: Documented Facts and Specific Conclusions Derived from the Case of Carietta White*, presents "facts" about telekinesis as well as a deeper history of Margaret White's troubled life.

It's an effective device, one that was also used by Michael Crichton for his 1969 breakthrough novel, *The Andromeda Strain*, and by Lawrence Sanders in *The Anderson Tapes* (1970), where literal transcripts of recorded conversations and other materials led the narrative. For fans of the film who haven't read the novel of Carrie, it's an exciting and intricate exploration of the same story.

GIVING *CARRIE* A CINEMATIC VOICE

BRIAN DE PALMA: I really fought to direct *Carrie*. A friend, a writer, told me about the novel; I remember going around to a bookstore on Eighth Street, and buying the hardback, reading it, and saying, "Wow, I could really make a terrific movie out of this." It finally went over to UA, and it was because of Mike Medavoy, who ran the studio and knew me, that I got the job.

As I remember, the screenplay was in pretty good shape, but we had to make things smaller than they were in the novel. My first idea was, well, we can't destroy the town, let's just destroy the high school, not only for economical reasons, but because high school symbolizes the adolescent world. And then there were a lot of things that came to me, like the end sequence, which we figured out when we got to it.

Carrie not only gave Stephen King a voice that resonates to this day, but it also provided Brian De Palma the platform to explore an emotional, primal, and compassionate tale told in blood. It also ties in with themes that echo throughout several films of the De Palma decade. Carrie is split, both victim and monster, angel and devil. The notion of sexuality is equally divided between discovery and repression, guilt and manipulation, punishment and death. The story also provided De Palma with a canvas to continue to flex his visual language. Split diopter shots merging foreground and background underline Carrie's desire to connect, and split screens define the horror and chaos at the prom.

Mothers were very central to Hitchcock's cinema. Equally, the towering mother figure in *Carrie* is also a perfect thematic fold in to this era of De Palma's works. In *Sisters*, Grace's mom harasses her about marriage and has no faith in her journalistic career; in *Dressed to Kill*, Kate is a conflicted mom and wife, and also complains to her shrink about her own mother coming in from Florida and ruining her birthday; and in *The Fury*, we will see how Gillian's mother is always traveling and doesn't understand her daughter's fear of making people bleed. Even in De Palma's semi-autobiographical *Home Movies* (the nonthriller/horror film of this prodigious decade), an eccentric mother is also quite present. But Mrs. White is, by far, the most lethal of all the mothers of this period and plays a central role in the destruction of her daughter.

NEW DISCOVERIES AND RETURNING TALENT

By the time Brian De Palma got to *Carrie*, he had already proven his incredible eye for casting. He is almost unrivaled in his discovery of many interesting actors as well as directing powerful performances from previous generations of talent. Most people forget that *Carrie* received Oscar nominations for Sissy Spacek and Piper Laurie—a rare and remarkable achievement for a film originally positioned as a Halloween B-horror movie. Through *Carrie*, De Palma would introduce (or re-introduce, in the case of Piper Laurie) a stunning assortment of actors.

BRIAN DE PALMA: George Lucas and I were both looking for unknowns, and because we were looking at everybody, we opened up the casting to any kid that wanted to come and try out for the parts in *Carrie* and *Star Wars* [1977]. It took weeks and weeks; we sat together and, basically, went through hundreds of boys and girls.

I knew Sissy because she was [production designer] Jack Fisk's girlfriend, and, ultimately, his wife. She had helped paint sets on *Phantom of the Paradise*. She had done a couple of films, but I had my eye set for another young actress I had

Clockwise from top left: Amy Irving as Sue Snell, William Katt as Tommy Ross, Nancy Allen as Chris Hargensen, and Betty Buckley as Miss Collins.

seen in a movie where she gets an abortion [Betsy Slade in *Our Time*, 1974]; she was very touching and moving, and I thought this girl was perfect for the part.

SISSY SPACEK ("CARRIE WHITE"): All of the young actors in LA wanted to be in this film. And I was feeling a little weird because I was only testing for one role. So, I didn't have as big a shot as everybody else did of getting in the film. I got this commercial and it just happened to be on the same day as the test.

I called Brian, told him about the commercial, and there was a long silence on the telephone, and he said, "Do the commercial." I hung up and it just made me so mad.

BRIAN DE PALMA: But Sissy thought about it, came in, and did the test.

SISSY SPACEK: I had re-read the book the day before the screen test and I think I rubbed Vaseline in my hair. I found some old sailor suit that my mother had made for me in seventh grade, I took the hem out of it, and I was really into it. I was feeling very sorry for myself, which was perfect for the character. So, when I went into the test the next morning, I don't think I even washed my face. [The hair and make-up team] saw me come in, they just ran for me because I just looked so awful and, of course, I told them no. I went into a corner and felt so bad at that point because I knew I was not Brian's favorite. And that worked for me, I just decided I was going to get it.

JACK FISK (PRODUCTION DESIGNER): Because I was working on the film, the next day I went to see the results of all the tests. And Sissy came on and just knocked people's socks off. She was waiting for me out in the parking lot in the car, because she was anxious to see how it went.

SISSY SPACEK: And he came running out and said, "You got the part. Ask for whatever you want," which was very little!

BRIAN DE PALMA: Casting a movie like *Carrie* has a lot to do with just your ability to spot young talent, and then give them a good part, like I did with Bob De Niro in *The Wedding Party* [1969], *Greetings*, and *Hi, Mom!* We spent a long time casting these roles, and I think we got the best group of young actors around at the time. They connected with the audience, and many of them went on to have long careers. I remember pairing them up, switching them around, trying improvisations, and, of course, they were very eager to try anything I could dream up, basically.

They were playing stereotypes of your high school, mythological figures. Amy Irving's character, Sue, has everything: She's the smart and good-looking girl. She's got the good-looking guy, the athlete with the golden curls, played by William Katt. And then we have the dark side. We have Nancy Allen as Chris, playing the manipulative, sexy villain, basically, and John Travolta playing the numbskull who gets manipulated by Chris. And the actors made such interesting creations off these stereotypes and gave them warmth, heart, and emotions.

AMY IRVING ("SUE SNELL"): I had never made a film before. I had grown up in the theater and geared my whole life toward being a stage actress. When I finished drama school in London, I came back to Los Angeles, where my parents were, and I immediately got an agent and started making the rounds while doing a production of *Romeo and Juliet.*

The screen test for *Carrie* was first, and Brian offered me the role, but then I had my screen test for *Star Wars*. It was a very difficult script—we're talking about R2-D2 and C-3PO. Brian sat me down and worked on the audition [for *Star Wars*] with me. And I said, "Why are you doing this? If I do *Star Wars*, I won't be able to do *Carrie*." And he said, "Amy, *Star Wars* is going to be a huge film. I think if you get it, you should do it." And I said, "You don't want me?" He goes, "No, I do. I want you. But I just think this would be amazing for you, and you'd be great as Princess Leia." I did not get the role but what a wonderful consolation prize to be in Brian De Palma's *Carrie*.

NANCY ALLEN ("CHRIS HARGENSEN"): Chris is the only role that I read for *Carrie*. The day before the audition, I stayed up all night to read both the script and the novel. For some reason, I understood Chris. I sympathized with her and could see that she was feeling like Carrie, but she was the type that would lash out. And it's just so much fun to get to play mean, and hateful, something you don't get to do in real life.

When I first met Brian De Palma that day at the casting session, I just immediately felt at ease. He was part of what we were doing. He'd say, try this, try that. I felt comfortable exploring and taking risks with the character. I didn't really know who he was. I knew the name sounded familiar and I had seen *Phantom of the Paradise*. I was just very excited to be there.

WILLIAM KATT ("TOMMY ROSS"): In the early seventies, I was playing all kinds of entertainment fields. I was in a band; I was working in the theater largely. I had been doing a few seasons at South Coast Repertory. I had worked down at the Mark Taper Forum, and I was bouncing all over the place, getting periodic day gigs, doing some voice-over work or being a day player on episodic shows. I first met Brian De Palma and George Lucas during their shared casting session. I read for Luke Skywalker, which I didn't get. I came back specifically for the role of Tommy, and I had a third audition where they paired us up. I remember doing a scene with Amy and another with Sissy. Amy and I had been dating so that didn't hurt that we were going to play boyfriend and girlfriend in the film.

P.J. SOLES ("NORMA"): I came out to LA, and it was just a magical thing that one of the first auditions I went on was this dual audition. I went in and I just remember, right away, Brian looking at me. I could just sort of tell that he liked me. And then George Lucas was just kind of stern-faced. Brian turned to him and said, "I'll put this one on my list."

BETTY BUCKLEY ("MISS COLLINS"): I had met De Palma when I went on an audition for *Phantom of the Paradise*. I was in my mid-twenties [and] a very serious young actress in town. I had only ever really wanted to be a theater actress. I never thought much about Hollywood. But I had some wonderful agents, and they sent me on this audition. By then, I thought Hollywood people were arrogant and pompous. So, I walked in with an attitude. And De Palma was intrigued by that, which I thought was amusing. He didn't cast me in *Phantom*, but he came to see me in *Pippin* on Broadway, and then he came to the acting class I taught. Eventually, he called me in to loop minor characters in *Phantom* and his next film, *Obsession*. I had this ability to do voices. I realized that Brian was getting into this pattern of casting somebody who looked right for the part but didn't have any real acting skills. And I told him, "No more looping." Months later, he called me for dinner; he gave me [the novel] *Carrie*, and said he wanted me for the gym teacher. It seemed like a small part, but I said yes. Later, I got the script, and the part was much bigger; it was a fabulous role. I was so touched by it. I just sat in my living room and cried. He had made this gift to me; there had been such a progression to our understanding of one another, at a time when nobody in Hollywood would have ever thought of me for anything. If it hadn't been for De Palma, I would have never done a movie.

BRIAN DE PALMA: The idea of Piper Laurie came from Marcia Nasatir. I had always been an admirer of Laurie, and I thought this was an interesting idea. I met her and told her how I thought the part should be played, and she amazed everybody.

PIPER LAURIE ("MARGARET WHITE"): I'd done *The Hustler* [1961] and I retired for fifteen years until I was asked to do *Carrie*. Fifteen years. To say I was bored with acting isn't quite accurate, but I was kind of fed up. It didn't seem very important. The Vietnam War had started and civil rights movement, and I was getting offers of the same part I did in *The Hustler*. It just seemed much more interesting to retire and live in upstate New York in Woodstock . . . When *Carrie* came my way, truthfully, I wasn't that enthusiastic about it. I no longer had an agent, but a wonderful woman who had been my agent years before called and said, "I have a script here, I'm going to send it up." So, I read it, and I just didn't get it. I was talking to my husband [critic Joe Morgenstern] that evening and he said, "You know, Brian De Palma has a comedic approach to just about everything he does," and I thought oh, that's the secret. I re-read it and I saw it was a satire, so I took the train into New York City to meet Brian De Palma.

BETTY BUCKLEY: I loved the role of Margaret White, and I am a great admirer of Piper Laurie. But I wanted to play that part so badly! I wasn't quite old enough for it yet but that was the kind of acting that I had aspired to be able to do, to play crazy people. Her performance was wonderful. So, I was really excited to get the opportunity to grow from playing Miss Collins to play Margaret White in the musical stage version (1988) of *Carrie* a few years later.

BRIAN DE PALMA: The cast was just a dream. They were committed and devoted to trying everything. They were afraid of nothing; they would do anything. It was one of those great cast experiences.

THE OPENING VOLLEY

LAWRENCE D. COHEN: In the original script there was a prologue to the film, which I was enormously proud of, and it was really one of the pieces that was in the collage of the book that ended up making its way into at least the script form. It was a sequence featuring a woman named Stella Horan, who had been a teenager when Carrie was a child. She looked back and remembered an episode when she was sunbathing next door wearing a bikini. Margaret White always referred to her as the "Whore of Babylon," and little Carrie, at six or seven years old, came by in the bushes and peered out at Stella in a bikini and was fascinated by her "dirty pillows," a reference to breasts. Margaret caught Carrie talking to this "Whore of Babylon" and started to scream and rant for her to come inside. She was shaking and screaming at Carrie and, as the child was begging for her to stop, out of the perfectly blue sky, came a hail of stones. It was a great idea and a wonderful prologue.

BRIAN DE PALMA: Originally, the film opened with a flash-back, which we shot and, ultimately, cut out. All I remember of it is Sissy Spacek as a young girl, looking through the fences of the house, her mom screaming at her, and Carrie brings on a hailstorm. Instead, it felt stronger to set up this world of adolescent failure and trauma, with Carrie being the butt of all the girls' anger, which starts on the volleyball court, and moves into the shower scene.

AMY IRVING: People always think that the shower sequence is the opening sequence of the film. But I would like to point out that the opening sequence of the film is a volleyball game, which took us so long to get the ball to keep going over the net! But then, yes, that sequence in the locker room, it's an amazingly erotic, beautiful sequence.

De Palma introduces us to the world of *Carrie* with a bird's-eye view on a volleyball game, as if we, the viewers, descend upon Carrie as she blows a shot at hitting the ball. Norma hits her with her baseball cap and Chris tells her to "eat shit."

P.J. SOLES: I was just supposed to go, "Carrie!!" and I said, "Don't blow it, Carrie. Hit it!" And I then hit her over the head with my baseball hat, which I wore in every scene. I had brought it to the audition and Brian had asked me to keep it for the film. In fact, the first thing he asked me when he saw me on the set was, "Did you bring your red baseball hat?"

Following the game, we are put in a voyeuristic position, in the girls' locker room, reminiscent of the opening of the game show in *Sisters*. It is both a sensuous and misleading introduction. Like the beginning of *Dressed to Kill*, De Palma lures us in as the camera moves in slow motion amongst the girls and ends on Carrie, still soaping up in the shower. Suddenly there's this strange angle on her as she drops the soap to the shower floor and blood drips between her legs. De Palma switches out of slow motion, removing the dreamlike quality of the moment as we lock onto the central motif of the film: a hand drenched in blood (it will return when pig's blood is dropped on Carrie at the prom, and it is the same bloody hand that grabs Sue at the end of the film). But in this moment, not only is Carrie seeing something she can't understand and immediately associating it with pain, but it is also a possible premonition that she's been cursed with blood, as her fanatical mother tells her later. Spacek's acting in this scene is incredible, not only courageous in that she is naked, but in the way she walks toward her classmates in horror and panic. She reaches out and grabs Sue Snell while she pleads for help. In a way, Carrie is choosing Sue, and that link will remain for the rest of the film. It's important that, from this point forward, neither Sue nor Chris ever directly interact with Carrie. But they're all part of her destiny, with Sue setting her up with Tommy and Chris orchestrating the bloody prom plot.

The crucial character of the compassionate gym teacher, Miss Collins (renamed from Ms. Desjardin in the book), is also introduced in this scene. Carrie grabs her by her shorts, leaving a smear of blood on them, and screams until Miss Collins slaps her to calm her down. Carrie's screams cause a lightbulb to burst, the first hint of the "power" that comes with anger and fear. Accompanying the moment are a few notes from Bernard Herrmann's score to *Psycho*—in which Marion Crane (Janet Leigh) is murdered in a shower! The homage is appropriately placed and used throughout the film, in lieu of sound design, to signify Carrie's powers.

The entire sequence conveys, at once, so many feelings, calling on taboos and something as intimate as a girl's first menstrual period, as well as cruelty and bullying. The cycle of blood has begun...

AMY IRVING: We all sat at lunch before we shot that, and nobody spoke. At that point, it hadn't been decided who was naked, what stage of dress each person was, so there was a lot of inhibitions going on. I knew I was already at my locker, so I felt

Sissy Spacek in the deleted opening scene, in which she played a much younger version of Carrie.

a little safer and wasn't as terrified as everyone else. But what came out of it, is so beautiful, especially for a horror movie.

SISSY SPACEK: It's interesting, that shower scene. Of course, I worried about it and wanted it to work, wanted it to be authentic, wanted to be able to lose myself in it and not think about being naked in front of the world. Brian and I had talked and there were certain parameters that he promised he wouldn't go beyond. I had a great deal of faith and trust in him, and he honored those agreements that we had.

AMY IRVING: Brian storyboards everything. I didn't know what a storyboard was then, but I do remember his little figures and him showing me exactly what was going to happen in a specific sequence. It was very well planned out, very well-rehearsed, and there were no accidents. It was all in his head. And written out very carefully.

THE DE PALMA DECADE

NANCY ALLEN: The shower scene in *Carrie*, as I think back on it, was interesting because we shot it early in the movie. In fact, I think it was the first week. Everybody knew what we had to do because Brian had walked us through his storyboards. It was at a school in Redondo Beach, and it seems like we were just sitting around in our robes for maybe six hours while Brian was shooting Sissy in the shower. We were all really scared, but in a way, it allowed us to bond.

Everything was choreographed, moment by moment by moment. Brian was very sensitive, and it certainly made the rest of the film a lot easier to shoot.

BRIAN DE PALMA: Sissy, who was the greatest trooper of them all, had to do all this naked soaping of her body before any of the girls got into the shower. So, we spent days shooting slow-motion shots of Sissy completely naked, doing all these close-ups, and I allowed everyone to watch dailies. They thought, "If Sissy can do it, we can do it, too!"

PAUL HIRSCH (EDITOR): Brian knows that to surprise an audience successfully, you have to mislead them. The intent of the scene isn't revealed until the moment you choose to reveal it. You think you're watching a scene that's about sensuality, with soft dissolves, and beautiful music, and suddenly, we come to this angry scene, which is—in fact—the payoff of the volleyball scene, where all the girls are acting out the hostility they feel toward this girl.

SISSY SPACEK: I went to Brian, and I asked about the scene. He thought for a minute, and said, "It's like getting hit by a Mack truck." He obviously wanted shock, and I went to [my husband] Jack, who we had decided would be in the shower with me, putting the blood in my hand because that was going to be out of frame, and I'd bring it out to see it. And I said, "Jack, Brian said it would be like getting hit by a Mack truck, what's getting hit by a Mack truck like?"

JACK FISK: She didn't quite know how to make sense of it. But I, as a kid, had been run over by a car. So, I started telling her what it was like to be hit by a car. It was at Christmastime; I was looking around at Christmas lights and everything was happiness and then I saw a car coming and then it was veering away and suddenly it hit me, then I was like trapped underneath and couldn't get out. And she was able to use Brian's suggestion and my sort of visualization from having been through it and brought it to Carrie's reaction to finding blood coming out of her body.

SISSY SPACEK: When I'm playing that scene, I am walking down a road looking at the Christmas lights and when I see the blood in my hand is when he looks over and sees the car. It sounds very bizarre. She's taking a shower, and it's all so wonderful, and then she sees the headlights coming at her and so that's what I was thinking. That's what was going on in my mind during the shower scene, step by step. And it really worked because I had something in my head. The blood was the car hitting me. That was a real big breakthrough for me. I wasn't in the shower; I was looking at Christmas lights. One of the wonderful things about Brian was that he would always bring me in or bring the other actors so I could see what didn't work out and we could figure out what would work.

NANCY ALLEN: I remember shaking. It was very disturbing to shoot that scene. I can't even imagine how Sissy felt at that point.

BETTY BUCKLEY: Brian establishes an atmosphere of trust so that you can give a natural response and play a scene to its full completion.

REACHING A BOILING POINT

Following the shocking locker room scene, De Palma leads us into the actual story and the different characters while constantly reminding us of Carrie's mounting powers. We find Miss Collins discussing the event in the shower in the principal's office. Carrie is seated outside, waiting to be brought in. De Palma immediately enhances the moment by having Carrie and the principal's secretary in the same frame, in focus, by using the split diopter lens. It conveys the deep humiliation and claustrophobia Carrie is feeling. And, in a near-surreal moment and using a similar technique, the principal notices the blood on Miss Collins's shorts, and appears embarrassed, probably thinking she is having her period, perhaps without realizing it. And upon calling Carrie into the office, the principal keeps butchering her name, leading to another telekinetic outburst that sends an ashtray flipping to the floor.

BRIAN DE PALMA: The powers were always an extension of her emotions, and they came out of rage. That was always the way I thought it would work; it had to be an emotional response. She just couldn't be making things float across the room. It had to be something she didn't quite understand, until she gets to the prom where she is humiliated and controls her powers.

PAUL HIRSCH: Brian has always been interested in film technique. And one of the techniques that attracts him is the use of split screen. He liked the idea of juxtaposing images from one side of the screen to the other side of the screen. So, he used what is known as a split diopter lens in which you can focus on something close on one side and focus on something distant on the other side. The effect is you have, in a way, a built-in split screen. He used it in the principal's office. And, again, in the classroom sequences when Carrie's enamored with Tommy's poem.

In the first draft, as Carrie is on her way home, she is taunted by a boy on a bike. We hear her inner voice saying, "Fall off that bike, split your head, fall off!" Immediately before her encounter with the boy, Carrie was also having quick flashbacks of the shower scene and concentrated on a mental image of Chris Hargensen, which shattered and then exploded into a green light. The way it was shot, with the boy riding between trees, finds its origin in *Greetings*, where three actors walk between columns in downtown New York City. The camera is placed alternately

Carrie, on her way home, is taunted by a young boy (played by De Palma's nephew Cameron).

on either side of the trees or the columns, and De Palma creates another type of split image where there are, literally, two separate points of view. Paul Hirsch has often referred to De Palma as a graphic artist, essentially an illustrator, who always tries to create something visually dynamic. In this case, he builds suspense and anticipation that something is about to happen. Carrie has shattered a lightbulb and turned over an ashtray. She looks at the boy and throws him off his bike, with the same *Psycho*-like music underlining her powers. De Palma makes that switch—from Carrie able to affect objects to now, hurting someone. De Palma's young nephew Cameron plays the boy on the bike, with Betty Buckley dubbing him, saying, "Creepy Carrie, Creepy Carrie! Ha ha ha!"

BRIAN DE PALMA: I had months and months to prepare this movie, waiting to get the money to make it, wrestling over the budget. I was sitting in my apartment, I had all these billboards up; I started to draw my little cards, and had the whole movie, every shot on a card, on the wall, around me. I sat there for months, moving them around and working out the whole visual design of the movie. I can't really think of any movie that I conceptualized so strongly visually and had so much time to play with the visual design of it before I shot it. I remember cards on my breakfast table, on my lunch table, on the wall, and things like the use of split screen, and split diopter, and slow motion worked out like a musical score. That's why the film has a carefully designed look.

Both Piper Laurie as Carrie's mother, Margaret, and Sissy Spacek received Academy Award nominations for their roles.

TWO MOTHERS

Motherhood is the heart of the film's conflict and there's a documentary aspect to *Carrie*, about American society of the 1970s. Carrie's mom, Margaret White, visits Sue Snell's mother (Priscilla Pointer), clearly traveling door-to-door, spreading religious rants, and collecting donations. Mrs. White is shown as completely cut off from reality, whereas Mrs. Snell is introduced as she watches a couple arguing in a soap opera on TV and drinks what appears to be alcohol in the middle of the afternoon. Mrs. Snell wears pants, whereas Mrs. White—dressed in a color opposite her name—is in a black cape, dress, stockings, and shoes, almost looking like a witch. When Carrie's mom comments, "These are godless times," Sue's mom replies, "I'll drink to that!" The exchange brings their opposite world views to light. How the two women treat their daughters is also different. Sue is clearly embraced by her mom, but Carrie is tortured by hers and forced to pray for punishment inside a closet, staring at a statue of Saint Sebastian, pierced with arrows, with his eyes wide open.

AMY IRVING: It was Brian's idea to have my own mother [veteran actor Priscilla Pointer] play Sue's mother. He had done that in *Sisters*, with Jennifer Salt's mother. He really liked that dynamic and he knew my mom's work. *Carrie* was the first film we did together, and since then, we made several films together.

PRISCILLA POINTER ("MRS. SNELL"): I found that Brian having cast me as a mother, and specifically Amy's, allowed for whatever was human to come out. That was, for me, an easy part to play. The problem would have been if I started acting. But in that scene with Piper Laurie, my perception was that there was a tremendous intensity. What she was bringing to the role was not on the page.

BRIAN DE PALMA: We tried to make Carrie's home feel like it was infused with religious fever, very claustrophobic and rigid. I remember that tapestry of *The Last Supper* on the wall, and we used candles, crosses, arches, and, of course, the horrible closet.

JACK FISK: I'd gone to art school in Philadelphia, and I lived in a small three-room house. It was one room on top of the other and they used to refer to those as Father, Son, and Holy Ghost. I started thinking, "Boy, how perfect for this movie." The mother was a religious fanatic, and her house is patterned after the Holy Trinity. That's pretty much where we started. Her world was created to be visually completely different from the rest of the film, in contrast with the gymnasium and Amy Irving's house. But then we had to find an exterior. I saw this one house in Santa Paula that had a vacant lot next door, and it was just bizarre. I couldn't figure out what was wrong with it. And the more I looked at it, I realized it was asymmetrical; things didn't line up. I fell in love with it instantly.

In building the interiors of Carrie's house, we made a conscious effort to make it a sort of Gothic church. I went all over LA looking for interesting artifacts to put in the house. That's how I found *The Last Supper* rug, which hangs on the wall.

We built the closet. I made the little Saint Sebastian and put arrows in him. That image became so strong that Brian got the idea of having Carrie's mom be stabbed and die in the same position as the statue.

It's worth noting that the LGBTQ+ community has adopted Saint Sebastian for both the portrayal of his strong and attractive naked physique and "his defying tolerance for pain." American author and professor Richard A. Kaye wrote in 1996, "Contemporary gay men have seen in Sebastian at once a stunning advertisement for homosexual desire (indeed, a homoerotic ideal), and a prototypical portrait of tortured closet case." His words perfectly conjure that statue of Saint Sebastian in Carrie's closet—most literally, a closet full of repression and punishment. While *Carrie* was never intended to be a queer narrative, like the statue itself, it has since been embraced by members of the LGBTQ+ community.

In the first draft of the screenplay, there was a note to use David Bowie's "Changes" while Carrie was in the closet. In the novel, as well as the first draft of the script, Margaret White kept a different object inside the closet: "the statue of a man sitting on a huge flame-colored throne with a trident in one hand . . .

[He had a] grinning face and the body of a man but had a spike tail and the head of a jackal."

After Carrie exits the closet and apologizes to her mom, she goes to her room, located in the attic—a place that generally symbolizes hidden and suppressed desires. She stares painfully at herself in a mirror, reflecting her own image and that of a drawing of Christ wearing a crown—made of thorns, but still alluding to the crown Carrie will soon wear at prom—pinned to her bedroom wall. Carrie then has another episode and shatters the glass. Her mother comes up and asks, "What was that noise?" Carrie dismisses her mom, and Mrs. White leaves. The camera pans to the mirror, magically pieced back together but clearly cracked, with the split image of Christ with Carrie, as though she's reflecting on the shattered image of her own faith.

BRIAN DE PALMA: You must thank the actresses for pulling this off. Sissy's playing the miserable, tortured, abused child of a religious nutcase; and both actresses brought a tremendous amount of reality and humanity to these characters. Piper is, at times, almost comical, but also quite real. Very difficult to do and to make believable without the whole thing falling apart. They're both very instinctual actresses. I remember having Piper on the set, and I would look into those eyes, and I would think, "What is this woman thinking? I don't have a clue." And then she would do a scene, and I'd be amazed every time. She had a very odd sense of humor and, to this day, when I run into her, we just smile at each other.

SISSY SPACEK: It's all over the top. But Piper was so amazing because she came in and just filled up that character with such power and it was just mind-boggling. She inflated that role. She filled it, so it was such fun to do battle with her, and to meet that power, no matter what we gave each other, it was a dance.

PIPER LAURIE: I didn't think of her as an evil person at all, but as innocent, someone who was just passionate about her child, and who wanted to save her child. As far as my look is concerned, in the description of the character, she had hair that was tightly pulled back into a bun, and I had assumed that's what I would do. Ordinarily, I never pull my hair back; I always just washed it and let it dry, and it was out, like you saw it in the movie. We were rehearsing and Jack Fisk saw me standing in the kitchen, surrounded by some sort of archway and he said, "Brian, come take a look; that's the way she should wear her hair in the film." I thought it was perfect. I won't have to worry about anything else; it'll be simple. It was pretty much agreed that she would wear dark clothes, except later in the film when Sissy comes back after the prom, I wore white satin; it was very feminine. As for the quality of Margaret White's voice, it wasn't anything that I consciously was aware of while I was doing it or something I prepared. It simply came out of the emotion of the moment.

SISSY SPACEK: *The Miracle Worker* [1962] was always a favorite film of mine. When I read the Stephen King novel, I got to the scene where she's dragging her into the closet, I thought of Helen Keller as played by Patty Duke. And so that inspired me and her just kicking and screaming, being like a child, that was what was in my mind during that scene.

In the first draft of the screenplay, prior to Mrs. White coming home, there was a scene where Carrie experimented with her abilities by moving her brush. Apparently De Palma shot—but deleted—a scene where Carrie removed a box from underneath her bed in which she kept her poetry, the fabric that she would eventually use to make her dress, a picture of Tommy Ross, and a snapshot of her father. Carrie also had a radio, which she keeps hidden from her mother. In the scene, the camera panned around the room, according to Sissy Spacek, in similar fashion to the dance sequence, with the camera doing a 360-degree movement.

DETENTION

De Palma has a very powerful approach to Miss Collins's speech, berating the girls for their behavior toward Carrie. It's a crucial moment during which there's clear tension with Chris when Miss Collins tells her to spit out her gum. "Where should I put it, Miss Collins?" asks Chris. "You can choke on it for all I care, just get it out of your mouth," Miss Collins replies, and then explains how the girls did a really "shitty" thing to Carrie, completely ignoring that the girl has feelings. But, of course, they're too busy thinking about their dates and the prom. As punishment, Miss Collins offers up her unique form of detention. De Palma switches his approach here, invoking comedy as the girls are forced to work out. The music supports the humor, slowing down as the girls are getting exhausted. But, ultimately, Chris remains defiant and Miss Collins slaps her. Chris tries to get the support from the girls but is left on her own, and screams, "This isn't over. This isn't over by a long shot!"

BETTY BUCKLEY: Brian would tell me what response he wanted from the actress, whoever it was that he was shooting a close-up of, and he would then tell me to get that specific response from them. In retrospect, it was a little manipulative especially when you have an actress as terrific as Amy Irving.

AMY IRVING: Betty Buckley and I used to commute to Redondo Beach together and I would share all these intimate stories with her on the car rides. And in this scene, Brian wanted me to tear up because Sue is the one with a conscience. So, he had Betty, off camera, saying all kinds of things to me—and she chose intimate stories I had told her! I'm literally reacting to awful things Betty's telling me! [*Laughs*] I'm completely out of character. I could have come to it on my own—and by the time we made *The Fury*, Brian knew not to manipulate me again!

NANCY ALLEN: Even though we had the rehearsals, from my perspective, we were still getting to know each other, and everyone thought I was that horrible mean character. That detention scene was a big deal because it's really when you see these two characters of Chris Hargensen and Sue Snell going in a different direction. And Miss Collins is really the catalyst. Betty Buckley was the den mother in a way, she really did seem like this authority figure. She was a bit older and had a different kind of maturity, maybe from doing theater in New York. I loved acting with her because she'd get right in your face.

BETTY BUCKLEY: Brian had this idea that I needed to slap Sissy in the shower scene. My inclination was just to calm her down and comfort her. But Brian said, no, no, she's hysterical. And that made sense. So, then we got to the scene where I've given the girls detention and, Chris is being a jerk and challenges me. I did a phony slap and Brian told me, I really want you to slap her. Nancy was excited about it—and he made us do it repeatedly.

NANCY ALLEN: Betty slapped me what felt like thirty times. I guess Brian wanted a particular reaction. Betty was great and we worked it out. But I did end up with a bruised ear after that.

BETTY BUCKLEY: Her poor little face was just red, and she was starting to duck the blow, she was anticipating it. Brian took me aside and said, slap her from the left side. I felt I couldn't switch hands and was afraid to hurt Nancy. So, I went to her and told her not to duck the blow, I said, "Don't flinch!" And that was the take!

HIGH SCHOOL RIVALS

The break between Chris and the other girls in detention lays the groundwork for what's to come. Chris and her boyfriend, the dark-haired, beer-drinking moron Billy, versus Sue and Tommy, the blonde Adonis. The former pair wants to harm Carrie, the latter to help, but neither realizes that their combined efforts will destroy her.

Both Sue and Chris use sex to get what they want from their boyfriends. Sue is studying while Tommy is watching TV; he's

Motivated by guilt, Sue plays a crucial, yet unintentional, role in Carrie's demise at the prom.

Chris seduces her boyfriend Billy Nolan (John Travolta) to help carry out the evil plan against Carrie.

clearly been "punished"—no sex until he agrees to take Carrie to the prom. He finally agrees. And Chris manipulates Billy by giving him sex—which eventually leads Billy to slaughter a pig and, following Chris's orders, empty the blood from a bucket above the prom stage. The back and forth between those two opposite worlds leads to the inevitable and tragic event at the prom; it's the good intentions that provoke the evil outcome, and it's all powerfully connected through the curse of sex and blood.

NANCY ALLEN: The car scenes with John Travolta were shot over a period of several nights. The entire floor of the car was just covered in beer. It smelled horrible. John, unlike Betty, really wouldn't hit me. [*Laughs*] But he was so much in character, he really was that "stupid jerk." I had a purpose in the scene; who wouldn't want to seduce John Travolta? Whenever John and I did a scene, we were very funny. I had no idea we were such villains until I saw the movie, because we were the comic relief on the set.

JACK FISK: One of my assistants on my early films with Roger Corman was Bill Paxton, who then became an actor and director. But at the time, he was great in the art department; he was one of the few people who would stay up all night and work on stuff with me. And his hobby was making 8mm films and exploring downtown Los Angeles. When we were looking for interesting locations for the film, I'd always call Bill and say, "What have you got?" And he told me about Farmer John's, which is a meat processing plant in downtown LA. He contributed a lot to the film, and he was never credited because of union stuff. [He is informally acknowledged in the film with the PAXTON REALTY sign seen outside Carrie's home.]

NANCY ALLEN: I remember the pigs. It was pouring rain and we were drenched. It was the most bizarre place. The whole place had murals with pigs. And that night, they served us hot dogs. And we just looked at each other and I said, "I don't think I can eat this." And John said, "No, I can't either." We just drove out of there and ate someplace else.

DIRTY PILLOWS

Carrie and her mother share a candlelit dinner, sitting at opposite ends of the table, with the *Last Supper* tapestry between them. The image hints at Carrie's own demise rapidly approaching. When she tells her mom that Tommy has asked her to the prom, Margaret White's reaction is to throw a glass of water in her daughter's face. Coming from such a religious fanatic, the gesture invokes a baptism. The water puts out the candles and the rest of the scene is played out in darkness. The scene ends

"We'll pray," speaks Margaret while holding her daughter one last time before stabbing her, in sacrifice for her own sins in the film's climax.

with Carrie and Margaret discussing her powers. Margaret tells her that's the Devil working through her, like it did her father. But Carrie maintains her father ran away with another woman, and that "everybody knows it." She asserts that she is going to the prom, and her mother can't stop her. The scene is relatable and powerful because Carrie is trying to make her mother accept the fact that she is different. Speaking to the queer reading of the film, this scene might as well be a discussion about sexual orientation between a kid and their parents, and a mirror into the sad circumstances happening in many homes. But in this moment, Carrie takes control of her destiny and identity. She embraces her powers and the fact that she is different.

SISSY SPACEK: Wasn't that [scene] amazing? Carrie turns a corner; that's her epiphany there. And Brian put us at the ends of a long, narrow table. And had a tapestry of *The Last Supper*. He had everything thought out so all we had to do was just work within the boundaries that he had set. But we had freedom within those boundaries.

On the evening of the prom, while Carrie waits for Tommy, Margaret makes a last attempt to stop her daughter from going, saying—as though she knows what will happen—that "they're all gonna laugh at you!" It's also in this scene that Piper Laurie delivers the instantly iconic and infinitely quotable line about Carrie's "dirty pillows." With her power, Carrie pushes her mother back to the bed and leaves. After her daughter has gone, Margaret utters to herself, "Thou shalt not suffer a witch to live," an Old Testament verse used to justify the persecution of so-called witches in centuries past. With this verse, Margaret White has cursed her daughter with a promise of death.

PIPER LAURIE: "I can see your dirty pillows"—that stuff was Stephen King. That line and the one about "after the blood comes the boys, like sniffing dogs," have given me such pleasure through the years. People get such a kick out of it. But I take pride in rescuing one of my favorite lines; Carrie has made her own dress and I say, "Red, I should have known it would be red." But the costume designer had decided to make the dress pink. Brian was going to change the dialogue, but I said, "No, no, in her head it's red." So, I got to say it; it was very "Margaret White."

Sissy Spacek has a contemplative moment on set before filming the prom scene.

THE TRAGEDY OF A HIGH SCHOOL PROM

Like the way De Palma structured sequences in *Dressed to Kill*, he had the prom play out as a dramatic and choreographed three-act play.

Act One: The Fairy Tale

As Carrie and Tommy enter the scene, the school band aptly plays, "...He's out of control, the Devil has got a hold of his soul." Two moments truly shine. First, Betty Buckley delivers the most moving monologue about her prom. In that moment, she reveals how awkward she once was, and we sense her connection with Carrie. In the background, we hear "Born to Have It All," the first of two songs by Katie Irving (no relation, despite the pure coincidence that Amy Irving's sister is also named Katie) begins, with lyrics written by producer Paul Monash's wife, Merrit Malloy. The song echoes the story of Carrie herself, "You were born to touch, born to want too much, let the bodies fall, you were born to have it all . . ." Carrie and Tommy then begin dancing, almost in their own world, as no one else seems to be around them. They slow dance to Katie Irving's "I Never Dreamed Someone Like You Could Love Someone Like Me" (also with lyrics by Merrit Malloy). This is truly an extraordinary moment that seems to belong exclusively to Tommy and Carrie. We do not see anyone else around them. It's quite similar to the embrace between father and daughter at the end of *Obsession*— in both cases, it creates a dizzying dreamlike quality, and truly captures us in the emotion of the moment. Through the camera move, De Palma includes us in the dance but, by going in the opposite direction of their motion, he also tells us that the outcome of the couple's embrace will not be as harmonious or as complete as it seems. And all this is underlined by incredible performances from both Spacek and Katt, who are so relatable. You are rooting for them and see the beginning of a possible romance, which makes the outcome of the prom even more tragic. Afterward, Tommy convinces Carrie to vote for themselves as queen and king of the prom, saying, "To the Devil with false modesty." Carrie marks off the ballot and replies as if misunderstanding Tommy and making a much darker pact, "To the Devil!"

NANCY ALLEN: The prom scene is, of course, the "moment." That's what the whole movie leads up to and you have everybody there—all your key players with their own agenda.

JACK FISK: The gymnasium and prom set had to fill a large space. And because of our budget we couldn't build a ceiling. To distract, I came up with the ideas of stars hanging down.

We built the set with 360-degree walls, but we did remove a section so Brian could bring in a crane. It was kind of a "fluid set" and the advantage we had was that you could pretty much shoot in one direction and just change the people around, turn things over, and it would look like you were in a different part of the gymnasium.

PAUL HIRSCH: Brian's approach to the prom scene was a combination of very long, tracking shots, followed by a slow-motion sequence, which is followed by a split-screen sequence.

BRIAN DE PALMA: We had this big Chapman crane on a soundstage, and you get in with this God's view on this world, you come down, and then you introduce all your principals. The studio got very upset with me because they couldn't figure out what I was doing. In fact, at one point, the head of the studio came down to the set and we had a big argument about it. And I said, [*Laughs*] "What do you want me to do, shoot a bunch of close-ups here? Will that make you happy? It's not going to work, we need this elaborate shot, or fire me." That was my attitude and, ultimately, he left me alone, and I did very complicated shots.

WILLIAM KATT: Sissy has this great ability to play both extremes. She can be this very repressed demure woman, which she played so effectively in the film. And she can also be this stunning, little, vivacious, gorgeous woman. It was easy to go there with her because she's such a fine actress.

BETTY BUCKLEY: The story I tell Carrie of my prom was something I made up on the spot. Brian would trust me to do that. I think Miss Collins herself was probably a version of Carrie when she was growing up; she wants to side with the underdog.

BRIAN DE PALMA: The idea of filming Carrie and Tommy by going around them in a circle as they're dancing was inspired by the ending of my film *Obsession*. It sets up that this is a very important emotional scene between the two of them. This was a combination of us running around them and putting them on a turntable. I don't know how we got over the vertigo of doing the shot. It gets faster and faster and faster and faster. It's the paradise moment for Carrie, Everything is perfect, and it's the last moment of ecstatic beauty until the fall begins.

SISSY SPACEK: The camera going around and around. Yes!! Yes!! It was wonderful. We always had the feeling of the prom, the romance, the music, and being swept away. It was exhilarating and romantic and magical. His shots are always so designed, but it never interferes with the moment that you're trying to capture.

AMY IRVING: Doing the kind of sequence all in one shot, the way Brian does it, had a continuity that a lot of films don't give you. I'm a theater baby so I'm used to going from the beginning of the story to the end; you never have to break from the reality. It's all happening. You don't have to use your imagination; you just stay in character and follow the moves.

Act Two: The Coronation

The entire sequence leading to the bucket of blood dumped on Carrie is one of De Palma's greatest cinematic displays. All filmed in slow motion, it takes us through several points of view—Carrie and Tommy, the prom attendees (with a focus on

Miss Collins), Chris and Billy under the stage preparing to pull the rope attached to the bucket, and Sue Snell who has sneaked in. Sue thought she had redeemed herself by setting up Tommy and Carrie, but soon realizes that she has, in fact, delivered them to the slaughter.

As the "winners" of the prom night are announced, De Palma's camera has traveled to the bucket, and frames it in the foreground, before it pushes toward Carrie and Tommy in the

The Queen and King of the prom—the dream before the nightmare.

background. They then proceed to the stage in slow motion. A piece of crepe paper floats from the rafters, toward where Carrie is standing, indicating the strategic placement of the bucket of blood, almost like a pointed arrow, making Sue realize what's about to happen. Sue tries to alert Miss Collins but, in a cruel twist of fate, the teacher thinks Sue is jealous and literally pushes her outside. As Miss Collins closes the door on her, Chris pulls the rope, spilling the blood. De Palma's grasp of this entire sequence is masterful, not only in the meticulous framing, but also in the editing by Paul Hirsch, with the measured intercutting between the different players. The suspense is enhanced by Pino Donaggio's score, which switches back and forth between lush and mounting tension, marking the transition musically from coronation to a baptism in blood.

SISSY SPACEK: I was a prom queen in real life. And I didn't have nearly so nice an outfit as I did in *Carrie*. But it was like getting an Academy Award. You're having an out of body experience between the time that your name is called, you go up, and you're on top of the world.

NANCY ALLEN: It felt like we were stuck underneath that stage for months! It was uncomfortable and it added to the tension. I was mesmerized when I saw it all put together, but filming it was tough. Pulling the rope is supposed to be almost orgasmic. I couldn't honestly say that I really understood it. Brian certainly was tuned into that and I remember it being just a release in a funny kind of a way. I like working with directors who are very specific, about how they're shooting the movie and what they want, if within the context of that, you have some freedom to explore. And on *Carrie*, I never felt for one minute, "Oh, this is really a horrible idea."

WILLIAM KATT: There's always that sense of apprehension when you're doing any kind of special effects gag because you never really know how it's going to turn out, and this bucket was falling from quite a way up. I must give them credit; they did let me feel it and I could tell it was made from cardboard. But I was nervous. And there was all that stuff that was going to fall, mainly all over Sissy. It was like this red Karo syrup. I remember her being very, very focused and into herself. Sissy doesn't act, she is one of those people who becomes that part.

NANCY ALLEN: The tone shifted on the set at that time. It was a lot more tension because of the special effects and the amount of people there. It was very tricky and disturbing.

BRIAN DE PALMA: The producer told me that one of the studio heads was very upset about the pig's blood and suggested that we change it to something else. And I said, "What are we going to use, blue paint? How about confetti? I don't think it'll have exactly the same effect." But there're two things about the blood. I had Jack Fisk pour the blood on top of Sissy, because I knew he'd do it carefully and lovingly. He had been there for the shower scene and had put the blood on her thigh and he was the one who "buried" her for the end scene. Once she got that blood on, Sissy went into a trance; it's hard to describe how she did it. The closest I've gotten to this was Al Pacino at the end of *Scarface*. She lived in this blood every day; it would dry quickly and got very stiff, almost like a cast. But it was effective and each time we would start rolling, she would go into that trance.

AMY IRVING: Sissy Spacek was extremely concentrated and separate from the group. She really needed to feel she was always an outcast, and she was not one to joke around at lunch and hang with the kids. She really threw her entire self into the character.

SISSY SPACEK: I was trying to imagine what it would be like and not to react like I knew it was about to happen. I remember being caught kind of mid-moment. The blood was made from Karo syrup and red food coloring. They warmed it up, so it felt like a heavy, warm, wet blanket. It was an amazing sensation. But, after, it started to dry and got sticky. My chin would stick to my neck, my arms would stick to my sides, and it was hard to get my dress off after we shot all day. If I sat down, I would stick to a chair. They had someone with me with a little spritz bottle, unsticking me. [*Laughs*] We did it maybe two or three times, because I had to get completely "redone." I kept to myself the whole time. It was very lonely. Every day, I would come in, they would curl my hair, they would do everything, and then they'd put this stuff on me. So, it was quite an ordeal. It was a very humbling experience.

AMY IRVING: I remember when the bucket fell and watching Sissy having to deal with this awful sticky stuff on her all day long. I remember [thinking] how uncomfortable she must have been. When the blood fell on her, just like everyone else, I was just stunned. The build-up to it had been so long that when we saw her get it, it was breathtaking. It was scary and it shut us all up.

Act Three: The Retribution

Once Carrie is soaked in blood, De Palma removes all sound, including dialogue, except for the dripping of the blood and the dropping of the bucket falling on Tommy's head, knocking him dead. A transition is marked by Mrs. White's voice off-screen, repeating, "They will laugh at you." From Carrie's point of view, we see everyone—no longer in slow motion—in a kaleidoscope

Possibly De Palma's most famous sequence of the era, Carrie is showered in pig's blood.

montage of images and a cacophony of laughter, the "plug it up" from the shower sequence, Miss Collins's "Trust me, Carrie," and the principal's "We're all very sorry 'Cassy.'"

De Palma employs several devices to stage the chaos and destruction, feeling at times completely surreal. For instance, when Chris and Billy escape before the back doors close in on them, there's no sound coming from the prom itself, isolating them, perhaps, from the real world. De Palma spins the sequence by using split screens, nearly disorienting us, but effectively depicting the mayhem. He has his images in red—using the colored spotlight above the stage—and then fire and flames. Most shocking and unexpected, especially for the readers of King's novel in which Miss Collins survives, is the teacher's death. After the carnage, as Carrie walks home drenched in blood, Chris and Billy drive toward her. Chris is behind the wheel—chewing that gum again—and De Palma cuts very quick shots (jump cuts) toward Carrie's face with the added *Psycho* music cue, using the same visual device he would wield in *The Fury* to indicate the power at play. The car flips over and, after another series of quick shots (jump cuts) toward Carrie, the car explodes. All bets are off, Carrie has crossed over into hell.

SISSY SPACEK: In the beginning, she was just a repressed young girl that just wanted to be like everybody else. Then, she's just like a flower unfolding, she was like a rose that bloomed. And she becomes this vulnerable, beautiful woman, there's translucence about her, but it was just a moment. Then, that hate is thrown on her, at a time when she is exposed, and she becomes a monster.

JACK FISK: Brian used to tell Sissy, it's a story of revenge. She's getting back at the bully who picked on her in the playground.

SISSY SPACEK: Brian would say, "Open your eyes wider." He knew exactly what he wanted me to do. It was very effective. I benefited from Jack being the production designer, because he had a huge amount of research that I was able to study. So many religious drawings and paintings that I used for body language. Because I could see the position I wanted to be in.

JACK FISK: I had a book of Gustave Doré etchings of Dante's *Inferno*; Sissy saw that and would mimic poses from the drawings.

BRIAN DE PALMA: I must mention [again] the influence of the play *Dionysus in 69*. Within the play, there were all these primitive rituals, the birth ritual when Dionysus is born, the death ritual when he is torn apart; it was just stunning. And maybe, subconsciously, I directed Sissy along those lines. I don't know if she ever saw *Dionysus*, but it's something that stayed in my mind.

BETTY BUCKLEY: Brian asked me to laugh at Carrie after the bucket of blood fell on her. I didn't want to do that because I didn't feel like it was true to my character. But Brian said, "That's what I want," and I did it despite myself. Later, when I saw it in context of it playing from Carrie's imagination, I understood what he was going for.

BRIAN DE PALMA: I used split screens during that sequence but, ultimately, felt it was a mistake; that technique is not good for action. It becomes gimmicky and it doesn't have enough visceral energy for a scene like this. So, in the cutting room, I kept reducing the number of split images.

PAUL HIRSCH: There was universal negative feedback about the split screen sequence. There were too many of them, it was confusing, and Brian was disappointed at the reaction. It was a challenge to reduce the number of split screens because Brian had shot scenes thinking only half the frame would be shown. So, it was difficult to find ways to replace them.

BETTY BUCKLEY: [Before I read the script] I didn't realize that my character was going to be killed. Nobody knew how the movie was going to end. I campaigned to Brian that Miss Collins should survive the disaster of the prom. And then when I found out I was going to die at the prom, I was like, damn. I was curious about how I was going to die. By then, we'd all bonded intensely, and we would show up for everybody else's death scene. And then we would all go out and party. But the idea was this basketball board device was supposed to come down, almost like a guillotine. The plan was to stop it right before it hits me. Then they replaced me with this stuntwoman for the hit and then, I came back in. Brian's directions to me were classic. He comes up to me and he goes, "I want you to vomit the blood and I want you to squirm like a bug on a pin." I'd never shot a death scene before, so it was very exciting and fun. Then, we all went out for margaritas and Mexican food.

P.J. SOLES: There was a stunt girl for me going against the stage and falling. But Brian wanted a close-up of my face. The water from the hose was supposed to just hit my cheek but, instead, the force of it was so strong that it went into my ear. And it broke my eardrum instantly. It was excruciating. [Members of the crew] rescued me.

SISSY SPACEK: Filming was safe and shot in a way that looked like the fire was closer than it really was. But one of the most frightening things was when I had to make the car flip. I was as scared as I've ever been. I wasn't in any danger, but you're so worried that you're going to do something that will screw up the stunt and that was upsetting.

BRIAN DE PALMA: This was a low-budget movie. Ultimately, it cost $1.8 million. And we had our stuntman, Dick Ziker, rolling in a car, by shooting it off this cannon, something he'd never done before. I remember the sun was coming up, the camera was set, Dick rolled six and a half times, came to the stop; it was perfect. That was a "wow" moment.

PAUL HIRSCH: When Nancy Allen and John Travolta try to run over Carrie, she looks over her shoulder and we did a series of jump cuts, into a huge close-up of her eyes to accentuate the power she was using to flip the car and make it explode.

NANCY ALLEN: I thought it was very unfair that my character had to die. She could have at least just learned her lesson! [*Laughs*] When the movie was over, I was sad. I had such a wonderful time making it. I don't know that I could say that I knew it would be a classic and that people would be talking about it, but, from the first dailies I saw, I knew we were making a good movie. You could absolutely feel it every single day on the set.

FROM PROM TO "HOMECOMING"

There's something devastating and inevitable about Carrie's coming home to her mother. She's welcomed by hundreds of burning candles, spread across the home as if Margaret White has known the outcome of the prom all along, with the candles symbolizing birth, death, resurrection, and sacredness. As mentioned earlier, Margaret had told Carrie before she left that she "might have known" her dress would be red. At the time, Carrie corrected her, "It's pink . . ." and, yet, Margaret was proven right.

Carrie climbs the stairs to her attic bathroom. As she enters and turns on the light, we see Margaret White hiding, completely still, next to the dress form that her daughter used to make her gown for the prom. It's a terrifying image. Carrie washes herself and emerges looking like the sad little girl we met at the beginning of the film. She is embraced by her mom, who delivers another insane monologue admitting how much she loved sex with her drunken husband. Announcing that the Devil has come home, she then stabs her daughter in the back. Carrie falls down the stairs and retreats to the corner of her "punishment" closet, now her only safe place, as Margaret hovers over, doing the sign of the cross with a knife. Flashing a disturbing smile, she marches on almost in a ritualistic manner, as if she is offering her daughter in sacrifice. With her powers in full swing, Carrie sends kitchen utensils flying into her mother's body, literally crucifying her in the kitchen entryway. In an inspired performance piece by Piper Laurie, Margaret White dies, moaning with pleasure, for what seems to be a long uncomfortable moment, until her last breath. She finally rests with her eyes wide open, in the same position as the Saint Sebastian statue Carrie prayed to in the closet. As the house breaks apart and is engulfed into the ground, Carrie grabs

In the novel, Carrie killed her mom by causing her to have a heart attack, but De Palma designed a much more spectacular death for her.

her mom's body and finds refuge inside the closet, only to die holding in her arms the mother who created her and, ultimately, destroyed her.

JACK FISK: I can't remember where the idea for all the candles came from. The main thing about working on a Brian De Palma film is that by the time you get to the end of it, you can do almost anything. He's got the audience accepting his conventions. People were so involved with the story, they didn't ask themselves, "How did she light seven hundred candles? Where did she get them?"

PIPER LAURIE: I was on the movie for three glorious weeks. When Carrie comes home, with all the candles lit around the house, it was stunning. And I remember being behind the door, and Brian telling me not to move. And, suddenly, I am revealed, standing there, all in white, in her wedding gown, I guess.

There was no improvisation in my scenes with Sissy. Most of them were quite rehearsed. Only one scene was not rehearsed, because it almost got dropped from the script—the speech about the truth about my sexuality. I brought it up to Brian's attention and he put it back in. We never rehearsed it, and I was glad because I wanted it to be as raw and fresh as possible. I think we did two takes. Brian was wonderful, and he let me do it my way.

SISSY SPACEK: One of the things that astounded me about Piper when she said those lines: It came from the depths of her soul. But one of the scenes I loved the most was when Piper stabs me. She has got the knife, she's holding me, and it's just so wonderful and she stabs me in the back! As I fall down the stairs, she's still coming at me with this knife.

LAWRENCE D. COHEN: I was having dinner with Marty Scorsese at Musso & Frank Grill in Hollywood when Brian arrived and stopped by our table. He was very excited with an idea he'd come up with of how Carrie should kill Margaret versus the way she did it in the novel—using her mind to slow down her mother's heart. Brian argued that the book's solution was literary, emphatically not filmic. He proposed Carrie use her telekinetic powers to make the kitchen utensils impale Margaret. I thought he was kidding—it would be comic and the audience would laugh seeing her looking like a pin cushion. Brian insisted it would be shocking, having seen a similar scene in the Kurosawa film *Throne of Blood* [1957]. He asked me to trust him and watch Kurosawa's movie. After seeing it, I realized that he was right. Piper's orgasmic sounds only added immeasurably to the effect.

BRIAN DE PALMA: When you're making horror or suspense films, you're always asking yourself, "How can I do this in a way that's not too upsetting or in bad taste?" While I'm conscious of what's going to work on film or not, I am always trying to come up with a strong image. And I got this image of the crucifixion of the mother. I was always questioning our big finish, "Mrs. White has a heart attack?" I kept on complaining about it. I came up with this other idea and everyone thought it was in poor taste. I just went ahead and did it anyway.

PIPER LAURIE: My elaborate death scene took a day to shoot. There was a steel grill made for my chest area and on it, there were wooden blocks with strategic spots where I was going to be stabbed. The utensils would travel along a wire until they hit me. As for the emotional aspect of her death, it was Margaret's triumph. It was ecstasy because she was going to be where she wanted to be. But that wasn't in the script. I felt it needed something else. Before we shot it, I said to Brian, "How about she loves it when she dies?" And he said, "Terrific, let's do that!" I wasn't sure what I was going to do; I just wanted it to be wonderful.

The production challenges involved with the destruction of the house inadvertently present an interesting layer to Carrie's own mythology. Originally, in the film (as in the book), Carrie caused a rain of stones to fall on her house. The plan was to have boulders destroy and squash the house at the end, but the effects didn't work. It was De Palma's decision to simply burn it down as it disappears into the ground. With this new ending, it is possible to see the house as a gateway to hell and the source of Carrie's powers, in the same way the Overlook Hotel possesses Jack Torrance in *The Shining* (1980), or how the haunted car takes over Arnie in *Christine*.

147

PAUL HIRSCH: In the original opening scene, a torrent of gravel falls out of the clear blue sky on to the roof of the house. This was designed to set up a scene at the end of the film. However, there were two problems. The gravel didn't look like gravel. It looked like rain, like water. And the second problem was when we were filming the ending. The conveyor belt that was supposed to drop the stones on the house jammed. They were running out of nighttime. Dawn was coming soon, and Brian said, "Just burn the house." So, that's what they did. Unfortunately, they had already shot the interior scenes where stones were seen coming through the ceiling and so forth, but somehow in the context of all the action, we got away with it. The idea was this prologue was going to establish young Carrie, upset, bringing gravel out of the sky, and then as a grown teenager, Carrie, more upset, big boulders out of the sky. That whole idea was lost from the film.

SUE'S NIGHTMARE

In the novel, there's a real psychic connection between Sue and Carrie. Toward the end, Billy and Chris escape the carnage, but Carrie catches up to them, she stands with a knife sticking from her shoulder (from the confrontation with her mother) and makes Billy's car explode. She then drags herself to the parking lot. Sue, seemingly, knows everything that has occurred and can tell Carrie is dying. She heads off to find Carrie and, as she runs, she gets her period.

But, for the film, De Palma had one last shock in store, with a key addition to the ending of his adaptation of *Carrie*. Sue Snell is recovering at home, and we then see her, holding a bouquet of flowers, going to Carrie's grave, which is basically where the house collapsed. But something odd is happening; cars are driving backward. Amy Irving was filmed walking backward, the cars going forward, and the film was then reversed to give a sense of something being "off." There's also a single shot on a FOR SALE sign in the shape of a cross, planted amongst the stones, with graffiti saying, "Carrie White Burns in Hell" and an arrow pointing directly to the ground, against a completely dark sky (though it was daytime in the previous shot). Carrie's bloody hand bursts through stones and grabs Sue, in the same way she grabbed on to her in the shower sequence. It's one of the best jump scares in cinema history.

AMY IRVING: There was no ending when I first read the script. I went to the book and knew that Sue Snell survived. But they hadn't decided for the film. There was a question about the ending and who was going to be in the last scene, which brought a bit of a competitive edge to the production. When I finally saw it on paper, it didn't seem all that scary. I thought, I may have won the lottery here and got the last scene, but I'm not sure how it's really going to work.

LAWRENCE D. COHEN: The ending of the movie is probably the most notorious change from the book. It was something that Stephen King adored in the picture and wished he'd thought of it. So, we got his blessing, but the book ended with the events being covered up by the commission, and then in another part of the country, there's a little girl moving marbles with psychic powers. And it was fine for the novel. In terms of writing the screenplay, I had a couple of different endings that would retain the notion of a twist. And just when you thought it was safe, it would still leave you with something. At one point again Brian came in, having had one of these epiphanies, and said, "I've got a great idea for the ending of this."

BRIAN DE PALMA: The nightmare was inspired by the ending of John Boorman's *Deliverance* [1972], with the hand coming out of the water. That image you can never forget. It felt right to me thematically. Sue Snell was never going to forget this; she was the one who had caused it all. As innocent as she was, she brought this whole horror upon her friends and herself, and the bloody hand clutching her in her subconscious will never go away. The idea of having Amy walking backward came to me. I knew I had to come up with something original and different. Suddenly, in the middle of the night, I woke up with the idea of how to solve it.

AMY IRVING: But shooting the last scene was one of the strangest experiences I'd ever had as an actress. I am coming off four years of drama school, and I'm very, very prepared, and suddenly, Brian is asking me to walk backward, and to make it look like I'm going forward. And then, to glide over these rocks barefoot. A lot of people don't catch the cars driving backward, but the way we filmed it gave the scene a dreamlike, otherworldly feel.

SISSY SPACEK: I insisted on doing my hand work in the last scene. Jack dug up a hole, put plywood, covered it all with pumice rocks, and then, I brought my arm up.

JACK FISK: At the right moment I would holler to Sissy. The rocks that were right around the arm hole were made of foam rubber so she wouldn't get hurt. And it all went smoothly.

NANCY ALLEN: We were all around when Brian was shooting the ending, but I never had a clue about what he was doing. So, yes, of course I just jumped right out of my seat when I saw it.

AMY IRVING: I remember Brian showed me the film after we shot it, and I was alone in the theater. I knew what was coming so it didn't scare me. I was very worried about that until I saw it with an audience in a theatre in Westwood, and everyone hit the ceiling when that hand came out, and they scared me! That's when I got the big scare. So, I really wouldn't come to me for advice when it comes to showing me a script and asking about the scares!

As Sue wakes up, she is comforted by her mother, a reversal from Carrie holding her own mom in death. The camera moves up—in the opposite direction from its descent in the opening volleyball scene—in a subjective shot reminding us that Carrie might just be watching.

AMY IRVING: Filming that last moment, when I wake up from the nightmare, was hard for my mom because she'd never seen me hysterical. I might have had my moments as a teenager, but to be holding me was emotionally difficult for her. We're very connected and close. Brian was able to tap into the whole mother/daughter dynamic of that moment.

PRISCILLA POINTER: She was so emotionally wrought that I was sure I called her Amy while we were filming the scene!

PINO'S MAGICAL FLUTE

One of the great revelations of *Carrie* was the soundtrack by Pino Donaggio. It's an incredible composition that divides Carrie's world musically between beauty and horror, with the perfect choice of the flute as part of Carrie's theme—an instrument appropriately rooted in primitive cultures and associated with the realm of magic. It is believed to be a conduit to the spirit world.

BRIAN DE PALMA: I listen to scores all the time because you need to build temp tracks. When Bernard Herrmann died, I had to find a new composer to work with, and I really liked Pino Donaggio's score to *Don't Look Now* [1973]. I called him up and we got together. To express Carrie's powers, we tried all kinds of sounds. But that shriek from *Psycho* was the only thing that seemed to work and so we literally duplicated it.

PAUL HIRSCH: To regard any of the music in *Carrie* as an homage to Herrmann is a little bit incorrect because we were simply applying the lessons we had learned from him in terms of how to make music effective in film. It wasn't particularly meant as an homage per se. Pino turned out to be a very felicitous choice because his music supported the warmth that Sissy Spacek brought, and created a very sympathetic character that the audiences could relate to.

The mood of the film—at least its conclusion—could have been much different. At one point, producer Paul Monash intended to have John Travolta sing a song over the end credits. Lawrence D. Cohen alerted Stephen King, who told Monash he couldn't have the guy who dumps pig's blood on Carrie sing over the end credits. Monash then suggested the Bee Gees, to which King replied, "No, I *really* don't think so."

FINALLY ROOTING FOR CARRIE

Reviews of *Carrie* were generally kind and, at times, euphoric: "*Carrie*'s ultimate triumph is spectacular beyond anything one is used to in this antique genre," wrote Richard Schickel in *Time*. Pauline Kael wrote, "*Carrie* is a terrifyingly lyrical thriller. The director, Brian De Palma, has mastered a teasing style—a perverse mixture of comedy and horror and tension, like that of

Hitchcock or Polanski, but with a lulling sensuousness." But– unfairly in my opinion–Kael found the music "modest, inof- fensive, and derivative." She also pointed confusingly to a few places where the film "seems to err in technique," yet concluded how De Palma "found his own route to a mass audience: his new trash heart is the ultimate De Palma joke."

Kael's review described the novel itself as "an unassuming potboiler." Stephen King declared in a 1979 *Take One* magazine interview, "I started to write her a letter about that. I was con- vinced that someone had told her the book was an unassuming potboiler, and that she hadn't read it. But she would immedi- ately have said, ' Of course, I read it; I thought it was an unassum- ing potboiler!'" Stephen King also felt the review ascribed to Brian De Palma some things that came directly from the book. For instance, Pauline Kael wrote that one good thing about the movie was that it discovered the junk heart of America. King agreed but said that a good portion of this element is in his novel as well: "You don't write a novel that could be subtitled *High School Confidential* without the thought foremost in your mind that there is a junk, kitschy part of America that's very compel- ling and that's fun to play with."

In *Newsweek*, Janet Maslin sadly deplored that "De Palma, who directed the recent *Obsession*, continually subverts the sense of detachment he seems to be indulging in too many fancy camera tricks," while the *Hollywood Reporter* truly understood the film, going as far as comparing a specific shot at the prom to something out of *Citizen Kane* (1941), hailing how *Carrie* made *The Exorcist* seem like a Disney family film, and emphasizing it marked "the final emergence of yet another major young talent, Brian De Palma."

The United States Conference of Catholic Bishops, on the other hand, slapped its "condemned" rating on *Carrie*, meaning they regarded the picture as morally objectionable for US Roman Catholics. In its repressed review of the film in the December 15, 1976, issue of *Film & Broadcasting Review*, the Conference summarized *Carrie* as "ludicrous and overdrawn." The Conference also "blessed" De Palma with this surreal, unwarranted quote, "Sick humor, it seems, has become the last refuge of the slovenly, untalented filmmaker."

BRIAN DE PALMA: At the time, I was having a battle with United Artists, the distributor, to not treat it like a tawdry pre-Halloween picture, and give it a decent release. But that was the year of *Rocky* [1976]. I couldn't get them to focus any attention on my "horror" picture. It was a limited release until they saw it was popular; then basically they got behind it.

BETTY BUCKLEY: I saw it first in a small screening room and I was just blown away by the ending. I just thought it was amazing. And then I took my husband at that time and a good friend of ours when it came out. When we got to the end of the movie, the two of them screamed and jumped up and backward in their seats. I laughed so hard. And I went to the movie several times with different sets of friends just to watch them react to the ending. It was so fun to watch people totally scream their heads off.

PIPER LAURIE: I was making another movie and missed the first screening. But my husband saw it and he called me to say, "It's going to change our life." I didn't see the movie until they had a sneak preview on Halloween eve, midnight, in Westwood. And I was very, very nervous. And, of course, when I was nominated, that was really a shocker. It was amazing. But, in those days people thought of it as a horror movie and it took a while before *Carrie* could build a reputation of being a classy movie for its genre.

AMY IRVING: To have been a part of *Carrie* is one of the high points in my film career. To work with a great director like Brian De Palma in a moment when he was doing some of his finest work and with some great actors at a time when they were so green and fresh is a big kick for me. I'm still more known for that role than anything else I've done. And I don't mind. Sometimes you get known for things that aren't special to you. This was a special experience and having your first film be that kind of success just doesn't happen to everybody. It's nice to be a part of that history.

PRISCILLA POINTER: It's marvelous that it's become a classic film, despite it being classified as a horror film. There was a tremendous amount of emotional involvement and truth—truth about young people and the madness that engulfed them all.

P.J. SOLES: *Carrie* is more than just a teenage horror film. It is about young kids trying to find themselves as adults in the world. They're making that transition and all the feelings of finding first love or wanting to be respected by your peers and not knowing quite where you fit in society; wanting to make a name for yourself.

BETTY BUCKLEY: Brian's vision was so specific, and yet there was this team atmosphere; and there was an exciting quality to it all.

NANCY ALLEN: It was my first big film, and it was such an exceptional experience that it made it hard to go into other movies after that.

WILLIAM KATT: It was an interesting part; Tommy was this conceited, self-indulgent jock jerk at the beginning of the film. And there was a real awakening during the film. It was terrific to play because it started one place and it finished completely somewhere else.

LAWRENCE D. COHEN: Watching the film being made, what was clear to me was that the performances were extraordinary, and that they would live irrespective of anything else about the movie. I felt we would scare the hell out of people. But I don't think any of us had the idea that, so many years later, we'd be having this conversation.

PAUL HIRSCH: *Carrie* was a real breakthrough for Brian. It was the first of his pictures that really had a great commercial success. It was an exciting movie to work on and it was the film that got me invited into *Star Wars*, which certainly changed my career.

JACK FISK: I really liked the story, but I liked the film better. And I liked it because I was working on it, because it was so much fun, and because Brian was so receptive to any ideas. You couldn't go too far with Brian. Sissy got unbelievable reviews. Piper Laurie got unbelievable reviews. It went from normal, everyday life to kind of unreal, in another universe. And I wanted the studio to put ads up for the Academy Awards. They said, "No, nobody ever gives awards to horror films." They weren't even going to try. But out of kindness to

Sissy, they said okay. "We'll give you four thousand dollars, and you can do it." A photographer friend of mine took all these pictures and helped me put together quarter-page ads. We always fought to get the outside edge of the page; it was just so striking because they were so different than the other ads. Sissy and Piper both got nominated; then the studio said, "We'll take over from here." And they went to colorful full-page ads.

SISSY SPACEK: Brian was the perfect person to take on Stephen King's story. There was something very modern and very hip about *Carrie*. And it stands up.

BRIAN DE PALMA: My first studio film, *Get to Know Your Rabbit* [1972], had been a catastrophe. So, the fact that *Carrie* was a hit was very satisfying at a time when I was surrounded by my contemporaries—George Lucas, Steven Spielberg, and Martin Scorsese—who were all very successful. I had no idea that *Carrie* was going to be thought of as a classic movie years later. But I knew I'd worked very hard on it, that it had an incredibly sophisticated visual design, that the performances were really good, and that it was a really great idea of a book by Stephen King.

TEENAGE MARTYR

My personal connection to *Carrie* runs deep. I've enjoyed a friendship with Steve King. In fact, I remember visiting the Louvre in Paris with him, and he asked me about my ambition to direct movies. And I said, "I want to make something like *Carrie*." It suddenly dawned on me that both the novel and the film had had an incredible impact. My fascination began when the film received the 1977 Grand Prix at the Avoriaz International Fantastic Film Festival in France, which, at the time, was the Cannes of horror and science-fiction cinema. No one under eighteen was admitted so I was just intrigued for several years by the poster, the juxtaposition of Carrie as the prom queen on one side and covered in blood on the other— the perfect split image that echoed De Palma's technique. The French title *Carrie au bal du diable* (*Carrie at the Devil's Ball*) was even more promising; it was meant to draw parallels to *The Exorcist*, which had been a gigantic hit worldwide. And not unlike *The Exorcist*, both the novel and the film of *Carrie* set a new bar in the horror genre. But it is unfair to qualify either *The Exorcist* or *Carrie* simply as horror. They're very much psychological stories that deal with very relatable themes.

For a teenager like me, reading the novel was also quite the experience. It felt taboo and—again drawing parallels to Regan MacNeil in *The Exorcist* masturbating with a crucifix—the talk of menstruation and public humiliation in *Carrie* felt very daring and primal. Growing up in an all-boys boarding school and having suffered through bullying pretty much during my entire experience there, I couldn't help but relate to Carrie. That is how powerful and identifiable the story was.

My first book on Brian De Palma led to the recording of an audio commentary about *Carrie* for the Criterion Collection in the early 1990s. And I was the first person to do a retrospective documentary on the film's twenty-fifth anniversary. A lot has been written and done on *Carrie* since then, but I take great pride in having been the first to revisit the film and its history through the novel, script, casting, production, release, and legacy.

Carrie: The Musical—a flop in 1988 with The Royal Shakespeare Company and then on Broadway—fared well off-Broadway and has gained more and more praise and cult status over the years. It is not only performed by legitimate theater, but also by students in schools. *Carrie's* legacy symbolizes teenagers who feel different, who are called freaks. She speaks for all of us who are different in the eyes of society. She is a sacrificial lamb, taking on the sins of her classmates. Although Carrie dies, she continues to live through the timeless nature of her story, as written by Stephen King and directed by Brian De Palma.

The original theatrical poster, featuring a striking image of the psychic twins Gillian and Robin.

THE FURY

—— 1978 ——

*Everybody thinks our careers
are carefully planned out. No.*

—BRIAN DE PALMA

(DIRECTOR)

THE STORY: Robin Sandza (Andrew Stevens), a young man with telekinetic powers, is kidnapped by covert government agent Childress (John Cassavetes) during a staged terrorist attack. Robin believes his father, Peter (Kirk Douglas), was killed in the attack, though Peter narrowly escapes. On the run and out for revenge, Peter seeks to stop Childress from exploiting Robin's abilities. He's aided by Hester (Carrie Snodgress), a nurse who works for the Paragon Institute, a research facility for young people with psychic powers that is collaborating with Childress. There, Hester meets a young woman named Gillian (Amy Irving), who is struggling with her own powers (and making people bleed)—she turns out to be Robin's psychic twin. Peter and Hester rescue Gillian from Paragon, though Hester is killed in the escape. Using her abilities, Gillian is able to locate Robin, who has gone mad from the experiments to which Childress has subjected him. Robin dies in a confrontation with his father, resulting in Peter taking his own life in despair. Childress sets his sights on Gillian now, who fakes a willingness to cooperate. But with the full fury of her psychic abilities, she leads Childress to an explosive end.

Following the success of the first Stephen King adaptation, De Palma turned to another seminal author of the era, John Farris. Hailed by Stephen King himself as "America's premier novelist of terror," Farris was—for a while—the youngest novelist in America ever published, at the age of twenty. "In the years of my adolescence and early adulthood," King wrote, "I did more than just admire his work—I adopted his career as both a goal to be reached and an example to be emulated." John Farris's first foray into supernatural horror came with *The Fury* (1976), at a time when the genre was entering a new and exciting era for authors like Farris, King, Peter Straub (*Ghost Story*, 1979), William Peter Blatty (*The Exorcist*, 1971), Thomas Tryon (*The*

Other, 1971), Peter Benchley (Jaws, 1974) and Frank De Felitta (*Audrey Rose*, 1975). Those novels were not only bestsellers, but they were also immediately snatched by film studios, often prior to publication, and adapted to the big screen.

PSYCHIC BIRTH

The novel by John Farris is fascinating, especially given that, unlike *Carrie*, the author adapted his own book to the screen. It provides a different experience by diving much deeper into the mythology of Gillian and Robin (with hints about past lives and supernatural gifts), as well as the history and purpose of the agency led by Childermass (Childress in the film), called Multiphasic Operations and Research Group (MORG). The novel is far more graphic, both in terms of violence and sexuality, and several characters, such as Gillian's parents, her friend Larue, and Raymond Dunwoodie, have much bigger roles. There's also a subplot with an elderly couple named Meg and Miles Bundy, former musical stars who befriend Hester, but are, in fact, spying on her. The Bundys were included in the original script but were eventually dropped. The script and film do retain the overall idea of psychic twins and a government agency grooming teens with special powers, but Farris does a great job at creating a cinematic path into the journey of the lead characters and how they converge toward one another.

The book reveals Robin has "married and fathered and otherwise loved" Gillian through many past lives. In this lifetime, they were meant to be brother and sister. When Robin died, strangled by the umbilical cord an hour before birth, he located another body so both infants could be born "while the conjunctions and the solar eclipse were in full force." But the kids stayed psychically connected and Robin would regularly "visit" Gillian through astral projection. Gillian, however, blocked her powers,

Amy Irving takes on the role of Gillian, a teen with psychic powers in De Palma's next evolution in horror.

though she does have blackouts, goes into a fugue state, and makes people bleed. Gillian leaves quite a few victims along the way, including her best friend, Larue, whom she inadvertently kills while experiencing the memory of Larue's half-brother's accidental death.

In the book, Robin has been raised by his ultra-religious aunt and uncle and doesn't know that his father, Peter, is an assassin/agent working for MORG. When Peter realizes what his son is capable of, he shares the secret with Childermass, who then proceeds to kidnap the boy and brainwash him. Robin is, ultimately, moved to the PSI Faculty, where he is sexually manipulated by Dr. Gwyn Charles, Childermass's niece, and transformed into a full-blown psychic weapon.

There're quite a few other secondary characters, including a psychic who senses Gillian's powers and a man who picks her up in a movie theater and asks her to perform S&M acts. Yet for all its imaginative weirdness, the general theme has to do with teenage angst. Both Robin and Gillian are fourteen-year-olds in the book and forced to grow up fast. The world of adults is perverted; while Robin is in control (in the beginning, at least), Gillian seems to refuse to grow up. The fact that she blacks out and makes people bleed is, possibly, linked to the repressed refusal of her own "bleeding" as she is becoming a woman. In both the book and the script, Farris gives his young protagonists all the power, something that speaks for the turbulent and rebellious 1960s and '70s, with the sexual revolution, events like the Kent State shootings, the civil rights movement. In many ways, *The Fury* is about young people taking on the power from the adult world and blowing up the system of past generations. During the book's chilling ending, in which Gillian kills Childermass, she finally embraces her power. Talking to herself, she says, "You're somebody I can live with."

I've enjoyed a friendship with John Farris and his son, Peter, over the years. For the first time since the novel and film released, John discussed the genesis of the story and his work alongside Brian De Palma.

JOHN FARRIS (AUTHOR/SCREENWRITER): In 1975, my career was ascending. I had already directed one movie [*Dear Dead Delilah,* 1972] and written a couple of screenplays. Two were based on my novels—*The Captors* and *When Michael Calls* for Fox and producer Larry Turman [who did *The Graduate,* 1967, and was a hot producer at the time]. Both received tremendous reviews. My career felt like it was in an upward trajectory when I wrote *The Fury*.

Several other authors emerged at the same time; William Peter Blatty and his novel *The Exorcist* predated *The Fury*, Stephen King, and Peter Straub. I'd argue Cormac McCarthy's early work [*Child of God*] was already doing horror, as was, of course, Shirley Jackson. Perhaps with the Kennedy assassination, the

Cuban Missile Crisis, and the whole tenor of the Cold War, Vietnam, Kent State, etc., we all lost our innocence, and art, in general, felt like it took a darker turn. A sea change in how people thought about the times they lived in.

Images always inspired me, and in this case, I had an image of psychic twins. I wrote a screenplay called *Paragon* about it, from which the novel *The Fury* evolved. But it lacked something, which was, "What is the disturbing thing that they did?" So, one day, I was looking out a train window on my way home to Scarsdale, thinking about turning *Paragon* into a book and I saw the image of a girl's face. I suppose it was somebody's reflection walking down the aisle and, somehow, it led me to the psychic twins making people bleed.

I recall the fiction around psychics, too, and in the tabloids, as well as the friendly neighborhood psychic with a sign out in the yard offering readings. People wanted to believe somebody could interpret their past lives, predict what was coming, and I wanted to take that a step further. I happen to believe there are true psychics out there. But I didn't do any specific research during the time I wrote the novel. I relied on what worked for the story regarding telepathy, ESP, and psychic phenomena. I fell back on an age-old bit of advice for fiction writing: "Never let the facts get in the way of a good story." To me, *The Fury* is *Dracula* . . . with Robin and Gillian as a modern synthesis of the Dracula legend.

If there is a political influence on *The Fury*, it would have been J. Edgar Hoover and the FBI, plus people just beginning to figure out the CIA wasn't on our side with respect to the Kennedy assassination.

I had published *Sharp Practice* through Simon & Schuster and took *The Fury* to the editor-in-chief, Michael Korda, who offered a deal that wasn't satisfactory. So, I called Bob Gleason, who had edited three of my books prior [*The Captors, When Michael Calls, Sharp Practice*] while working at Trident Press / Simon & Schuster and recently had become managing editor at Playboy Press. He offered me a much more favorable deal and I took it. Bob liked everything I wrote, and he told me *The Fury* would be a lead title, and same with my follow-up novel, *All Heads Turn When the Hunt Goes By*. Playboy went all out, and just missed it becoming a bestseller in hardcover. But it was a bestseller in paperback, especially once the film came out and the reviews were quite good.

In fall of 1975, my agent, Bob Bookman, at ICM sent *The Fury* to producer Frank Yablans's office. Two assistants [one of them, my future wife, Maryann] read the book, and both wrote positive coverage and recommended it to Frank. Frank got on the phone to [Fox production head] Alan Ladd Jr. and said he had a book he wanted to option. Bob chimed in and said I would write the screenplay, which was okay with Frank and Fox since I'd written and sold a few scripts already and directed a feature—I wasn't a novice, in other words. All of this happened prior to the book's release.

After it was optioned, I prepared a 125-page treatment for Yablans's benefit and interest. We didn't have a director yet. Frank approved the treatment, and I went to work in the summer of '76 on the screenplay. When I adapt any book—my own and others—the only thing I care about is: "Does this work as a movie?" Many novels can't make that jump. Blatty could do it. There are things that have to be cut, other things that have to be invented, but screenwriting is a specific language. If a scene or character isn't absolutely necessary, it simply has to go for a script to work, even if it's a "helluva" good scene or character. It's all about staying one jump ahead of the audience and moving the movie along.

In September 1976, I finished my version of the script, and it was greenlit prior to signing a director.

BRIAN DE PALMA: After the success of *Carrie*, the best offer I had was *The Fury* through Frank Yablans. Frank was at Filmways when we made *Greetings* and *Hi, Mom!* In fact, Frank was the guy who pushed for *Greetings*. He literally went around the country, forced theaters to play it, and made it a hit. And now he was a producer over at Fox. They made me the best offer, and I said, "My God, with a big budget?" *Carrie's* budget was $1.8 million. Did I want to make another telepathic horror movie again? Not particularly. But then Frank said, "We got Kirk Douglas and John Cassavetes." I thought, "Well, let's do this."

JOHN FARRIS: Both Frank and Brian had great script sense and input. Frank's feedback was mostly, "This doesn't work, this works, what can you do to make this work better?" Brian is a film director, so his sole focus was making the movie right in accordance with his vision. By the time he got to *The Fury*, he was pretty clued in on what works. Our discussions and conversations about the script revolved around what he wanted to emphasize in the script, not so much if it worked, but how he could focus visually on a scene to make it better. The notion of the psychic twins was a challenge. Brian and I kicked ideas around on how to make the "psychic" element more visual and we felt we were wasting time trying to explain it. We simply had to get on with it. Brian's imagination is incredible, one of the best I've ever seen with a filmmaker. *Sisters* is one of the scariest horror films ever made. But I was also impressed with how he worked with actors, giving them everything they needed to be good.

BEST THERE IS

De Palma assembled an impressive cast, pairing veterans like Kirk Douglas and John Cassavetes with a new generation of actors, including Andrew Stevens and Carrie Snodgress (who, similar to Piper Laurie in *Carrie*, made a return to the screen seven years after her Oscar-nominated performance in 1970's *Diary of a Mad Housewife*). De Palma's "regulars," who had worked with him on previous films, also appeared, including Amy Irving, Charles Durning, and William Finley. *The Fury* also marked the first of several appearances for Dennis Franz, in a small comical role (which was originally proposed to Durning, who apparently preferred the meatier part of the lead psychiatrist at the Paragon Institute).

An all-star assembly joined the crew, including director of photography Richard H. Kline (fresh off the 1976 remake of *King Kong*), production designer Bill Malley (*The Exorcist*), costume

On the set of The Fury *(from left): actor Kirk Douglas, editor Paul Hirsch, and De Palma.*

designer Theoni V. Aldredge (*Network*, 1976), and editor Paul Hirsch, marking his sixth collaboration with De Palma.

PAUL HIRSCH (EDITOR): I remember I met Brian for lunch, and he started telling me the story of *The Fury*. Now, I must explain that Brian has a taste for horror and Grand Guignol kind of stuff, but that's not me. I'm not really a big horror guy. But he started telling me how characters grab hold of people and make them bleed, and then at the end, he says, "[Childress] blows up!" I thought to myself, "Are you kidding me? This is what you want to do?" [*Laughs*] It was so unlike my own sensibility, but Brian had recommended me for *Star Wars*, and here I was coming off winning an Oscar for it, and there was no way I could turn him down. We had done five pictures together; he was the only director who had ever hired me before I worked on *Star Wars*. But still, I was a little dismayed about working on another horror picture.

ANDREW STEVENS ("ROBIN SANDZA"): I had a general audition when George Lucas and Brian De Palma were casting *Star Wars* and *Carrie*—I did an audition with Harrison Ford, and I didn't get [*Star Wars*] at all. *Carrie* resonated with me, and I thought it could be terrific. But I was maybe eighteen years old at the time, and they were casting people who were in their mid-twenties to play high schoolers, like William Katt. So, that was my first encounter with Brian. And a few years later, through Frank Yablans, I auditioned for *The Fury* and I ended up getting offered the role of Robin.

AMY IRVING ("GILLIAN BELLAVER"): I didn't understand career trajectory. I really thought once I did my first film then I would just do one film after another, and it would just all happen. And it didn't. After *Carrie* I just was like, "What's next?" Then, one day, I got two scripts, *The Fury* and *Big Wednesday* [to be directed by John Milius]. And, suddenly, I had my whole family reading both scripts because I had to decide. *The Fury* was not necessarily the movie I would go see first; I would have gone to see the surfing movie. I hate going to horror films; I barely made it through watching *Carrie* and I have no interest in being scared. But *The Fury* was Brian De Palma, and I knew it's a different animal when a horror film is put in Brian's hands. It's not a B movie, which normally horror films were. He elevated the whole genre, in my opinion. So, I chose him.

DENNIS FRANZ ("BOB"): I was a stage actor in Chicago. Auditions were being held there and this big-time Hollywood director, Brian De Palma, was coming into the city to direct a movie. At that time, there wasn't a lot of filming done in Chicago; this was a big deal. I was a huge fan of *Carrie* and I read for the casting director, Lynn Stalmaster. I got a call back and read for a couple of people—one was De Palma, but I didn't realize it. He didn't introduce himself and I didn't know what he looked like. But that's how I got cast, and it started a nice long friendship and working relationship with Brian.

The Fury is set in motion by a strong opening credit sequence and a score by John Williams that defines the universe we are entering. The score carries us into Israel, where we meet father and son, Peter and Robin, at a beach resort, sitting at a table after a race in the water. During that scene, we learn that Robin has supernatural gifts; he is "different," and thinks of himself as a freak who belongs in a zoo. Like Carrie White, Robin fights against his natural gifts, only to grow into them. Though

171

Mrs. White forced her daughter to repress her powers, Peter tells Robin to embrace what makes him "different."

Originally, as written in the shooting script dated 8/11/77, this sequence was to be a flashback that came in during Peter's first secret and intimate encounter with his girlfriend, Hester, in her van. And it started as a race between Peter and Robin, not in the ocean as in the film, but in a pool, in Tangier, Morocco. (Shades of that scene are still in the dialogue when Gillian asks Peter when he last saw his son and he mentions the competitive spirit of their swimming together in a pool. Clearly, the script changed after this was filmed.)

By placing the sequence at the opening of the film, we immediately get a sense of the stakes and the fact that Childress is a destructive force who will stop at nothing to get what he wants. Without that opening scene, Childress would have appeared as a much lesser threat.

The camera work in the scene invokes *Carrie*. While the camera did counter circles in that film to show the imminent disaster as Carrie and Tommy danced, here, the camera does half circles, back and forth, as Peter and Robin are having what turns out to be their last conversation. (A similar approach is used when Gillian and Hester are sharing a dessert at Paragon, again with half circles, announcing the impending doom and Hester's death.)

Following this opening scene, which also establishes John Cassavetes as Childress, Peter's former colleague at a secret government agency, the resort is attacked. It's all a setup by Childress to get Robin and to eliminate Peter. Childress even has the attack filmed so he can later brainwash Robin by forcing him to relive the traumatic event; the manipulation through images is truly an ironic look at the function of cinema as weapon. Peter, in fact, survives the attack, grabs a machine gun, and wounds Childress in the arm. This powerful sequence gets the plot in

Childress (John Cassavetes) pretends to protect Robin (Andrew Stevens) but has, in fact, designs to use the young man's psychic powers for his own gain.

motion. (In the earlier draft of the script, this scene was set at the ferry terminal of Tangier Harbor.)

PAUL HIRSCH: It's very interesting [to watch Kirk Douglas and John Cassavetes]. Kirk was great in the first couple of takes, then would lose some freshness. On the other hand, Cassavetes wouldn't get warmed up for ten takes. He'd come in and he'd sort of walk around, walk through it, and then he would get going, and deliver a marvelous performance. They had two very different styles of acting.

BRIAN DE PALMA: John, basically, did it as a job and his attitude was, "I'll say my lines and just get me outta here." Originally, his arm was supposed to be cut off completely. John said, "No way am I doing that. I'm not having my arm cut off. I'm gonna put it in a sling. I'm not wearing one of those things where you have to have your arm strapped to your side during the entire movie." And when we had to do a body cast to blow him up at the end, he hated it. I thought he was gonna kill us.

Kirk is very concentrated, and he was pushing himself to do all this kind of action stuff that obviously he had done when he was ten or twenty years younger. It played effortlessly, but he was working hard.

ANDREW STEVENS: During the swim race, I thought, "This is Kirk Douglas. He's going to kick my ass." Brian said, "Action," I start swimming, and left Kirk three yards behind [as scripted]!

CURSED BY BLOOD

Gillian Bellaver (Amy Irving) is then introduced as a teenager struggling with the discovery of her powers. We meet her walking on the beach with her friend, Larue (Melody Thomas,

Kirk Douglas as Peter Sandza in the opening sequence of the film, which sets in motion the search for his son.

who had played a younger version of Tippi Hedren's titular character in Hitchcock's *Marnie*), being followed by Raymond Dunwoodie (William Finley). Dunwoodie is a psychic hired by Peter to track down his son and, by pure coincidence, he connects with Gillian via ESP, revealed later to be Robin's psychic twin; as convenient as it may seem, it's a very small "psychic" world, where all the characters are somewhat connected by destiny and a sense of a general subconsciousness. (Originally, Dunwoodie had a much bigger part. He is being stalked by Childress's organization and is shot after he calls Peter to tell him about Gillian.)

Later, Dr. Lindstrom (Carol Rossen) and her nurse assistant, Hester, from the Paragon Institute visit Gillian's school to provide biofeedback training to demonstrate how a person can regulate brainwaves to gain control of their own body. Part of

Between shots, Irving hangs out with actor William Finley, who portrays the eccentric psychic Raymond Dunwoodie.

the experiment involves controlling a toy train, and Lindstrom invites Gillian to try. Gillian puts on electrodes and immediately gets the train in motion but—suddenly—has a vision of a bloodied dead woman in front of her classmates during the test. (We will discover the victim to be Dr. Susan Charles, played by Fiona Lewis; in the script, the vision was of the same character, just coming out of a bath and wrapping a towel around herself.)

AMY IRVING: I wanted to know what it felt like to be in a receptive state. And that's where they said, "Well, we can send you to this clinic." I went there to learn how to work on my biofeedback. You want to get into the alpha and beta stages. And they taught me, through different techniques, how to do that . . . That was just part of the homework. At the time, I was definitely experiencing weird things, but I don't think it had anything to do with the film. I think I was probably stressed. It was scary going into this new adventure.

We soon learn Gillian can make people bleed with her mind, an ability she's yet to learn to control. At the school cafeteria, when classmate Cheryl bullies Gillian into "reading her mind," Gillian reveals that she knows Cheryl is pregnant. Cheryl grabs Gillian's hand, demanding to know how she knew. Distressed, Gillian inadvertently causes her nasty classmate's nose to bleed, starting a cycle of blood that will continue throughout the film. (We also learn Gillian made her own mother bleed by reopening a wound.)

Gillian joins Paragon under the supervision of Dr. McKeever (Charles Durning). As she trips on the stairs, she grabs for the doctor's hand. She immediately has a vision of Robin trying to escape and, ultimately, falling through a window. McKeever had sliced his hand on the broken glass of the window, a wound Gillian reopens before running away, leaving a bloody handprint on the wall as she cries out, "Don't touch me anymore! Please, don't touch me!"

Unlike the book, where Gillian and Robin have lived several past lives, the film presents them as bonded in a psychic world apart from the physical world they inhabit. Their journey is connecting the worlds. But this connection can also be seen as Gillian being the good twin and Robin as the dark side—they're split and must unite as one.

Reflected in the filmmaking is De Palma's now-familiar split diopter—he uses it to remind us that the duality exists on a plane that's not necessarily two-dimensional but, rather, an equal level. The most effective use of the visual device is after Gillian had the vision of Robin running on the stairs. She is sedated and reveals how she saw him attempting to escape from

Horror at hand: Gillian makes people bleed in this French lobby card of the film.

Paragon. It's the first time she acknowledges her psychic bond, though she doesn't remember it later. Gillian is in the foreground of the shot, with Hester listening in the background. The fact that Hester is the link to Robin and Peter makes the revelation—and the technique—all the more binding. But it also underlines the two realms of Gillian's existence, one conscious and the other subconscious.

This reveal leads to one of the most powerful scenes of dialogue in the De Palma oeuvre, as McKeever explains that, in primitive societies, people like Gillian and Robin would be perceived as prophets but, in our modern world, they're exploited and transformed into weapons—they're so far ahead that our society, ultimately, destroys them. This explanation could easily apply to Carrie White as well. McKeever is defining the tragedy of horror, where all three characters are linked and cursed by blood. Robin, Gillian, and Carrie go from "freaks" to "monsters" as they're threatened by those who wish to exploit them.

In the mythology of *The Fury*, Gillian's psychic connection to Robin evolves to an even bloodier event, when Dr. Lindstrom shows Gillian photos of the young man. She falls into a trance and, in a masterful piece of acting by Amy Irving, literally becomes Robin as he is forced to relive the assassination attempt on his father. As Robin/Gillian's rage mounts, the girl grabs Dr. Lindstrom's hand, causing her to bleed through her fingers, mouth, nose, and ears. The scene climaxes with Gillian staring at Robin's reflection in a glass table—they look at each other in a powerful stare of recognition that practically transcends time and space.

UNLIKELY HITCHCOCK CONNECTION

One could look at *The Fury* as a supernatural psychic version of Hitchcock's great thriller *North by Northwest*—in both cases, you have a traitor and an undercover-type government organization, as well as secrets being traded (with Hitchcock, it's microfilms rather than the trafficking of human beings with special skills). Kirk Douglas stands in for Cary Grant as the man on the run; John Cassavetes for James Mason as the villain. By spying for Peter, Hester is Eva Marie Saint's double agent. And both films are done with cinematic set pieces and humor. Wit is present throughout *North by Northwest,* and De Palma purposely hits a similar note, beginning with the sequence in which Peter has to escape from his hotel room in boxer shorts and lands in the apartment of a nagging couple with an elderly mother.

The humor continues as we begin another of the film's exciting action set pieces—a chase in which Peter—disguised as an old man—highjacks a brand-new car with its owner, a cop played by Dennis Franz, and his partner, in tow. Franz's cop comically freaks out throughout the sequence, praying that nothing bad happens to his new car.

BRIAN DE PALMA: I hate car chases and I had to do this one on a sound stage, basically, after we shot the beginning of it on Lower Wacker Drive in Chicago. And I tried to make some half-fast car chase. I think William Friedkin's car chase in *The French Connection* [1971] is the best ever shot—period. He had the greatest idea to tie in the bad guy riding the elevated subway, and the cop pursuing him underneath, dodging all this stuff on the ground and trying to get to a stop where he can run up and, maybe, get the guy. It's great because you have a very clear geography. I constantly talk about how the audience has to be oriented spatially, or all this action means nothing.

SOPHISTICATED COMPOSITIONS

Within a few years, John Williams visited, among others but most significant, the ocean with *Jaws* (1975), the skies with *Close Encounters of the Third Kind* (1977), and a galaxy far, far away with *Star Wars*. With *The Fury*, he explores the supernatural, but through a classic symphonic approach that gives the film further characterization through music. The music is complicit in the depiction of Robin and Gillian's powers through a theremin-like ARP sound. The main theme truly stands out. Nearly a march, it gives an imposing voice to De Palma's vision.

Williams also displays a great variety across the score. For instance, he uses a bucolic cue when Gillian is playing in the park with a dog and, in complete contrast, carousel music that goes out of control, speeding up alongside the action when Robin sends a merry-go-round flying with his powers. There's genuine emotion in the music when Peter and Gillian reflect on memories of Robin after Hester's death. And it's the score that accompanies Gillian's powers when she makes Childress explode at the end.

In her review of the film, Pauline Kael referred to the opening title cue as "otherworldly, seductively frightening." And stated most precisely that the music clearly established that this was "visionary, science-fiction horror," and not at all a gross-out slasher film, an important distinction given the era. Basically, like De Palma himself, it's John Williams bringing class and order to the genre and, ultimately, giving his own appreciation to De Palma's artistry through music. Like the film itself, the score is not as well-known as others of Williams's works. Shortly after *The Fury*, John Williams did the score for John Badham's *Dracula* (1979). As with this film, he contrasts the horror with a romantic and tragic musical composition full of pathos and emotions.

BRIAN DE PALMA: John is such a great composer. I think *The Fury* is one of his best scores. Steven [Spielberg] and I used to talk about John all the time. Of course, he's a great admirer of Benny Herrmann. I remember being with Steven at the recording session for *The Fury*; it was just amazing.

PAUL HIRSCH: I had the sense with *The Fury* that John was writing music expressing an inexorable force that was pulling these characters along in this drama, leading to a doomed finale. There's a driving sense in the music of pulling the audience through an unhappy world.

THE GREAT ESCAPE

The most impressive sequence in the film is Gillian's escape from the Paragon Institute. Paced to John Williams's epic score, the suspenseful sequence clocks at just over five minutes—mostly in slow motion and with few sounds (car skidding, gunshot, glass shattering). Gillian in her white, flowing nightgown and barefoot. As she rushes out of the building through a back door, Hester is running behind her. This jubilant moment of freedom intercuts with a guard, disguised as a doorman, coming after Gillian, and Hester, literally, knocking him down as she runs into him. A car—with two villains, including producer Frank Yablans in a cameo role sitting in the passenger seat—pulls around. One of Childress's henchmen, Robinson (J. Patrick McNamara), who was "jogging" in the park, is now alerted and runs to the scene while both Gillian and Hester move toward Peter, waiting in a cab. The geography is perfectly designed with different points of view. As Peter shoots the driver of the car, it skids and hits Hester. She lands on the hood of a parked vehicle, shattering the windshield. Peter sees Hester's mangled body, and De Palma does his signature jump cut (which he had

Hester (Carrie Snodgress) is killed while helping Gillian escape from the Paragon Institute.

used earlier to signify Gillian's power when she held McKeever's hand) to get us closer to the victim and reveal the blood on her face. Amy Irving delivers an incredible—and silent— performance, reminiscent of Sissy Spacek's at the prom in *Carrie*—she has raised her hands in horror in a similar way Carrie did when she was showered in blood. Peter's devastating realization that he unintentionally killed Hester is interrupted by the henchman assaulting Gillian. Peter turns around and shoots him. Holding his gun, Peter faces Gillian for the first time—with her hands in that same helpless position. Putting his gun away, Peter carries Gillian to the cab. The image of Peter carrying Gillian in her white gown looks like something out of a macabre fairy tale, with Prince Charming saving the princess. That entire sequence is breathtaking and so cleverly orchestrated. It's De Palma and John Williams (and the cast) at their best, creating a visual and musical ballet.

BRIAN DE PALMA: The escape from Paragon was about geography. You've oriented the audience previously; there's this street with the park at the end of it. One guy is on the roof. There's another guy by the adjacent building. You know where everything is. By the time you get to Gillian escaping from the Institute, it's simple. She's running up the street. Peter is at the other end of it with a gun. You slow everything down so the audience can absorb all the different juxtapositions of all the angles. They never get lost. It's all carefully established. Of course, this was inspired by the genius of Hitchcock in the crop duster sequence in *North by Northwest*. Hitchcock evolves the sequence slowly; he keeps the audience interested until the plane comes after Roger Thornhill [Cary Grant] and starts shooting at him. The same thing is true of the scene in *The Fury*. It's also

Peter rescues Gillian from Paragon, in the film's best sequence, literally a cinematic ballet orchestrated and designed by De Palma.

true of the scene I did in *The Untouchables* [1987] where you orient viewers to the grand staircase at the train station, the baby carriage, and eventually the shoot-out. I preach this over and over again and nobody seems to get it. Every time I see a shoot-out or people running around, you don't know where anybody is. It's bang, reaction. But you have no idea where they are in relationship to each other.

JOHN FARRIS: Brian was there with the sun that morning and he didn't waste a second of film. And Amy Irving gave it everything she had for what was a physical day of shooting. [As she was barefoot] I remember thinking, "God, I hope Amy Irving doesn't stub her toe."

AMY IRVING: During the escape sequence, they were doing a shot of me on the street. I was pushing myself with a hysterical performance. Brian took me aside and said, "In this shot, you're the size of a pinkie fingernail on the screen. You mustn't emote so much when you're so tiny on the screen." And I said, "From now on just put your hand up and show me the framing so I can modulate my performance accordingly." And he replied, "Yeah, because you're not going to survive past twenty-five at this rate!" So, he taught me how to conserve my energy and emotions and hold out for the close-up. It was a real workshop for me learning about how to act on film. And he protected me through it.

PAUL HIRSCH: The escape scene from Paragon in *The Fury* was not cut to music. That was all the rhythms of the editing or derived from the rhythms of the action contained within it. I had this idea to use a dissolve, usually meant to indicate the passage of time, but in this case, I used it to indicate the passage of great emotion. I'm not sure it was entirely successful. But, with John's score, there's this magic that comes when you put music against picture. It's very exciting.

The escape played out very differently in the original script (and in the novel). As mentioned, on the page, there was an elderly couple, Meg and Miles Bundy, who lived in Hester's building and "used to dance in musicals in the 1940s and '50s." They're almost like the neighbors in *Rosemary's Baby*—sweet, but nosy, and ultimately, deadly. They are following Hester's every move after giving her a pair of earrings embedded with a transmitting device. In that draft of the script, Hester is not present at Paragon for the escape. Rather, Gillian and Peter find refuge at her place after. The elderly couple then break in and fire on Hester with a silencer; Peter strikes them using boiling cooking fat and, ultimately, shoots them both. That subplot was never filmed, and Hester's death was merged into the escape sequence.

ROBIN UNLEASHED

After the escape from Paragon, Peter and Gillian are on a bus (clearly filmed on a sound stage as indicated by the rear projection seen through the back window; in fact, you may notice that the same footage projected is looped several times). In a sweet moment accentuated by John Williams's melancholic music, Peter talks about Robin and how they competed swimming, and Gillian goes on to explain how she is connected psychically to Robin. She lies and says Robin is okay to reassure Peter. Only later does she reveal Robin is in trouble—and she is the only one who can track him down. In the script, the pair then boarded a cabin cruiser, with Gillian using her psychic abilities to locate Robin. The sequence was dragging and, ultimately, left on the

In one of the film's most disturbing moments, Robin makes his girlfriend Susan Charles (Fiona Lewis) bleed to death without touching her.

cutting-room floor. Instead, we cut directly to nighttime with Peter and Gillian arriving at the estate to stage the rescue.

Inside the mansion, Robin levitates Susan and makes her bleed to death. (Originally, Robin raped her, but that, too, was cut.) Gillian and Robin psychically connect, with De Palma using the jump cut device. One can't help but appreciate the "artistry" involved with Susan's death as she revolves around and around, but the scene notably presents Robin's transformation into a monster—just moments before he is about to be reunited with his father and meet his psychic twin. That is the tragedy of *The Fury*.

AMY IRVING: There was one moment [outside the mansion] where I was being chased by dogs and one of them bit me and Brian stopped everything; he really panicked. It wasn't bad but I said to him and to Paul Hirsch, "When you cut this film, I want that bite in it. I don't want you to cut until I get bitten because I don't want these teeth marks to be for nothing." And you, literally, see me get bitten in the film.

Childress sends Peter to Robin, where he discovers the carnage—Gillian's initial vision at school of Susan's bloodied body now fully realized. Peter soon finds Robin, suspended in the air in an evocative and near-mythological framing. Robin attacks, and the force sends them through the window. Peter grabs his son before he falls over the roof, and both are hanging. Peter begs his son to hang on but, in an act of self-destruction, Robin forces his father to let go of him. After Robin hits the ground—in a last moment of perfect union before his last breath—he transfers his powers onto Gillian while she holds his head. The fluorescent blue stare of his eyes is now reflected in hers. Defeated, Peter throws himself from the roof. The moment originally included Peter still alive, giving the finger to Childress, who then grabs a gun and shoots him. The scene was trimmed down, but we still see Childress handing the gun to one of the security guards.

Critics of the movie found it bizarre that, in one scene, Robin can levitate and, in the next, he is hanging off the roof, seemingly unable to save himself. De Palma argued at the time that Robin injured his head when he went through the window, affecting his abilities. (In fact, the scene on the rooftop, which was shot first, was supposed to have Robin in full makeup, with a head injury and a lot more gore.) But it is also very clear in the acting that Robin has a death wish. He knows what he has become; and like Carrie before him, he realizes death is the only escape.

ANDREW STEVENS: I learned a lot on that picture, especially from our director of photography, Richard Kline, about the synergy between the dolly, the camera marks, and the actor. Also, I had several hours of long sessions with, whom I later came to realize was, the dream team of makeup: Dick Smith, who was the grandfather of special-effects makeup; a kid named Rick Baker, Smith's prodigy, who would apply the prosthetics Smith created; and a great makeup artist named Bill Tuttle. We had made makeup tests for the pulsing veins on my forehead. There were air tubes that went running through my head, down my back to a squeeze bulb. I would control the throbbing of these veins, and you had to be careful enough to make it read on camera, but not burst the bladder inside the prosthetic. And Brian would say, "Okay, give me your look, do the veins!"

PAUL HIRSCH: I had difficulty with the scene where Robin is torturing Susan; he makes her bleed, lifts her up in the air, starts to turn her faster and faster. She's pleading for him to stop as she spins around. At one point, Fiona was replaced by a mannequin, and we would cut to places in the room getting splattered with blood. It was so disturbing. And my way of dealing with it was to get a piece of red gel over my screen so I couldn't see the blood; it was all neutralized by everything being the same color. It was difficult but it's all part of the game.

JOHN FARRIS: I saw rushes of Susan's death and I thought it was terrific, despite the challenges. Fiona was a soggy mess before the day was over, but she was a real trooper. This was before the days of heavy CGI, so what you saw in rushes was what you were going to get. It was very uncomfortable for Fiona to do that scene, as Brian did numerous takes from various angles. The effect of Fiona turning didn't always look right so it had to be done a few times. The scene really speaks to the collaboration between the director, the effects team, and the actor.

At the end of the novel, Gillian smothers Childress with sheets and then makes him bleed in a bathtub. But the author created a much more impressive death for his villain, one that recalls the finale of *Jaws*. In Peter Benchley's original novel, the shark sank, dead from its wounds after being harpooned; it was Steven Spielberg who pushed for a more powerful ending in which Brody (Roy Scheider) shoots at an oxygen tank in the shark's mouth, causing a bloody explosion. The change, of course, worked superbly. Embracing a similar concept, De Palma delivered a scene that begins with Gillian waking up the morning after Robin and Peter's deaths. Childress gives a speech, "apologizing" for what's happened and trying to create an alliance. Childress comforts Gillian and—in an act that feels almost sexual (she moans in a near-seductive way)—she starts to kiss Childress. But suddenly blinds him (captured with jump cuts to his bloodshot eyes and tears), invoking mythological tales of gods inflicting blindness upon mortals as punishment. Childress tries to grab Gillian, but she defiantly sends him "to hell." Rallying the power she has accumulated through Robin, and with jump cuts toward the fluorescent blue stare, she causes Childress to explode. The scene was filmed with a dummy conceived by Rick Baker and loaded with explosives by special-effects artist A.D. Flowers, and shot twice, using a total of eight cameras, with a speed ranging from 800 to 1500 frames per second to capture slow motion. The first time they attempted to shoot the scene, the film broke in four of the cameras. The room had to be completely re-dressed and cleaned and, a week later, they tried again. That time, seven out of eight cameras worked. Most effective (and impressive) was a shot

"You go to Hell!" With her powers in full swing, Gillian causes Childress to meet with an explosive end.

showing Childress's head falling to the ground, eyes wide open, staring lifelessly.

Two alternate endings were written but never filmed. One had a young boy wearing electrodes psychically experiencing Childress's death while interacting with a toy train. Upset by the vision, he tears off the electrodes and, as he leaves, we see that he's in a scientific lab in Russia. Another alternate ending had a young man on a bus, holding on to a pole, also mentally witness-ing Childress's demise. As his face registers shock and horror, he has unconsciously grabbed someone else's hand, and made that person bleed.

But what De Palma settled for is the best possible and most shocking way to conclude the film; a last shot drenched in blood, the reversal of the curse that plagued Gillian, now and forever in full control of her destructive powers.

JOHN FARRIS: I never did like the bathtub scene in the novel. I wrote something else that wasn't very climactic; none of us liked it. Brian and I were sitting in Frank's office, and it popped into my head. I just said, "She blows him up." And Frank said, "Yeah, go write it."

We were at the Fox lot and all I remember was how tedious it was to set it up properly. None of us had any idea how it was going to work out. There was a dummy, the effects/pyrotechnics, and all those camera operators. It's strange, hours and hours of tedious setup and triple-checking everything and it was over in an instant. And it was up to Paul Hirsch to put it all together. But that scene seems to have a huge impact on filmmakers and audiences. People had never seen anything like that before.

I was looking forward to seeing the finished product. I finally saw a completed cut in a screening room in New York, where Paul was editing. There were a lot of people, executives from Fox, Brian, Frank, and me. My reaction was that it really worked. The finale puts it over really big. The reaction in that screening room was very positive. In Frank's office, an execu-tive got on the phone with Alan Ladd Jr. and said, "We've got a winner here." I can still watch the film today and marvel how it has held up over the years.

ANDREW STEVENS: I saw it at a cast and crew screening on the Fox lot. What did I think? I thought it was very different from the previous several projects I'd done. But I didn't know what audiences would think.

TEMPERING THE FURY

Reviews on *The Fury* were, again, divided. There was the De Palma crusader Pauline Kael, who wrote in *The New Yorker* that the director "seems to extend the effects he's playing with as far as he can without losing control. This inferno comedy is perched right on the edge." On the other end, Vincent Canby, in the *New York Times*, called *The Fury* a film that "got out of hand," and the New York *Observer's* Rex Reed labeled it "one of the worst of all time." *The Fury* was also condemned by the United States Conference of Catholic Bishops for violence and "its unremitting depiction of bloodshed and its affront to human dignity," citing the use of "an aging couple trapped in a crime-ridden environment and obliged to care for a disabled mother as comic relief." Still, the film found a cult following that remains strong today, especially in Europe where De Palma continues to enjoy a prosperous and solid reputation.

JOHN FARRIS: Originally, the film was scheduled to open in June or July, and the producers of *Damien; Omen* II [1978] convinced Fox that they needed the summer slot and *The Fury* got bounced to early spring. So, it opened in March during a snowstorm in the Midwest. You couldn't have picked a worse time to open the film, which cost everybody [including Fox] a lot of money. It opened well [not terrific but well].

The Fury was a good story. That's what carried it through the decades. Why is *Dracula* still around? Because it was a good story. But the line in *The Fury*, "What a culture can't assimilate,

A fantastic image of De Palma framing and blessing a shot with Cassavetes and Irving during the last scene of the film.

it destroys," absolutely still applies today in both good and corrupt societies. It definitely captures the theme of *The Fury*.

BRIAN DE PALMA: *The Fury* did okay. I did a lot of interesting things with it and I had a great time with the cast. There're some really nice sequences in it. During those early years, the most fun I had on a set was *The Fury* because Frank did a very good job producing it. I had all these great characters and Chicago in the summer was a lot of fun. I believe in good producers like Frank. It's like Marty Bregman on *Scarface* and *Carlito's Way* [1993]. George Litto was also a very good producer. Makes your life so much easier.

AMY IRVING: I just moved on. To this day I have no idea which of my films did well, and which did not. I don't read the reviews and I don't pay attention to box office. It doesn't matter to me. My work is done. But my son, Max, when he was about two and a half or three years old, caught the film on TV. He freaked out when he saw my scene with Charles Durning on the stairs; we had to show him a bottle of ketchup and tell him the blood was fake! But for years I could not wear red fingernail polish because the idea of blood and my hands freaked him out so much.

JOHN FARRIS: I took a long time between *The Fury* and writing the book sequels—*The Fury and The Terror* [2001], *The Fury and The Power* [2003] and *Avenging Fury* [2008]. But, one day, I got to thinking about what happened next [after I killed off everyone] and thought, "What if Robin didn't die?" I had a three-book deal with Tor Books, and it was advantageous to create a quadrilogy around *The Fury* mythology.

The Fury was supposed to be followed by *The Demolished Man*, based on the 1953 classic sci-fi novel by Alfred Bester, concluding an unintentional trilogy about psychic powers. The story was about the rivalry between two men—and one of them deciding to murder the other with the aid of a

---

first-class "Esper," a mutant with extrasensory perception. It was, basically, a procedural set in the future. De Palma's script adaptation did the book justice and merged the idea of psychic powers with voyeurism in the form of reading other people's minds.

De Palma had planned to have many scenes split in three images, essentially for the mind-peeping sessions, further evolving his approach to literally illustrate the thematic—the peeper would be seen on the left, victim on the right side, and the victim's thoughts dead center.

John Farris also worked on the project, but because of the complexities of the script, *The Demolished Man* was put aside; De Palma abandoned it as he got involved with *Home Movies*, and then *Dressed to Kill*, with both films dealing with voyeurism, but in the present day.

ON THE VERGE OF ADULTHOOD

I remember *The Fury* coming out in France with an ad campaign underlining it as the new "shocking" film from De Palma. And after the success of *Dressed to Kill*, it was re-released and played consistently in Parisian movie theaters. In fact, I went to see it several times over a period of a month and grew to appreciate the film more and more. Although it may lack the emotional and more subtle touch of *Carrie*, *The Fury* has improved with age; it is clearly the path to De Palma's grander-scale filmmaking on all levels. He is working not only with high-caliber actors and stars of the moment, but he also offers a grand spectacle, while staying true to his cinematic style. Interestingly, *The Fury* is also witness to and part of a seventies movement in horror cinema that showed kids' and teenage angst; it's about the fear of being different, about the clear division with the dangers of the adult world, and how they take control of who they are. It's about their revenge on the world at a time when we've seen young Americans rebelling at the bloody events at Kent State in 1970, or being sent to war in Vietnam. Viewed from that perspective, *The Fury* remains a testament to tragic, turbulent times.

THE
TRAGEDIES

Brian De Palma's films all have a tragic angle—
so far, casual sex has led to murder and psychic powers have caused destruction. But with
Phantom of the Paradise, Obsession, and *Blow Out,*
the tragedy is grand opera, played out against
heightened emotions and the complexities of the
human soul. We're in De Palma's heart.

William Finley is the titular Phantom in De Palma's cult classic, the horror-rock opera Phantom of the Paradise.

PHANTOM OF THE PARADISE

———— 1974 ————

*I got the idea for Phantom of the Paradise
from listening to a Muzak version of a Beatles song
in an elevator. It was "I Want to Hold Your Hand,"
and I thought, my God, they can take something
so original, so exciting, and turn it into pop.*

—BRIAN DE PALMA
(WRITER / DIRECTOR)

THE STORY: Swan (Paul Williams), a powerful record producer, is about to open a new music club called the Paradise. He has stolen the unfinished rock opera written by Winslow Leach (William Finley), a young, naive, and unknown composer, who gets framed on drug charges and is locked up in jail. After he hears this music performed by a group called the Juicy Fruits, Winslow escapes, but while attempting to destroy Swan's recording, his face is accidentally smashed by a record press, leaving him disfigured and without his voice. Winslow dons a mask and a cape and becomes the Phantom of the Paradise, intent on getting revenge against Swan. But Swan protects his empire by striking a deal. He offers to restore Winslow's voice if Winslow completes his rock opera. Swan also agrees to allow Phoenix (Jessica Harper), the woman Winslow loves, to perform the songs. The two men sign a contract marked in blood, but Swan doesn't fully honor his end of the deal—he hires Beef (Gerrit Graham), a coked-up singer, to perform the rock opera. But after Winslow electrocutes Beef during the concert, in front of a delirious audience, Phoenix finally makes her triumphant debut. Swan tortures Winslow further by seducing Phoenix. Winslow attempts to take his life—stabbing himself—only to discover he can't die, an unseen clause in his blood contract with Swan. Winslow learns that Swan is under a contract as well, one he made with the Devil that assures him everlasting youth and success. But once Winslow learns Swan plans to murder Phoenix during their televised wedding, he rushes into action. He destroys the videotaped contracts, thereby robbing Swan of his immortality. Phoenix is spared, but Winslow stabs Swan. As a result, Winslow's self-inflicted wound reopens and he meets his tragic end, having saved the beauty from the beast.

Despite its horror/supernatural elements, *Phantom of the Paradise* is very much a satire that reflects De Palma's humor. It's closer in style to his earlier films, *Greetings* and *Hi, Mom!*, but also resembles *Murder à la Mod*. William Finley plays a bizarre prankster in *Murder à la Mod*, and the character is pure training ground for him; his gangly, pantomime body language performance carries over to *Phantom*. As the title character, Finley informs the type of film we're dealing with; he is a comical, yet tragic, figure. He straddles both the absurdist horror and slapstick comedy reminiscent of Buster Keaton. Even his disfigurement scene is comical—inadvertently starting a record press, slipping on a vinyl record and getting his face smashed in the machine.

Murder à la Mod is, arguably, De Palma's first horror thriller. It's memorable for its bold approach and convoluted plot. Its story is told three times, in different styles, and from three different points of view. The plot itself is unimportant, but the visuals aren't—especially the shocking and graphic murder of a young woman who is stabbed through the hand and eye with an ice pick—it's the forebearer to both Kate Miller's elevator death in *Dressed to Kill*, and the ice pick serial killings in *Blow Out*.

REMIXING THE CLASSICS

Though *Phantom* was a box office failure in America, it became an instant cult classic in France, where it played continuously for several years and won the Grand Prix at the Avoriaz Fantastic Film Festival in 1975. I remember buying the soundtrack album and learning the songs' lyrics by heart, singing along to perfect my English. Over the years, the film has deservingly been recognized worldwide as a rock parody of the horror classic *The Phantom of the Opera*, remixed with elements of *The Portrait of Dorian Gray*, *Beauty and the Beast*, and *Faust*.

Showtime! The Phantom shines the spotlight on the performance below.

But the "Devil" is truly De Palma's singular vision for the film, which melds dark humor, the exploration of the double, pre-MTV musical numbers, and—beyond the satire—a reflection on the struggle for artistic integrity. One can easily recognize De Palma himself as Winslow Leach, a composer whose work is stolen, bastardized, and ripped apart by Swan. The end is tragic for both men, but the work—the songs—remain. As we will see again in *Blow Out*, where the heroine dies but her screams "survive," *Phantom* celebrates the immortality of art while underlining the sacrifice it entails.

BEFORE PARADISE

Phantom of the Paradise began as *Phantom of the Fillmore*. The revised draft quoted here, credited to De Palma and his *Sisters* co-writer Louisa Rose, is dated 6/12/73. The first page opens by quoting the American rock band the Byrds: "So you want to be a rock 'n' roll star?" The story begins in the late fifties. Swan is named Spectre in this draft and is unseen during the first few scenes. Philbin (played by George Memmoli) is a sleazy music manager who lost a lawsuit against one of his clients—a star singer named Annette—and has come to Spectre for justice. (The character is named after the silent movie actress Mary Philbin who starred in the 1925 film adaptation of the novel *The Phantom of the Opera*.) Spectre tells Philbin it's time to look for a new sound and they conduct auditions at a school gymnasium. Winslow Leach (named after De Palma's favorite Drama teacher Wilford Leach), a bullied teen, performs his Faust ballad, which impresses Spectre. (We later find out Annette went to a dentist who, acting on Spectre's orders, instead of pulling out a tooth, removed her tongue.)

Philbin visits Winslow's home—he still lives with his mother, who thinks Philbin has come to meet her younger son, Norman, a science genius. The brother and the mother tell Philbin that Winslow suffered from "infantile sensitivitis," an inflammation of the senses. The brother says, "Any external stimuli caused excruciating pain. They had to wrap the creep in wet gauze for five years." (This, potentially, was a nod to another horror classic, *The Mummy*, 1932.)

As scripted, De Palma wanted to film at the Fillmore, a movie theater built in Fillmore, California, in 1916 during the silent film era. In the script, it is described as a gothic cathedral turned into a rock opera palace, complete with a recording studio located in the bell tower.

As in the film, Spectre steals Winslow's opera. Winslow is thrown in jail, where his teeth are pulled out, but he succeeds in a rage-fueled escape after hearing his opera performed on a radio by The Juicy Fruits, a band from his school. Winslow is disfigured by a record press, with the scar an the impression of a 45 rpm record, and the mask he wears was to be in the image of Spectre. However, the final film presents Leach assuming an aspect of his antagonist in another way—Swan replaces Leach's destroyed voice with his own—he makes Leach his double, but in voice only.

BRIAN DE PALMA: After Winslow is disfigured and his voice is destroyed, I came up with the idea of Paul Williams dubbing Bill Finley. Swan, the egomaniac that he is, gives him his own voice. And that's what we did.

PAUL WILLIAMS ("SWAN"/COMPOSER/LYRICIST/SINGER): The kind of work behind a mask that Bill Finley did was just so stunning. With one eye he could convey his heartache. Me doing his voice is an idea that evolved during the shoot; his voice is ruined, Swan is rebuilding it, and what would he consider the perfect voice? His own, of course. And as the composer and songwriter of the film, it gave me the opportunity to sing a song for it.

The script appeared to have a fun self-reference to *Sisters*, in which Philbin lies to Phoenix about the relationship between Winslow and Spectre, claiming they were twins. He explains, "They were very weird, conjoined twins 'cause they joined at the head. Well, right after they were born the doctors separated them and gave Spectre all the brains and good looks and left Winslow with nothing. Well after that Winslow turned rotten and Spectre tried to do everything he could for him, but nothing did any good."

Throughout the script, Spectre is filmed by a documentary crew; there's a secret screening room—run by a projectionist who pretended to be blind to get the job—where Spectre views the footage. This projectionist reveals to Winslow that the "film is the secret to Spectre's beauty. It gets ugly instead of him." If the film is destroyed, Spectre would be finished.

The climax of the film takes place in a park at a free concert during which Spectre intends to marry Phoenix. But Winslow destroys the film, Spectre loses his looks and is stomped to death. Winslow's face, on the other hand, is back to normal but the wound to his heart when he attempted suicide reopens. He staggers on stage, where Phoenix is about to start singing. She has gone mad and rejects him. She loses her voice because of the deal she made with Spectre, but goes on with her performance anyway.

BUILDING THE BAND

By the time De Palma makes *Phantom*, he has forged his incredible eye for casting, a tradition he would carry throughout his career. He has a natural talent not just for finding the right actors, but also at getting their best performances. Here, De Palma and William Finley reunite for their sixth film together (counting the short *Woton's Wake*, 1963, and the filmed performance of *Dionysus in 69)*. Finley understands how to approach Winslow, which is both tragic but on the edge of satire. Casting Paul Williams is an inspired choice; he embodies Swan's duality of both godlike figure and the Devil. The quality of his discernible voice adds to the character's ambiguity. Just like her character's name—Phoenix—Jessica Harper displayed little doubt that she'd rise, emerging as an actress with a bright future after *Phantom*. Of all the characters, she has a clear journey and transformation, from naive to empowered when she sings, to seduced after she replaces Beef on stage. But De Palma is also quite adept at underlining the importance of the entire cast, including courageous performances by George Memmoli as the

Swan (Paul Williams) has found his new star in Phoenix (Jessica Harper).

rather sordid Philbin, and Gerrit Graham, in his third film with De Palma, portraying the extravagant Beef.

BRIAN DE PALMA: We had a hard time trying to get a group. Our first idea was to get Sha Na Na, but that didn't work out. It was a group that did fifties songs.

PAUL WILLIAMS: I was at A&M Records as a staff writer. I was having a nice rush with success and A&M decided to get into the film business, placing music and songs in movies. They hired someone to run that side of the company, who connected with Brian. They talked about me, and I got the script. And it was a chance for me to satirize all the different kinds of music I love.

Brian was very contained. He was so focused that there was not a lot of talking. I can still picture him lost in thought, kind of coming back to the surface and looking at me, going, "You know, there's something about you that could work for Swan." And I said, "No, no, I can't do that," but then I just realized, "Oh, my God, yeah. I would love that." It's a bit over the top but I just loved it.

BRIAN DE PALMA: Paul and I got on very well; he could write all the different versions of the [main] song, in all the different styles. I also liked the way he acted so I said, we'll make you Swan, and Bill Finley will be the Phantom.

JESSICA HARPER ("PHOENIX"): It was the kind of script that was so dependent on the characters and their performances in the film. I had seen *Sisters*, and I always loved the actors Brian chose, like Bill Finley. He had a great quality for that role of the Phantom. He played a kind, geeky guy, with those thick glasses. He's one of those actors who had an innate sweetness and that, at least in my opinion, instantly inspired empathy and made him a great choice for that role. Someone else might have taken a different direction that would be more expected. But I think that was often the case with Brian.

BRIAN DE PALMA: [For the role of Phoenix] we auditioned singers; Linda Ronstadt being one of them.

JESSICA HARPER: I was working in the theater in New York at that time. Richard Foreman offered me a role in this musical called *Doctor Selavy's Magic Theatre*, at the Mercer Arts Center. It was one of those things that happens in New York when a play gets a rave review, and everybody in town goes to see it. I got a lot of exposure, including to Brian De Palma. I was summoned Uptown to meet with Paul Williams, by whom I was sort of awestruck because he had already achieved greatness with his songs. I was asked to come up and sing for him; I sang "Superstar," which had been performed by Karen Carpenter.

I was trying to channel the Carpenters because she was Paul's muse, and I thought if I could pull that off, it might help. I guess he liked me.

PAUL WILLIAMS: I heard Jessica sing the song, before the actual audition, when she was waiting to come in. I thought she was great. Then she came in, sang it for Brian, and I asked her to do it again, just like she had done it outside. I told her to sing it to herself. She was just so wonderful and had that amazing innocence. She was just perfect for the role. We all fell in love with her.

JESSICA HARPER: Brian called me later and said, "Let's go to Hollywood for a screen test." They put me up at the Chateau Marmont; I was just absolutely dazzled by all this. I spent a sleepless night before the audition because I knew that my competition was Linda Ronstadt, which was pretty daunting, to say the least. I auditioned in a studio in Hollywood. It was on camera, and I had to sing and act. It's a blur because I was extremely nervous.

The evening after the audition, I remember going out to dinner with Brian to Musso & Frank Grill, a place that still exists and reeks of Hollywood history. He had a friend join us, who was jumpy and edgy—turns out his name was Marty Scorsese. Halfway through dinner, the costume designer Rosanna Norton joined us. She took me into the ladies' room and measured every inch of my body—which I thought was either a unique form of assault or a good sign. [*Laughs*] After I flew back to New York, I got the phone call that Linda Ronstadt was keeping her day job, and I was going to be Phoenix. I was just blown away with excitement because this was my first film, and it was an incredible role, singing this gorgeous music.

BRIAN DE PALMA: Gerrit Graham, I had used in *Greetings*, and *Hi, Mom!* He's a great improviser. He's very bright. He's got a real edge. Everyone did their own singing except for Gerrit. Betty Buckley auditioned for *Phantom of the Paradise*, and she gave an incredible audition, but I didn't think she was exactly right for the part. Needless to say, she was very talented. And when I got *Carrie*, I encouraged her to move to California, and got her a part in the film.

The stars weren't just on screen. And the film begins with a voice-over by none other than *The Twilight Zone*'s Rod Serling, setting the supernatural tone of the story.

BRIAN DE PALMA: We just went after Rod Serling and he did it. I met him in a recording studio, he read the stuff, and was

Beef (Gerrit Graham) is introduced at a press conference.

very quick. He did a lot of voice-overs. He had that great kind of voice that works for that genre.

THE HOUSE THAT JACK BUILT

With *Phantom*, there is a sense that De Palma is having fun with the look of the film. The world of the Paradise itself (with its elaborate musical numbers), as well as the other locations, contributes to the film's stylized approach. The look altogether spells out, on one hand, vibrant realism and, on the other, more fantasy.

JACK FISK (PRODUCTION DESIGNER): I went to LA, met with Brian, and I remember he was kind of an imposing figure. He had already done quite a few films, and I had been working with people who had done no movies, or just one or two. I remember he looked at me and said, "What have you

Decades before there was reality TV, there was the staged live wedding of Phoenix to Swan, officiated by Philbin (George Memmoli).

done?" [*Laughs*] I mentioned *Badlands* [1973], but no one had seen it yet. And the other things I'd done were just exploitation films with Roger Corman. But for some reason, he accepted me as the production designer / art director, and we started working together.

When I first went into his office I looked around and there were three-by-five notecards on all the walls, and little stick figures, crude drawings, and he had mapped out every shot in the film. And oh, my goodness, I'd never seen that before. But it gave me a great guide. I just knew where we were going, and what was important.

BRIAN DE PALMA: I immediately connected with Jack. We got the same sense of humor . . . He is very talented, as we well see.

JACK FISK: I had complete freedom as far as the design of the film. I had a friend, Jodie Tillen, who was a costume designer and said, "If it's a story about selling your soul to the Devil, you can't use black and red." I said, "Well that's exactly what I'm going to do." [*Laughs*] I'm a contrary person but things kept developing in that way; it grew and became fun . . . Everything got fantastical; I designed Swan's desk as a big gold record, his bed was a turntable, the hallways were curved like grooves of a record.

I was doing a lot of it myself and then I had some construction pals who helped with building the sets. I never knew what Brian thought until one day, while everybody went to lunch, I was bricking up the doorway to the set where Swan had locked Phantom in. I'd never laid brick before, the grips came back, and they were making fun of me, and Brian told them, "Shut up, Jack's making this film look beautiful." That was the first time I had heard any kind of message from him about what he was thinking of the design. It just felt so great. Brian often said that whenever he worked with me the sets were always wet. [*Laughs*] That's because I never wanted to give up. You just keep working until the last minute, until they push you off, and then you go, "Okay, you can shoot it."

BRIAN DE PALMA: The fact that he's still doing this today is unbelievable. He did *The Revenant* [2015], can you imagine? Yikes. [*Laughs*] For us, he designed the sets and the look of the film.

JACK FISK: My girlfriend then was Sissy Spacek, now my wife of fifty years . . . I was getting a little behind getting the sets ready and I needed help. I was scrambling and in over my head. It was too big a film for our budget, too big for the kind of crew I had. So, Sissy stepped in and started sewing together the sheets that were going to make up Swan's turntable bed. She stayed up all night sewing those, and then we made her the set dresser. She came to Texas with us, and we got her family involved. Her one cousin was helping me paint sets and others were making dummies for Beef's big musical number. It was a family effort. Even her mother came out when we were shooting. I was sweeping the stage—I was doing everything at that point in my career— but she was so proud and happy to see me working there.

JESSICA HARPER: I love that Brian cast Sissy Spacek in *Carrie* [after *Phantom*]. I remember she and Jack were such an incredible couple, very much in love with each other, and with each other all the time.

JACK FISK: Brian was patient with me. Because he storyboards everything, I learned that he could move quickly. It seemed like he was always waiting for people. He sat in his chair with a cup of coffee, waiting, like, "Come on, I've already done my work." But on one occasion, he had moved ahead by a day and, generally, I was lucky to have stuff ready on the day of shooting. He showed up to shoot the part with the judge behind the bench, with the big American flag, and then he wanted to go into a dressing room set that Sissy and her cousin were still painting. I told Brian, "We'll be ready tomorrow, as scheduled." And he said, "Okay." Then he went home. [*Laughs*]

BIRD'S-EYE VIEW

A bird motif is present throughout the film. It starts with Swan's record label, Death Records—a dead sparrow (widely viewed either as a good or a bad omen).

JACK FISK: The first day of work, I went out of my house in Topanga Canyon, and I looked down on the sidewalk, and there was a dead sparrow that had hit itself against the window. It was in perfect shape but dead. I thought of it in terms of a songbird; you always think of birds singing. I took it to work with me, I had a friend shoot it with a process camera and we made that the logo for Death Records.

Of course, there're the names like Swan—as in "swan song," but also an image that is part of the on-stage set design within the film, and Phoenix as portrayed by Jessica Harper, who survives and rises from the ashes. Even Winslow's one-eyed Phantom's mask is in the shape of a bird's head. In the finale, dancers are dressed as crows, and Winslow uses one of their headpieces to stab Swan.

The traditional symbolism of birds is twisted to represent both creativity and destruction, life and death, hope and

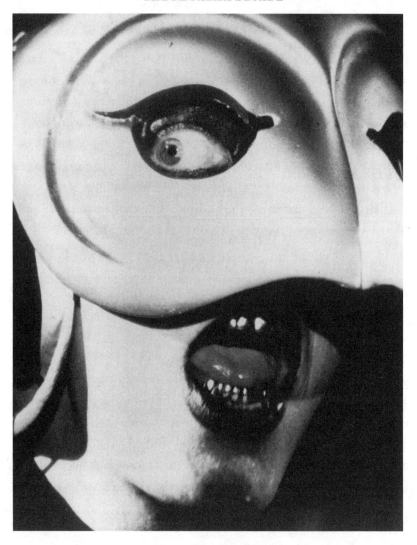

The beak shape of the Phantom's mask echoes the film's bird motif.

despair—just like the story itself. We're shown a world ruled by the
Devil, yet these characters remain—literally—birds of Paradise.

JESSICA HARPER: The costume designer, Rosanna Norton,
wanted to embrace this bird theme. I wore a wonderful, feath-
ered coat and, you couldn't tell, but there were bird designs
printed on the pants. There's no reference to birds in my

costume in the final scene. I needed to be able to move, so, I took it upon myself to adjust the costume, shall we say, and I took some things from the rack that Rosanna had chosen for other characters; she was not happy about it at all. It wasn't very professional on my part, I have to say. But the chorus girls are all in feathers, and they look incredible.

Through Winslow's character, De Palma looks into devices of cinema, like he would later do in *Blow Out*, exploring how films are dubbed. But here, as Winslow starts haunting the Paradise, De Palma introduces a Hitchcockian theme of building suspense. Using the split-screen technique, he offers different points of view when Winslow puts a ticking time bomb in a propped car as it rolls on stage for a rehearsal. De Palma is embracing Hitchcock's famous description of the difference between suspense and shock. A bomb is under a table with two people chatting; suspense keeps cutting back to the ticking bomb, but shock is having it explode unexpectedly.

Then, there's the shock of Beef in the shower and, as in *Psycho*, a dark figure approaches behind the curtain, slices it with a large knife. But instead of stabbing, Winslow uses a toilet plunger to silence Beef and threaten him. De Palma earns a laugh as he turns this reference around, creating a universe unique to his film.

BEHIND THE MUSIC

PAUL WILLIAMS: Larry Pizer was the great cinematographer on the film, but Ronnie Taylor, who became an Academy Award–winning DP with *Gandhi* [1982], was the camera operator. He did that amazing handheld shot from the point of view of the Phantom, which starts outside the Paradise, goes

backstage, up the stairs, and ends inside the wardrobe stor-
age room where he selects his leather outfit, finds the one-
eyed mask, and puts it on, literally, over the lens of the camera.
This was done in one shot before the Steadicam [existed], and
it is spectacular.

The musical numbers get increasingly more sophisticated
through the film and participate in the overall storytelling.
Phantom opens with The Juicy Fruits performing "Goodbye,
Eddie, Goodbye," on a simple stage over the opening credits.
The song—a sad tale of sacrifice—tells the story of a talented
singer who commits suicide so that his memorial album goes
to the top of the charts and pays for an operation needed by
his sister.

*The Beach Bums rehearse a rendition of "Faust," now entitled "Upholstery," unaware
that Winslow has hidden a bomb on stage.*

PAUL WILLIAMS: I wrote a lot of the songs while I was opening for Liza Minnelli at Harrah's in Tahoe. I wrote during the day while I was performing two shows a night. It was an interesting time in my life . . . I wanted my own road band to perform all the music in the film. I was comfortable with them. I knew I'd get what I wanted from them. They were so creative and so good. Then, for The Juicy Fruits, The Beach Bums, and The Undeads, we put together Jeffrey Comanor, Archie Hahn, and Harold Oblong. They were fabulous. Archie was perfect as the lead singer for "Goodbye, Eddie, Goodbye."

The next song, "Faust," is filmed in 360 degrees around Winslow at the piano. Swan is listening behind a two-way mirror but all we see of him are his whitegloved hands. His music manager, Philbin, is talking to him, but literally speaking straight to camera, breaking the fourth wall, and putting us in the position of Swan. We're forced into the position of the antagonist as he tells Philbin that Winslow's "Faust" is the new sound for the Paradise. We then hear "Never Thought I'd Get to Meet the Devil" play after Winslow discovers Swan wanted just the song, not Winslow himself.

Phoenix's audition, "Special to Me," has its own unique approach. As she sings, "Damn all evil that takes possession until your pipe dreams become obsessions," she also breaks the fourth wall, stares straight to camera, directly at us.

JESSICA HARPER: We recorded in Los Angeles and sang to playback. For my first song, that choreography was just me messing around, and that was my actual Bella hat that I wore a lot in those days. Again, I'd just decided, randomly, to wear it, much to the costume designer's concern, I'm afraid. And, as I exited the stage in the scene, I decided to throw my hat and to flap my arms; I just made up what has become known, by many fans, as the chicken dance. [*Laughs*]

"Phantom's Theme (Beauty and the Beast)" is accompanied by a beautiful montage and sung in Swan's voice, offering "All the devils that disturbed me and the angels that defeated them somehow, come together in me now."

PAUL HIRSCH (EDITOR): Brian didn't have time or a second unit to do the montage sequence. Both Gerrit Graham and I wanted to do it, but I got the assignment. I designed the shots and figured out how to do them. Most of it was against a black limbo backdrop. I first had to cut ["Phantom's Theme (Beauty and the Beast)"] down because it was too long. I got it to a reasonable length and then the idea was to illustrate something that can't be illustrated, which is somebody writing a song. How do you make that visual? That was the challenge. And so, I resorted to images that cinematic artist Slavko Vorkapich had used in his montages in the thirties to indicate time passing. Candle burning down, calendar pages, and we had a clock made from a gold record, spinning much faster than normal. Then, I had Jessica dressed in a feather boa against black. For the notes traveling across the screen, I worked with an optical house, I wrote the notes myself and they transferred them to some kind of plastic transparency. The trick was to make sure the notes you were seeing on screen were the notes you were hearing. It was very tricky, but it worked out. We had Bill Finley writing and playing the music within the scene, eventually being asleep at the end. I had him holding a black plastic pen and Brian said, "We'll never see it. It's not going to show." And he suggested a big feathery quill which I thought might be over the top. We couldn't find one at the time and he didn't insist. But that would have been a nice touch.

Ultimately, the most remarkable number is Beef's "construction" song, à la Frankenstein's monster entitled "Somebody Super Like You," with an impressive set straight out of 1920's *The Cabinet of Dr. Caligari* (featuring The Undeads dressed and made-up to reflect the angles and shadows of the décor). It is a surreal moment that transitions into the next song, "Life at Last," which blares the lyrics "I'm the evil that you created," and culminates with Beef's electrocution on stage. His death leads to Phoenix's triumphant performance of "Old Souls."

PAUL HIRSCH: My work as a trailer editor prepared me for the musical scenes because trailers are all about rhythm, it's just sort of dance-like. But I was not trained as an editor by anyone.

The Undeads perform "Somebody Super Like You," Beef's "construction" musical number.

I invented my own way of doing everything. Obviously, there was a whole history of Hollywood musicals before *Phantom of the Paradise*. I didn't know any of it and, if I had known more, it would have been a lot easier for me. But here I was on this low-budget film. I had to work out my own ways of cutting these musical numbers, particularly the one with The Undeads, which interacted with the audience, then Beef's performance, with his electrocution on stage and Phoenix taking over. There was a lot of footage. I had to figure out my own way of handling it all and keeping it all in sync. I didn't have a music editor on the film. I didn't know there was such a thing as a music editor, so I didn't even know to ask for one! Instinctively, I wanted to make sure I had the best possible angle on every line of every lyric and maintain sync and pace. You're making this spectacle as impressive as you can.

PAUL WILLIAMS: I'm so proud of that whole "Somebody Super Like You" sequence. Archie Hahn was just magnificent in it. And there was a guy named Art Munson who did that whole guitar opening that takes you into the song. It was so strong, just great musicians.

The one thing I've always had to live with is the fact that I chose a different voice for Beef on "Life at Last." I knew exactly the quality I was looking for and chose Ray Kennedy to do the singing. And then I saw Gerrit in that shower scene, when you hear his actual voice, I went, "Oh, Jesus, he's really good, he can sing." There're one or two occasions in my life when I replaced a voice and I wish I hadn't. The other time was Jodie Foster as Tallulah in *Bugsy Malone* [1976].

JACK FISK: A year before *Phantom*, I was working on *Messiah of Evil* [1974], directed by Willard Huyck. He and his wife, Gloria

Katz, told me about *The Cabinet of Dr. Caligari*. I rented it on 16mm with a projector and watched it. I was just knocked out because here were painters doing what I do, and they did it so beautifully. The sets and the lines on the faces came from that, trying to be expressionistic. It came organically from *The Cabinet of Dr. Caligari*, mixed with *Frankenstein* [1931]. For that number, we built the stage out into the audience. When I was an art student at Pennsylvania Academy, I worked as a carpenter at the Theater of Living Arts in Philadelphia, and I worked on a play in the sixties where we built the stage like that, with the audience in the scene. And I borrowed from that experience.

PAUL WILLIAMS: The mood for "Old Souls" had to do with my mother. The lyrics, "Our love is an old love, we're older than all our years, I have seen in strangers' eyes familiar tears," were written about my mother's death. She died of cancer around the time. My dad was killed in a car wreck when I was about thirteen years old, and I was shipped off to live with an aunt and uncle. I was away from my mom and my younger brother for all my high school years and then reconnected with them. As a result, the song has a somber element that connects to the drama of the loss. The melody was very much inspired by how I felt at that time. It's my favorite song. It's interesting because it's never had a life outside the movie. I've written some B-minus songs that have been recorded a bunch of times, but not this one. I always thought that was the song that was going to have a big life outside the movie, but it didn't.

The last song, "The Hell of It," plays over the end credits and bookends "Goodbye, Eddie, Goodbye." This time around, we hear, "We've all come to say goodbye, born defeated, died in vain, super destruction you were hooked on pain and tho' your music lingers on, all of us are glad you're gone."

PAUL WILLIAMS: "The Hell of It" was written for Beef's funeral. That song was a take on composer Nino Rota, who did many of Fellini's scores. When the casket was being lowered into the grave, there were cables hooked to a hearse, and there was Swan at a mixing board recording the whole thing. In the script, it said that as the casket is being lowered into the grave, a mother pushes her little girl forward. The girl runs, jumps up onto the casket, and starts tap dancing. But we could not find a cemetery where we could shoot this scene, and we were running out of money, so Brian said, "We're cutting out that funeral. But I'm going to use 'The Hell of It' in a montage sequence for the end credits."

THE DARK SIDE OF THE INDUSTRY

In a twist of life imitating art, the movie's theme of corporate giants attacking artists was carried out in the real world as the film was beset by numerous lawsuits. The band Led Zeppelin sued over the name "Swan Song," which was their record label. Additionally, their manager, Peter Grant, perceived Beef's death on stage as a send-up of the accidental electrocution on stage of Scottish guitarist Leslie Harvey in 1972, which he had witnessed. Due to the lawsuit, the filmmakers were forced to remove any visual references to Swan's original record label name, which was seen multiple times throughout the film. Using crude matte techniques and editing, the film was reshaped to avoid the lawsuit.

PAUL HIRSCH: The film was picked up by 20th Century Fox and there was a lot of excitement about it. And then, suddenly, the production was threatened with lawsuits. The film was originally titled *The Phantom*, but King Features Syndicate, who owned the comic book character The Phantom forced us to change the title to *Phantom of the Paradise*. Then, Universal claimed infringement on *Phantom of the Opera* and we had to give them points in the film. And we were instructed by Led Zeppelin's manager to remove all the shots showing the label Swan Song. I was obliged to recut the picture—sometimes in a brutal fashion—and employing crude optical techniques to cover the image when I couldn't simply cut it out. I am thrilled that audiences have enthusiastically embraced the film despite these flaws, but for me, I've never gotten over them.

The film feels like an indictment of not only the music business, but also the madness infused in concert audiences. Drugs

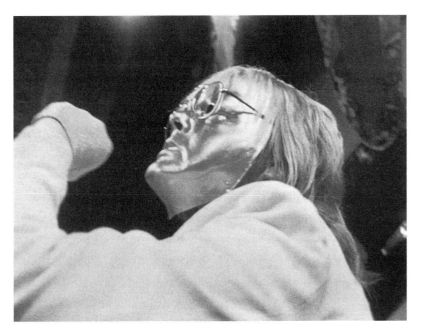

Swan wears a mask of his own at his marriage to Phoenix.

impacted artists and audiences alike. We're only a few years out from the stabbing of a man at a Rolling Stone concert. In *Phantom*, we see the audience participating in the building of Beef, as the singing group picks out dummy body parts hidden amongst the crowd. When Beef is electrocuted, the audience goes wild, thinking it's part of the act. And at the end of the film, similarly, there's no divide between audience and performers—all are together. No one except for Phoenix realizes that Winslow is dying while Swan is being carried out like a sacrificial lamb. You witness the audience going mad, taking off their clothes, and, literally, turning the Paradise into a hell of sex, drugs, and rock 'n' roll.

PAUL WILLIAMS: My favorite line in the movie—and in some ways the heart of the movie to me—is when Swan plans to have Phoenix shot during the wedding celebration on stage, I say, "An assassination live, on coast-to-coast television? That's entertainment!" To me, that's the heart of the story.

THE PHANTOM EXPOSED

Vincent Canby of the *New York Times* called *Phantom of the Paradise* an "elaborate disaster," while also criticizing what he perceived to be a failed attempt at humor. But *Variety* and Kevin Thomas of the *Los Angeles Times* got the film's outrageousness and underlined—with some reservation—De Palma's ingenious directing. Pauline Kael's comments were somewhat discreet, but mostly announced her personal connection and understanding of the De Palma touch, while Gene Siskel of the *Chicago Tribune* simply did not get it and labeled the film "childish." The film was ultimately nominated for an Academy Award for Original Song, Score, and Adaptation.

Swan's true appearance is finally revealed, to Phoenix's horror.

JESSICA HARPER: I just went to the movie theater like every-body else in New York. I went to the Upper East Side, and I remember standing and looking at the marquee, and I just couldn't believe that such a thing had happened, that I was involved with a film that was now playing in a movie theater. Seeing the movie was very affecting. It had a sad ending, and I reacted to it like your average moviegoer; I was really captured by the emotional arc of the story. I really went with it.

JACK FISK: They were selling it as a rock musical, but it's really a horror film. And, of course, you only get one chance to open a film.

BRIAN DE PALMA: Bill Finley and I went to see it when it opened in New York, and nobody was there. I mean nobody went. The Westwood showing in LA was a little better, but it basically died. I have no idea why. Maybe it was too crazy.

Mixing genres. Who knows. But then, it won a big prize at the Avoriaz International Fantastic Film Festival in France; the French tell me it played in Paris forever. And it was bigger than *Jaws* in Winnipeg!!

At the time the film was released, a puzzling novelization by Bjarne Rostaing was published, which—though roughly following the plot and characters—omits the supernatural angle completely. The most notable departure is the opening to the story. We're introduced to Winslow in Dunphy, Maine, studying under an alcoholic "mafia-lounge piano player," who dies in a freak accident. Winslow then moves to Manhattan with his electric piano, where he composes a modern opera version of *Faust* called *Foster* and meets Phoenix in a seedy hotel. The novel retains *The Phantom of the Opera* elements but, inexplicably, drops the pact with the Devil and the *Dorian Gray* angle.

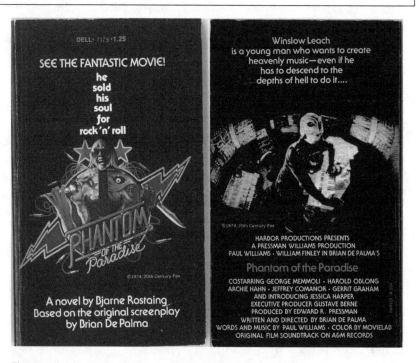

The novelization was published at the time of the film's release.

An ad highlighting Paul Williams's Academy Award nomination for Original Song, Score, and Adaptation.

LIVING FOREVER

The concept of preserving eternal life and beauty is central to Swan, but is also reflective of the artist, the director, and cinema at large. It is the symbolic power of filmed images, and how they can freeze someone in time, preserving them for eternity. Like most of the De Palma oeuvre, *Phantom of the Paradise* is a film that would later be re-evaluated and embraced. Undeniably, the film has had a journey like Winslow's own composition within the story—ignored and bastardized at first, but now immortal.

PAUL WILLIAMS: *Phantom* is the little movie that just sort of plopped out onto the screen. And one of the real gifts was that it was not even a moderate hit. If it had done well, it probably would have disappeared, but the fiery enthusiasm of people who loved the movie and couldn't believe that other people didn't know about it created this self-generating promotional thing. The reason I worked with Daft Punk was because of

Phantom of the Paradise. The two guys met in a theater in Paris. They saw it like twenty-five times, and they wound up getting the masks, which evolved into robots. Around 2013 or 2014, they called me, and we make an album together that wins album of the year. And I'm currently doing *Pan's Labyrinth* [2006] for the stage for Guillermo del Toro, because of *Phantom.* Brian De Palma gave me a gift that was much larger than I realized at the time. I was just floored because it was a chance to do both things that I love to do around film: composing and acting.

JESSICA HARPER: The film has accumulated a huge fan base over the years, very oddly. I had one man come up to me and say he'd seen the movie a hundred and fifty times. Maybe it was ten years ago, this Phantompalooza, they called it—a big revisiting of the movie in Winnipeg—and Paul and other cast members were invited to come and perform a mini concert before they screened the movie. People were lined up around the block, and it was really a big deal for these dear people. I did some singing with Paul; I threw my hat into the audience and did a little bit of the "chicken dance." All I had to do was flap my arms and people would go insane. It was very cool. And speaking of these little pockets of fandom around the world, I was walking through Paris about fifteen years ago, on Place de la Madeleine, and there was an electronic shop. I was walking by, and I heard myself singing. *Phantom of the Paradise* was on a screen perched in the window of this electronic store. It was wild.

PAUL HIRSCH: *Phantom* is great because it's so whacky and it's got all that fantastic music in it. There was a lot of experimentation in it. I have this expression—trial and success, instead of trial and errors. I was trying stuff out and, finally, it worked.

JACK FISK: I learned a lot [on *Phantom*] because I knew nothing. [*Laughs*] There's so much to learn. I learned about preparation. I learned to think about scenes before we shot them. Even working with directors in the future who didn't storyboard, I would always have a plan of how a set could be used. And I think that came from Brian's preparation.

JESSICA HARPER: I'll tell you a funny story. I knew an actor in New York named John Rothman. He'd been in a million plays, and I met him before I got *Phantom*. He had a little brother named Tom who was, at that time, at Brown University in Providence. Tom went home to Baltimore for Christmas and John took him to see *Phantom of the Paradise*. When I came on screen, John leaned over to Tom, and said, "See that girl? I know her." As Tom tells this story, at that moment, he thought to himself, "Wow, well, I've got to get to New York where the girls look like that!!" [*Laughs*] And in about fifteen years, Tom and I were married!

BRIAN DE PALMA: It was devastating when it opened and didn't do any business. It's like you can't believe it. You say, "Oh, my God, what am I going to do now?" The same thing happened with *Blow Out*. It was a disaster when it first came out. But, fortunately, you're rescued by time.

PLAYING ON REPEAT

There was something very comforting about *Phantom of the Paradise* always being available to see in movie theaters while I was growing up in Paris. Before the days of video rentals, being able to experience *Phantom* constantly on the big screen was always a treat. The album played constantly in the Bouzereau household, with my older sister and me learning the songs by heart. While the film fits thematically within the decade between *Sisters* and *Blow Out*, it operates as the satirical element closer to De Palma's earlier works. But it also establishes an operatic style De Palma would develop, and it is much bigger in scope than it seems. The madness at the closing rock concert nearly prepares us for Tony Montana's demise in *Scarface*, literally ten years later. But it's the tragedy of Winslow that always pulls at the heart strings; the Phantom is both hero and villain, monster and artist, genius and victim. He represents the archetypal tragic romantic type that De Palma would continue to explore in *Obsession* and *Blow Out*.

I saw the film a few years after it came out, at one of the small Paris theaters that played it continuously since its release. Because I knew the songs, I found myself singing along with the film. At the time, I was blown away by how different it was from *Obsession*. It really awoke in me the idea of a director exploring such different genres and sensibilities, yet having connectivity through his visual style.

Geneviève Bujold tackles dual roles in De Palma's emotional tribute to Hitchcock's Vertigo.

OBSESSION

—— 1976 ——

Whether you're a novelist or a painter or a filmmaker, you're always inspired by the masters that came before you. You get ideas from them; you build on their ideas.

—BRIAN DE PALMA
(DIRECTOR / STORY BY)

THE STORY: Michael Courtland (Cliff Robertson) is a successful businessman and land developer. He lives happily in New Orleans with his wife, Elizabeth (Geneviève Bujold), and their daughter, Amy (Wanda Blackman). After a party, where Michael is toasted by his partner Robert "Bob" La Salle (John Lithgow), his family is kidnapped. The blackmail attempt ends tragically with the deaths of Elizabeth and Amy in a car crash. Sixteen years later, Michael travels to Florence on a business trip with La Salle. He returns to the church where he met Elizabeth, and sees a young art historian named Sandra Portinari, who looks exactly like his wife (also played by Geneviève Bujold). They fall in love and return to New Orleans to get married despite the disapproval of his psychiatrist and colleagues.

The night before the wedding, Michael dreams of the ceremony, where Sandra speaks to him as if she were Elizabeth, saying how she came back to give him a second chance to prove his love. When he wakes, Michael discovers the same ransom note that claimed his wife and daughter—Sandra has been kidnapped. Michael begs La Salle to lend him the ransom money, borrowing against a large property they own together. La Salle seemingly agrees but substitutes blank paper for the bank notes. Surprisingly, it's Sandra herself who comes to collect the money, and we discover she is, in fact, Amy, Michael's daughter. She was not killed in the accident, and convinced by La Salle that her father didn't care about his family, she was sent to Italy, where she plotted her revenge. La Salle staged everything to swindle Michael. But Amy realizes her father is not the man La Salle led her to believe he was, and she attempts to kill herself on her flight back to Italy. After a confrontation with La Salle, Michael stabs him in what appears to be self-defense, takes the money, and runs to the airport, intent on killing "Sandra" as well. He spots her being brought out in a wheelchair; he draws a gun while a guard tries to stop him. In a scuffle with the guard, the suitcase full of money opens, with the bills flying out everywhere. When Sandra sees Michael brought the money, she runs into his arms. Michael realizes that Sandra is Amy. Father and daughter embrace.

Hitchcock's *Vertigo* was always problematic to me—I saw it when it was re-released in the 1980s, after it had been removed from distribution for several years. I could never quite understand how it lacked the logic I identified with Hitchcock. The story begins with a chase on rooftops—Scottie (Jimmy Stewart) slips and is hanging on to a gutter. He's unable to move, suffering from vertigo. His partner tries to grab him but falls to his death. The camera stays on Stewart as he looks down below while hanging, and we fade to black. The next scene picks up with Scottie and his friend Midge (Barbara Bel Geddes) chatting about the incident, and his vertigo. I just kept asking myself, "How did he get off that roof?" The whole film seemed full of contrivances and coincidences. Even the techniques—like the animation used for when Scottie has a nightmare—employed by Hitchcock were, at times, strange and jarring. *Vertigo* remained an enigma to me until I concluded that the whole film is set in purgatory. Scottie died at the beginning, and the entire story is his second chance, his choice between heaven and hell. He is, literally, hired by the Devil, Gavin Elster (Tom Helmore), in his office, to follow Elster's wife, Madeleine (Kim Novak). The film is about Scottie's journey to conquer and ascend to heaven, which he does, as the last image shows him advancing on the ledge of a church, at last, contemplating a leap to freedom and peace.

Obsession embraces the same dreamlike qualities as *Vertigo*. (The first draft even starts with a quote from *Vertigo:* "If I'm mad, that would explain it.") But *Obsession* operates on a much higher level, staging the story straight out of the Greek myth of

Myrrha, who had sex with her father and gave birth to Adonis. And *Obsession* embraced the concept, with Amy seducing her father for revenge.

BRIAN DE PALMA: Paul Schrader [who wrote the *Obsession* script] and I had just recently seen *Vertigo* at the LA County Museum. This is, I guess, around 1974. We went out to dinner together and we were both just astounded by the movie. We sat at Musso & Frank Grill and, basically, came up with a scenario modeled on the plot of *Vertigo*. Then, I went home and wrote up what we had discussed. It came down to a five- or six-page treatment. Paul and I talked about it some more. He took the treatment, and, from that, he wrote the screenplay. He did it quite quickly as I remember, and I was knocked out by it. I thought it was really good and that the changes we had made on the idea of *Vertigo* were very effective: the way the mother and daughter looked so much alike and were played by the same actress; Florence; New Orleans; the mystical spirit world . . . He had done a really good job in evoking all that.

The original script was entitled *Déjà Vu* [a term that would eventually be used in the voice-over for the trailer]. But we realized that no one would understand what it meant; it was a French expression, and people might think it was a foreign film. I don't remember how we came up with *Obsession* but I know there were all kinds of lists of different alternate titles and that was one of them.

PAUL HIRSCH (EDITOR): The first time I read the script for *Obsession*, it was called *Déjà Vu* [and then *Double Ransom*]. I was very excited about it because—first, remember, in those days—I was happy to do anything at all. I had only done three pictures. No other director was offering me jobs but,

nevertheless, when I read the script, I found it to be very compelling. It had mystery, and romance, and surprises. It was just
a wonderful screenplay. There were obvious similarities to
Vertigo, in the sense of a man in love with a woman he believed
to be dead and finding someone who looked just like her. But
the picture became more and more like *Vertigo* as we made it.
Even more than just the thematic material, in large part due to
the music by Bernard Herrmann, who had scored *Vertigo*.

BRIAN DE PALMA: *Vertigo* is a fabulous story, especially the
whole idea of creating this romantic illusion with Kim Novak
to torment Jimmy Stewart. There was a very funny story that
Bernard Herrmann told me once when he went to see some of
the rushes on *Vertigo*—he was very taken with Kim Novak. He
had dinner with her, and Herrmann told Hitchcock she was
not at all what he expected, who then said, "That's what you get
for going out with my illusion!" Directors are very aware of the
illusions they create up on the screen. Hitchcock was a master
at it. And that's what *Vertigo* is all about.

FINDING THE MONEY

At this stage in his career—after *Sisters* and *Phantom of the
Paradise*—De Palma was gaining in his reputation as a horror film director. He left behind the literal social satires of the
sixties and a disastrous comedy in Hollywood for Warners
titled *Get to Know Your Rabbit*, which starred Tommy
Smothers, Katharine Ross, and Orson Welles, and taps back into
his Hitchcock mode with *Obsession*.

GEORGE LITTO (PRODUCER): I had retired from the agency
business; I made one film with Robert Altman, *Thieves Like Us*
[1974], and I was very eager to make my next film and I loved

From left: Director of Photography Vilmos Zsigmond, Producer George Litto, and Director Brian De Palma.

Obsession. So, one night I went to my wife and told her to sign some papers. And she said, "Am I signing my house away? Do you like the movie that much?" I said yes. I pledged all my assets to the bank including my house, they lent me the money for the film and then I went to some financing people I knew.

BRIAN DE PALMA: George Litto had sold *Sisters,* that's how I first met him. I liked him immediately and asked him to become my agent. After George got out of the agency business, he wanted to become a producer. George had a long, hard struggle in raising independent money, it took years. It was very difficult, and, ironically of course, *Obsession* and *Carrie* came out the same year in 1976, even though *Obsession* was made the year before. But George worked very long and hard putting together these different groups of financial entities. The budget was like a million two, or three. It was very inexpensive, even at that time. But he, ultimately, pulled it off and we finished the film, and he sold it to Columbia.

VILMOS ZSIGMOND (DIRECTOR OF PHOTOGRAPHY): Everybody had to work for less money, but the producer, George Litto, gave us a piece of the action and I got a half percent of the profits. I'm still getting checks in the mail after all this time. Because I had deferred my salary until the film came out, I made more money on that movie than on most films I was working on at that time.

HERRMANN'S MARCH

Maestro, a little supernatural music, please.
—Note to the composer from the original
first draft of the script by Paul Schrader

I first saw *Obsession* at the Balzac theater near the Champs-Elysées in Paris the week it came out. Attracted by several elements, including Geneviève Bujold, who I knew from *Earthquake* (1974), and the campaign teasing a film experience akin to Hitchcock, I had no idea this film was about to introduce me to a brand-new cinematic world as the first De Palma film I ever saw. Bernard Herrmann's ominous near-religious (and posthumously Oscar-nominated) score provided an immediate and near-brutal entry to the film with its overture. It was phenomenal; a slide show history of the romance between Elizabeth and Michael Courtland flashes on the screen, with the pair in Florence in 1948, intercut with shots of the church where they met. We then find ourselves transported to New Orleans in 1959 at the party celebrating the couple. Their nine-year-old daughter, Amy, embraces her father, and they begin dancing to a beautiful waltz, one that could be deemed imaginary as the camera swirls around them. We don't know it yet, but that is the very last time father and daughter will be together. This movement—both the dance and the music—will be reprised at the end when they're finally reunited. From the beginning of the film, De Palma has set in motion a narrative that has more music than dialogue and that is paced to the score. Music is as much a character in the story as the actors. Herrmann inserts himself into the romance and the tragedy of the story. The entire opening is phenomenal.

As mentioned earlier, I was familiar with Herrmann at the time—first through his score for François Truffaut's *Fahrenheit 451* (1966), based on the 1953 sci-fi classic novel by Ray Bradbury. That film was my first realization of the weight that music could have in cinema. The march-like music in *Fahrenheit 451*, accompanying firemen on their way, not to put out fire but, to burn books, was nothing short of masterful. Herrmann's work isn't the only connection between *Obsession* and *Fahrenheit 451;* the latter's lead actress, Julie Christie, played two separate roles, much like Geneviève Bujold.

PAUL HIRSCH: I remember at the time, there was still some controversy between Brian and the producer as to who was going to be the composer for the film. The producer wanted a young composer named John Williams who had experience in jazz. His attitude was, well, we're shooting in New Orleans, which is a jazz city, so we should have a jazz score. Brian and I really felt this needed a much more interior, psychological kind of score as opposed to one that was descriptive of the location. So, we felt we had to, as we did on *Sisters*, demonstrate to the producer that Benny's music was right for the film. There's a sequence in Florence in which Michael has met Elizabeth in the church and he follows her back to her home from a distance. There're some beautiful shots of the Ponte Vecchio at sunset and so forth. And we took the love theme from *Vertigo* and laid it over this long, wordless sequence of Michael following Elizabeth. The producer came in and looked at it. He asked, what is that music? Is it *Romeo and Juliet*? And we said no, it's Bernard Herrmann.

GEORGE LITTO: I'll never forget when Brian and I were in London casting and he wanted me to meet Benny Herrmann. Before the meeting, Brian had told me that Benny didn't like producers, and that he could get crotchety and argumentative, "So, just be nice to him, George." After our meeting, Benny turned to Brian and said, "You know, Brian, for a producer he's okay." [*Laughs*]

BRIAN DE PALMA: When we moved on to start working on *Obsession*, I sent Bernard Herrmann the script and he was dying to do it. And then I remember when he went to the first screening before he scored the film, he came out, he was crying, and he said, "It's a wonderful movie, Brian, and I heard the music." While he was watching the movie, he had heard the music in his head.

PAUL HIRSCH: Benny, among his other gifts, helped us design the titles. He felt there was a need for a main title that acted as sort of an overture to set the psychological mood for what the audience was going to experience. And he, basically, dictated what he wanted the images to be. And he told me how long he wanted a shot of the church and then he wanted to show the slides [of Elizabeth and Michael when they first met in Florence]. And he wrote the music to match the design of the images.

BRIAN DE PALMA: I watched *Obsession* recently and I thought the score was a little overbearing. It's a great score, but we're not used to listening to music blasting away like that. It seemed so big now, even to me. But Benny loved the movie. He loved Geneviève. She is the movie. And he was greatly inspired by it. And it's one of his great scores. But we don't really have that tradition of orchestral music anymore where the score takes over.

STAGING THE CRIME

The original script began from the point of view of two kidnappers, named Sam Addikof and Charlie Knossack, who are disguised as caterers outside the Courtland home, where friends are celebrating the tenth wedding anniversary of Michael and Beth (rather than Elizabeth in the final film). We're clued into the backstory as the kidnappers read a newspaper with the headline, "Courtland-Simon firm to purchase new Pontchartrain."

Inside, the party guests are shown photos of how Beth and Michael met in Florence. Beth is shown on a ladder, sketching Madonna and Child in the Santa Trinita church (slightly less striking than the Basilica di San Miniato al Monte, the location chosen for the film). We meet Michael's insurance company partner, Bob Simon (later changed to La Salle), and Michael's secretary, Jane, who is infatuated with her boss—and affectionately refers to him as "Cap." Michael gives Beth a gold heart-shaped locket with a photo of Beth and Amy, their young daughter. The girl—half asleep—joins them at the party, trotting into in her mother's arms. For a moment, the script indicates, "They do look like Madonna and Child, or, rather, standard- and miniature-size versions of the same Madonna." Amy then gets into her father's arms, with "the camera circling counterclockwise, as they both spin clockwise." The party concludes and the guests leave. As Michael and Beth are about to go to bed, Amy is heard crying. Beth goes to her daughter's bedroom. Michael waits a beat, and then looks for his wife. But both Beth and Amy are gone, and he finds a ransom note on the buffet table in the living room.

The kidnapping evolves slightly differently. There's a strange funny bit with Inspector Brie and his assistant, named Camembert—both named after cheeses—and, rather than taking a ferry to a point of delivery, Michael throws the briefcase (with fake bank notes and a transmitter) from a train (a big wheel boat in the film), as requested by the kidnappers. The outcome of the kidnapping is the same as in the film, with both Amy and Beth seemingly killed in a car crash. We then cut to 1973; Courtland has refused to exploit the Pontchartrain property. No estates were ever built, and Michael even refuses to sell the land to an oil company. Instead, he has built a crypt where rest the ashes of Michael's wife and daughter. As Michael is about to leave on a business trip to Florence, Jane tries to discourage him from going, knowing the emotional toll it may have on him. After visiting his family crypt, he asks Jane to come with him to Italy. The character of Jane is more developed in this first draft of the script. In many ways, she is like Midge (Barbara Bel Geddes) in *Vertigo*, who once dated Scottie and remains in love with him; there's a scene in which Scottie takes offense to Midge painting herself as Carlotta Valdes (a figure that, supposedly, has possessed Madeleine); Scottie declares, "It's not funny," and walks out. Similarly, in *Obsession*'s script, Jane takes a photo of herself in the same pose that Beth was in when she and Michael first met. Nearly identical to Scottie, Michael utters, "This isn't funny, Jane. This isn't funny at all."

PARTY GUESTS

The opening party introduces all our main characters in one fell swoop. It's an exciting cast that mixes different acting styles. For better or worse, Cliff Robertson brings a classic old Hollywood touch to the character. Geneviève Bujold, with her Canadian roots, is spectacular in her "roles." She shows vulnerability and beauty and plays with both an Italian and an American accent effortlessly. She's also a puzzle. We know it's no coincidence that she looks like Elizabeth. Is she good or bad? What mystery is she hiding? And then, of course, John Lithgow, who brings his stage experience to La Salle, and delivers his lines generously, as if he is performing for an audience sitting right there. It's all perfect for the role of the Champagne villain, who overcompensates his sleaziness with misplaced charm.

GEORGE LITTO: Cliff was an Academy Award winner for *Charly* [1968]. Geneviève was nominated for an Academy Award as *Anne of a Thousand Days* [1969]. Vilmos Zsigmond was well established. Though this was a story that the major studios were not enthusiastic about, to have all these quality people involved was a big asset. I had an agreement with Brian; I wouldn't pick actors, but I'd have to approve them. We had Cliff and Geneviève but, when it came to the third name, Brian suggested John Lithgow. He came in to read with Cliff and blew us away. I thought he was one of the great unrecognized performances in any film I've ever seen. The way he played the younger partner and turned into the older partner, was incredible.

CLIFF ROBERTSON ("MICHAEL COURTLAND"): I was doing a movie in England and my agency in London said, "A young director came over, specifically to talk to you about a movie."

And I said, "Well, that's very nice. When is he going to be here?" They said, "He'd like to see you on Saturday." I explained that Saturday was sacred, because I'm a pilot and, on the weekends, I used to go to fly. Also, I had my young daughter with me and, basically, had no time to meet movie directors on weekends. But they insisted, and I ended up meeting Brian at the Dorchester Hotel at noon, and we talked until about three. We immediately connected. I asked him why he wanted me in the film, and he said I was right for the role. He had seen a film I had written and co-directed [J.W. Coop (1971)] and said, "I liked your directing and I think we can work well on this movie." My agent was rather cynical, and he told me, "Cliff, they all say that. They just want you in the film." But I disagreed and thought Brian was honest. And he kept his word. We would quietly discuss scenes and I suggested they cast my good friend Patrick McNamara, who is such a great talent. I was delighted to work with Geneviève and with John Lithgow in one of his earlier roles.

BRIAN DE PALMA: What was so great about *Vertigo* was that Jimmy Stewart was a star. We couldn't get a star. We were a low-budget, independent movie. And, as much as people may have liked the role, nobody knew who Paul Schrader was; they hardly knew who I was. And they didn't respond to the material, so we tried and tried and tried. Ultimately, the one person who did respond was Cliff Robertson. Cliff was a very experienced actor, but he had also directed, so he had very specific ideas about the way he thought he should look, which presented some problems. Cliff liked to carry a tan all the time. That's the way he thought his star image was. And he was playing this guy who's supposed to be living in a house for over fifteen years, haunted by the death of his family. So, we had a few struggles with trying to get the right shade of makeup on him. And, as good an actor as he was, he's not Jimmy Stewart. I think he is one of the great deficiencies of *Obsession*. Jimmy Stewart and Kim Novak, what a great mix they were in *Vertigo*! Geneviève Bujold, I don't think was matched by Cliff Robertson.

JOHN LITHGOW ("LA SALLE"): Cliff was a handful. He was a real education. This was my second major film role, and I had never experienced old-time, Hollywood star self-aggrandizement. That was Cliff. He seemed only interested in his close-up. That was it. He just did everything he could to screw up everybody else's performance in favor of his close-ups. I was startled by that. I'd never even conceived of this as a way to work as an actor on film. But he was also very pleasant. Outwardly, like the ultimate company man. He wasn't fooling anybody. Everyone on that whole crew said, "Oh, that's Cliff; he's up to his tricks again." He had endless makeup tests, with Brian trying to persuade him not to wear this deep, deep bronzer. And then on the first day of shooting, he shows up with that makeup on again. Brian said, "We're just going to have to shoot." Cliff played by the rules of old Hollywood. His best performances were things like *Three Days of the Condor* [1975], where he was a little bit out of story, roles where you didn't quite trust him. [*Laughs*]

VILMOS ZSIGMOND: Cliff was getting a little bit older, and he was very thoughtful about how he looked on film. And he was always checking himself in a mirror; he didn't trust me 100 percent, especially at the beginning of production. He tended to turn his head toward the light because that softens your face. It never bothered me. But when I lit the interior of the church, I put candles on the wrong side; we rehearsed the shot and, instead of looking at frescoes, he kept looking the other way. Brian pointed it out and Cliff argued that his character would not be looking that way and so on. I realized what was happening, so I pulled Brian aside and told him to send Cliff to his trailer. I relit the whole thing. When Cliff came back and saw the new staging of the light, he told Brian, "I think you're right—I should be looking at the frescoes." And he was right in a way because he wanted to look good. Many stars will do this. At least, with Cliff, I could shoot both sides of his face—certain actors can be photographed only from one side—which helped me. Cliff was interesting, and we were allies.

Geneviève Bujold is as ethereal in real life as she was on film. There's a vulnerability, yet determination, that was immediately identifiable, something that made her perfect for the dual roles of Elizabeth and Amy/Sandra. You can tell how dedicated she was to the role, as it was not an easy one. As Elizabeth, she had to convey sophistication and sensuality without any dialogue. As Amy/Sandra, she had to have an Italian accent and convince us (and her father, Michael) to believe she was a look-alike. She starts as Elizabeth, transitions to Sandra, and ends as Amy— essentially three very different roles and performances.

BRIAN DE PALMA: I always thought Geneviève was wonderful. I had seen a few of her movies. I wanted someone foreign, with an accent. She has a magical presence and could play the mother and the daughter. She had the kind of face that could look both young and mature. And I think her performance is a revelation. She really carries the movie.

GENEVIÈVE BUJOLD ("ELIZABETH COURTLAND / SANDRA PORTINARI / AMY COURTLAND"): I had to take on an Italian accent. The language is very musical and watching the film again, I noticed how soft and nice I sound. I must have listened to some tapes at the time, but I do remember getting into that right away. It came easy.

BRIAN DE PALMA: Cliff began to realize that Geneviève was going to steal the show. So, he was not too helpful with her. In many of her scenes, I am off-screen playing them with her. Especially the scene when Michael sees her in the church. We shot his close-up first and then for the reverse shot on Geneviève looking down at him, he was so unhelpful that I sent him home and took his place off-screen. That was very unfortunate. Geneviève sensed it as well and got very angry. There I was, basically trying to keep them as the loving couple. By the time we got to the sequence at the beginning of the film where she's supposed to be going to bed with him, Geneviève didn't want to kiss him. It was tough, even though she was quite justified in her feelings.

CLIFF ROBERTSON: Geneviève is so bright, and so instinctive. Take after take, she comes up with fresh things on every take.

GENEVIÈVE BUJOLD: I would have loved to work with Cliff again just to check him out a second time. I think I was carrying some of Amy in me. We didn't always see eye to eye. But the film is beautiful, and he's great. Everyone's good in the film.

The different physical aspects of Bujold's characters, developed by visual consultant Anne Pritchard, are simply striking. For instance, when Michael first sees Bujold as Sandra restoring a painting, she is wearing white and is filmed in slow motion. Both elements contribute to making her feel like an apparition.

And as the relationship between Sandra and Michael evolves, she wears almost exclusively black, as if to hint she may be in mourning, or perhaps, a manipulative black widow. There're a couple of instances where she wears a cream-color coat, the same shade as the nightgown Elizabeth wore the night she was kidnapped. The costumes are integral parts of the perfect design of the different characters Bujold plays.

BRIAN DE PALMA: Anne started as a costume designer on *Obsession* and when our [production designer], Jack Fisk, was unable to come on the movie, she took over the whole design of the film. She had a very definite visual idea in relationship to Geneviève and her transition from mother to daughter. Clothes were very carefully picked; the colors were orchestrated going from Florence back to New Orleans, and her choices gave the picture a very feminine design. Hitchcock's

De Palma on location in Florence, capturing the spirit of the world of Obsession.

Vertigo was very masculine. Locations like Ernie's Restaurant, and the Redwood Forest were all very masculine because it's Jimmy Stewart's story. *Obsession* is very much dominated by Geneviève's character. And that's what gives it all those feminine tones, and feminine locations like Florence and New Orleans. That's the real difference between the two films.

GENEVIÈVE BUJOLD: Anne Pritchard was my friend. She was based in Montreal, and Brian and George agreed to hire her. I trusted her. I was looking at the film recently, to prepare for this interview, and everything I wear in the film feels timeless. It's beautiful, classical, and just the right note. At one point, I wore this red beret that I, myself, would never wear but it was so right for the character.

Obsession was the first film John Lithgow did with De Palma, establishing a decades-long relationship that continued with *Blow Out* and *Raising Cain* (1992).

BRIAN DE PALMA: I first saw John Lithgow in Princeton in the early sixties, at the McCarter Theatre, in a French farce with William Finley. He's great, flamboyant, interesting, funny, evil . . . He can play many colors.

JOHN LITHGOW: Before I'd even seen Brian De Palma, I first heard him. It was him laughing hysterically in this audience of about thirty people in an auditorium that held two hundred. I asked everyone, "Did you hear that insane person?" And it was Brian. He came backstage and hung with his gang. I barely remember meeting him, but I certainly remember his laughter. Then things started happening. I got a call from him when I was a student at Harvard to come down to New York to audition for Wilford Leach, who was doing a play at Lincoln Center. I drove all the way down there just to meet Wilford Leach and Brian in an apartment. Of course, I couldn't drop out of college to do this thing. But I was so flattered that I heard from Brian, who just watched me playing this lunatic philosopher in a Molière one-act. A couple of years later, he urged producer Paul Williams [no relation] to see me for *Dealing: Or the Berkeley-to-Boston Forty-Brick Lost-Bag Blues* [1972], which ended up being the first movie I was ever in. Then time passed and, voilà, I got another call out of the blue from Brian to be in *Obsession*. And I went right from my second Broadway play, *My Fat Friend*, to Florence, Italy, to be in the film. It was really Brian who got me going. He is entitled to the credit, or the responsibility, for that. When we started on *Obsession*, I remember Brian fixed me up with a friend of his, someone from New Orleans. And I simply listened to him. I hung with

John Lithgow plays La Salle in his first of several roles for De Palma, here with Zsigmond.

him. And he coached me a little bit on certain sounds. But to me it's a pretty hokey southern accent. It's the same one I pull out of my kit bag whenever I play a southerner.

THE DE PALMA TOUCH

Except for split screens, *Obsession* showcases nearly every single one of De Palma's trademarks: split diopter, slow motion, long tracking shots, sequences designed to music, and 360 shots (including one that marks the passage of time simply through panning, clever editing, and a dissolve as it begins on Michael in 1959 and ends on him in the same spot in 1975). But there're also the locations. One of Hitchcock's signatures was using specific cities and monuments in his storytelling (such as Mount Rushmore in *North by Northwest*, The Royal Albert Hall in 1956's *The Man Who Knew Too Much*, etc.). Like him, De Palma took full advantage of Florence and, through dialogue and music, brings in religious and poetic layers to mark the allure of the city. He approaches New Orleans, similarly, including a wink to the depravity of the French Quarter; when Michael and Sandra first drive through town, you can spot a building with dark windows, spelling out "Adult Books, Magazines, Movies."

BRIAN DE PALMA: We didn't have any money; we had to shoot the film very quickly. We went from Florence to New Orleans to Los Angeles. We were constantly trying to figure out ways to be as economical as possible. At one point I remember George looking at me, with tears in his eyes, and saying he would lose his house if we didn't finish the film on schedule. He had really put himself on the line.

VILMOS ZSIGMOND: Each new film is a new experience! For me, locations are the most important things; they make it happen. In this case, Florence and New Orleans determined what the film should look like. One of the challenges was to make Cliff Robertson and John Lithgow look younger in the first part of the film; diffusion helped us. But then, we realized we couldn't just have that look for half the movie. So, we used diffusion throughout but less in the second part. I relied on my experience filming *McCabe & Mrs. Miller* [1971], where I used heavy diffusion. But for *Obsession*, I didn't want to be so heavy, and I used fog filters, something I did a lot in my early films. Brian was very stylized in this movie. He wanted to move the camera all the time. I enjoyed learning from Brian; he would sketch things out for himself. He would have to explain it all to me but, somehow, I always understood what he was trying to do.

BRIAN DE PALMA: It was all carefully planned out, but as always with making movies, things happen, and you've got to improvise. I remember once, we were walking in that square in Florence trying to figure out how to shoot the statue of David and we finally figured out to shoot it framing the sculpture's ass in the background!! Took us hours trying to figure out.

GENEVIÈVE BUJOLD: Just before Brian would say, "Action," Vilmos suddenly would just sort of perk up, start running, and go adjust a little something just like an elf, before "the gift is offered." He's a great artist.

PAUL HIRSCH: The strongest visual motif in *Obsession* is the church. It's in the main title and it's the place where he finds the woman, he thought he had lost, and it's the mausoleum he's built for his dead wife. It becomes the motif of the wedding cake when they marry in the dream sequence. It's these visual motifs that interest Brian so much.

BRIAN DE PALMA: When we went to Florence, we had picked all our locations and then found out that somebody had shot a pornographic movie, pretending to be a regular film, in one of the churches. As a result, the Vatican had shut down any requests to film inside churches across the country.

GEORGE LITTO: I had a very important lawyer friend in Rome; I called him and we made a compromise that we could shoot outside the Basilica di San Miniato al Monte in Florence.

BRIAN DE PALMA: Luckily, we were able to shoot the exteriors, with its dramatic stairs and the marble, but we couldn't

Michael (Cliff Robertson) returns to a church in Florence accompanied by his business partner La Salle (John Lithgow).

go inside. So, the interior church is shot at a different location, which I found literally within a couple weeks, just racing
around the hilltops. Fortunately, I'd gone to Italy when I was in
college and had trailed it on a scooter all through the regions
of northern Italy. I remembered this church in the town of San
Miniato and we were able to shoot the interior there.

PAUL HIRSCH: *Obsession* is the first widescreen film Brian
did, and he really took advantage of the size of the frame
especially during a dialogue scene in Florence in which John
Lithgow was having a conversation with Cliff Robertson. The
camera travels back and forth between them, creating tension
between the characters.

BRIAN DE PALMA: Going back and forth in that shot allowed
me to rack focus on the square with the statues outside the
window. Basically, the environment and the locations dictated
composition and the horizontal image gave the film grandeur
and elegance.

VILMOS ZSIGMOND: Brian likes to keep scenes flowing for
a long time, as long as he can make it happen and as long as
the actors can keep it up. The widescreen allows [for] fewer
cuts. Today is a totally different style; everybody is cutting
like crazy. If your shot is longer than two seconds, people feel
there's something wrong! It's a music video style and we certainly didn't do that in this film. Brian is a very stylish director
who wants to have the audience always somehow participating
in the story. He likes to do interesting shots, and he's doing this
because he'd rather tell the story with continuous movement
than cuts.

BRIAN DE PALMA: I'm very concerned with the way space and architecture are used in movies. There are many ways that you can make your scene extremely vivid by dynamic use of a specific space. It's a lost art and there are few directors who know how to do it today. In my case, I acquired that skill by making short silent movies in the late fifties. Today, directors tend to use sound to carry the narrative and they don't know how to tell stories purely in visual terms. Movies are a series of pictures. All that other stuff is just garnishing. That's why I have long visual passages in my movies.

THE DIVINE TRAGEDY

At one point in Florence, Sandra explains to Michael, "You know, as a child, I used to go to the church where Dante came to watch Beatrice—Beatrice, la bella donna—sitting with her father. And there, over there . . ."

"I'm her father?" Michael asks after she moves him in position.

"No. The young Dante, twenty-three years old, would stand and watch Beatrice, and here, in between, sat the 'lady of the screen,' a lady Dante pretended to love so Beatrice would not be embarrassed by his continual gaze," she replies. And she then concludes, "You still love Elizabeth, don't you? That's why you want me."

Curious to find out more about this tale, I looked it up and found out it refers to Dante Alighieri, the famous Italian poet and writer (*Divine Comedy*), who first saw (and fell in love with) a woman named Beatrice when he was nine years old. She became the principal inspiration for his *Vita Nuova* (*The New Life*), a text Dante never completed after she died at the age of twenty-four. Beatrice, presumably, didn't know of Dante's passion for her and yet became one of literature's most famous figures. In a fantastic bit of subtext, Sandra says her last name is Portinari, which

Bujold and Roberston on location in Florence for the slide show and opening credit sequence.

happened to be Beatrice's last name! In this scene, Sandra points out that Michael is still in love with his dead wife, who is symbolically the woman in-between. He is still looking at her because he is afraid of loving another woman. The depth here is extraordinary and part of what makes De Palma and Schrader's story so effective on multiple viewings.

The scene closes with Sandra asking Michael how Elizabeth died, to which he replies, "I killed her." Rather than Sandra demanding an explanation, or Michael telling her what he means, the statement just hangs. In the script, Michael goes on to say, "I killed her and if you want to sit down a moment, I'll tell you how." (During production, De Palma discovered that leaving the question unanswered was much more impactful.) But, in the screenplay, then cut to Michael and Sandra sitting in a museum restaurant; he has told her the whole story and she tells him he shouldn't feel responsible, that it wasn't his fault. She asks him how his wife talked, laughed, and "What did she do when she was angry?" Michael excuses himself to the men's room and Sandra investigates his wallet, sees a photo of Beth, and is stunned by the resemblance—an action that may have been deliberate to mislead viewers.

COMING HOME

After Michael and Sandra return to New Orleans, she discovers the house in which she was raised. Bart De Palma (the director's brother and an artist) painted the giant portrait

De Palma framing a shot on Bujold, in front of the painting of Elizabeth and Amy Courtland.

of Elizabeth and Amy seen in the living room, as well as other paintings throughout the house. A beautiful sequence connects present and past as Sandra enters the parents' bedroom, which has remained locked since the kidnapping. It evokes Alfred Hitchcock's *Rebecca* (1940), where the second Mrs. de Winter (Joan Fontaine) is eventually shown Rebecca's bedroom by Mrs. Danvers (Judith Anderson), and all that belonged to her as if she were still alive. The gothic aspect of *Rebecca* is very much present in *Obsession*.

As Sandra enters the bedroom, De Palma begins a 360-degree shot. As the shot progresses, it reveals that Sandra has opened an armoire with Elizabeth's clothes—which possess a ghostly, floaty movement—before landing on Sandra further in the room, reading Elizabeth's diary. That 360-degree shot precisely connects Sandra to Amy (and Elizabeth) and echoes the movement used at the beginning of the film, when daughter and father are dancing together. De Palma then dissolves to Sandra putting on pearls, and looking at herself in a mirror, moving her hair to look more like Elizabeth. Another dissolve is followed by Sandra digging into a chest and tearing up the ransom note that had been published in a newspaper. We end on her reflection in a small hand mirror, framing only her face and, at that point, resembling Elizabeth exactly. The next scene shows Michael and Sandra walking by the church, where their wedding is to take place. Sandra's hair is now coiffed like Elizabeth's, and, as mentioned earlier, she wears the cream-color coat in the shade of the nightgown from the beginning of the film. The transformation is nearly complete.

BRIAN DE PALMA: The whole movie was like being inside a cylinder; the characters are brought around and around to the same obsession through the years. So, I tried to put or use as many of these 360-degree pans as I could motivate. Also, it's a very slow movement, which fits the discovery of secrets—the unpeeling of things—and that's best done through languorous moves.

DREAM OR NO DREAM

The film speeds toward its conclusion with one masterful scene after another, beginning with a dream sequence in which Michael and Sandra get married and have a cake in the shape of the church in Florence, with Sandra fully transformed into Elizabeth, complete with the necklace and the dark gown she wore in the opening scene. Ripples over the images and an echo on the dialogue combined with diffusion further sell the dreamworld De Palma had already so brilliantly realized in *Sisters*, although in a different visual style. But the sequence originally played out differently. In the first draft of the script, Sandra slept in Amy's bedroom until the wedding night, when she and Michael consummated the marriage. And what followed was much more inspired by *Vertigo*; Sandra appears to be possessed by "Beth," even taking Michael to the crypt to show him that his wife's urn is empty. "I am Beth. I am no longer in there. I am here," she tells him.

CLIFF ROBERTSON: It begs the question, did he ever have slight suspicions, doubts, or questions, that maybe, even though it was very complicated, he knew, but went on anyway, because he'd really fallen in love with his daughter . . .

PAUL HIRSCH: The sequence of events was that Michael had planned a big church wedding and, one night, he says to Sandra, "Let's just get married right here tomorrow." And she says, "What about friends?" He replies, "I have no

A moment deleted from the film to appease the studio.

friends." We cut to an exterior of the house with a big padlock on the front gate, and we cut inside as they're being married. They cut the cake shaped like the church. Then we dissolve to a shot of Sandra at night in the bathroom, looking
in the mirror, terribly anxious. The door opens and Michael
comes in. He says, "I waited so long." He lifts her up, carries
her over to the bed, and we dissolve to a close-up of Michael
asleep. When executives and possible buyers saw the movie,
they thought, "Oh, my God, this man and his daughter slept
together. She slept with her father in order to get revenge
for what she perceived as an abandonment when she was a
child." They had enjoyed the picture, but they couldn't han-
dle this. We were getting turned down at studio after studio,
so Brian, who was in despair, would ask, "What are we going
to do?" Then I thought, well, what if it never happened?
What if he dreamed the whole thing? Brian called the producer, who rejected the idea. I was so convinced that this was
a good idea that I sat down and wrote the producer a letter.

I detailed all the reasons I thought it would work. My idea, essentially, was removing the shots of the exterior of the house with the padlock on the gate, Sandra in the bathroom, and Michael carrying her to bed, but adding a shot of him sleeping so he could be "dreaming" of the wedding ceremony and cake. I sent the letter, and he ignored it. About two months later, he called me up and said, "You know, I just re-read your letter. I think it's a great idea and I have discussed it with Brian. We want to go ahead with this." So, we did it and we also added a ripple dissolve with a candle effect to make it appear even more dream-like. We recut the music and turned it into the version that it is today. And it was that version that Columbia agreed to distribute. To this day, however, Brian would say the other version was better. For Brian, the edgier it is, the better for him.

BRIAN DE PALMA: I always felt that he should have married her for real, he should have taken her to bed and that, in fact, is what flips her out. She succeeds in carrying off her vengeance, but she falls in love with the man she knows is her father. She has played it to the point where she has become her mother. But that's the compromise we had to make and, strangely enough, very little was changed but it does affect the movie a great deal.

The second "kidnapping" plot takes us to the reveal that Sandra is, in fact, Amy. She regresses to childhood, with Geneviève Bujold playing the nine-year-old Amy in the flashback of the kidnapping. Then, there's a high angle shot that makes Geneviève appear to shrink when recollecting being taken to the airport as a child, but it's her little-girl lost performance that sells the moment. The effect is absolutely devastating and the film's true emotional revelation—one that

De Palma would try to reproduce—unsuccessfully—in *Carrie*, with Sissy Spacek playing herself as a young girl. Bujold's portrayal of the layers of her character, at first as a look-alike to Elizabeth, then as Elizabeth's ghost, and then as Amy in two separate timelines is a tour de force of acting.

BRIAN DE PALMA: I realized that if I shot Geneviève against the body of her mother at a certain angle, she could pull off playing the little girl. And then, you cut to Geneviève as the mother looking down at her. She played both parts and it was quite remarkable to see.

GEORGE LITTO: I was very concerned that the audience would be confused; we talked about it and Geneviève said, "Don't worry about it, George, it will work." I thought we could always go back and reshoot, but when Brian did it, I saw it totally worked.

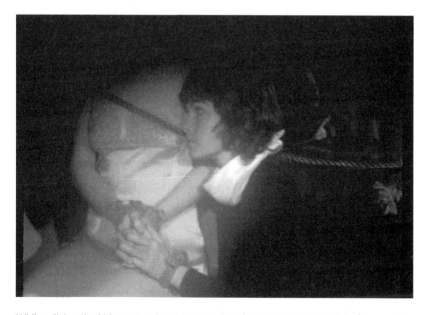

While reliving the kidnapping, Bujold masterfully played her character as a young girl.

VILMOS ZSIGMOND: Obviously, you cannot do that with makeup. It would be ridiculous. But by selecting a high angle, making the camera look down, we actually sold the idea that she was a child.

JOHN LITHGOW: What I really remember is that I didn't know what was going on. I was so new to movies, and Brian used the camera in such unusual ways that you just had no idea how this was going to pan out. But I knew it was kind of fantastic. I cannot remember when I first saw the completed film, but I do remember being overwhelmed by it. I didn't know we were doing this.

PAUL HIRSCH: Brian is always looking for a visual motif in each of the scenes and sometimes he goes to a point where the logic isn't quite there to support the visual, and he bends logic at times to support the visual. He's most successful—which is most of the time—when the audience isn't really aware of it. And it was a great idea using Geneviève as a child and as an adult.

After discovering that the money wasn't there, Michael meets La Salle in his office at night. No one else is around. At that point, La Salle confesses his contempt for his partner, saying how rich they could have been, how Sandra was in it with him from the start, and how she's going to Rome with her share. The only things La Salle doesn't reveal is how he plotted the original kidnapping or that Sandra is Michael's daughter. The original script was different from the way De Palma played up the confrontation between La Salle and Courtland: Michael goes mad and stabs La Salle with a pair of scissors, and as La Salle lies dying, he confesses, "I arranged it all. She died; it all went wrong." Michael then grabs a letter opener and a pointed paper holder and stabs La Salle with both, basically killing him three times. He leaves the office and returns to the crypt where Elizabeth's ashes have reappeared in the urn. Two policemen arrive at the crypt to arrest him.

CLIFF ROBERTSON: [When I attack John] I might have gone over the top on that one. I remember John saying afterward, "Gee, Cliff!!" [*Laughs*] That can happen to an actor. John is about six foot four, he's strong, and of course, he's a very good actor. But when I overcame him, I may have gone a little too far; better too far than not far enough. And he was a delight to work with. He and I had more fun off camera. We kidded around; just sitting around, we'd play different characters, spontaneously. He's so bright and funny.

JOHN LITHGOW: I remember there was a big quarrel between Brian and Cliff about my line in that scene, something that would trigger his anger. Cliff absolutely rejected it or insisted that I say something else. So, they set up a close-up of me saying the line that Cliff insisted that I not say. And everybody's job was to keep Cliff away from the set so he wouldn't know we were doing this. That's what it came to.

The first draft of the script continued with Sandra on the plane, flying back to Florence. Holding a drink and in a catatonic state, Sandra is sitting next to a woman "who resembles her when she'll be fifty." Suddenly, two men skyjack the plane. They threaten the woman next to Sandra, ripping a locket from around her neck. Sandra remains catatonic through the whole thing, as the men start firing their guns, and the plane crashes into the ocean. Sandra is floating amidst the wreckage, La Salle and Michael, holding the briefcase, swimming toward her. The briefcase bursts open revealing blank paper money. Still in the water, Sandra slashes her wrists with a letter opener and the script reveals that this sequence was a dream.

We follow Michael being sentenced to spend the rest of his natural life in a hospital for the criminally insane "until such a time as he shall be deemed fit to return to society." We then jump to 1985, when Michael is released. He is greeted by his secretary Jane and his shrink, Ellman. The crypt is now surrounded by oil wells; Michael is a rich man. He returns to Florence to find Sandra still completely in a state. At St. Ann's, a Catholic mental health hospital, Michael (pretending to be Charles, Sandra's brother-in-law) meets with the head doctor, Father Fabrini, and learns Sandra relentlessly paints portraits of the Madonna with Child—some fully formed, others without faces. Fabrini suggests that the only way to bring her out is to restage the kidnapping. Complete with two orderlies dressed as thugs, and behind a two-way mirror, Michael witnesses the whole thing until he steps in with a briefcase full of money. Amy finally speaks, "Daddy! Daddy! Mommy, look, Daddy's finally come with the money!" It's only then that Michael—and the audience—realize that Sandra is Amy. The script concludes:

> Sandra stands up, and Michael and Sandra embrace in a long tender kiss. They begin to turn slowly clockwise while the camera tracks around them counterclockwise.

PAUL HIRSCH: Brian felt when he read it that it was too many beats. He just compressed the ending, a change that was not greeted warmly by Paul Schrader. But I think Brian had the right instinct. It was time to end the picture.

BRIAN DE PALMA: It would have made the movie three hours long. Strangely enough, the person who substantiated what

I was feeling instinctively, was Bernard Herrmann, who just said, "Oh, that stuff in the future, just get rid of it. It doesn't work." He also felt that, musically, it was something that would be difficult to do. I did think that it was an incredibly audacious idea, and it was our original intention. But, ultimately, the script had more of a two-act structure.

Schrader would go on to write and direct a film entitled *Forever Mine* (1999) that explored what he felt *Obsession* should have been.

HAPPILY EVER AFTER?

Obsession has De Palma's happiest endings of this period of his work. Michael and Amy embrace and the camera swirls around them, reprising the 360-degree shot from the beginning of the film, as well as the waltz musical motif by Bernard Herrmann. But this time the tempo is upbeat, not at all the "valse lente" (slow waltz) from the opening. It now comes full circle. In that glorious moment, the music overpowers the dialogue— Amy repeating, "Daddy! Daddy!" and Michael saying, "Amy"— confirming that the score is a character with a voice (or voices as the chorus crescendos in that last cue, as in some kind of grand opera). And rather than closing with end credits, De Palma freezes on father and daughter looking at each other lovingly and smiling.

VILMOS ZSIGMOND: We shot the sequence at Los Angeles International Airport. The whole first part of the scene before they embrace was shot in slow motion. There were big fluorescent lights and when we saw the dailies, they were pulsating. We thought, "Oh, my God, we have to re-shoot!" Then we looked at the footage a second time and the effect was great! So, we

Father and daughter reunited—the emotional ending of Obsession *featured an unforgettable score by Bernard Herrmann.*

decided to keep it. For the second part, we had to circle around them in a very tiny place.

BRIAN DE PALMA: I'll never forget that shot. It was the cameraman and me, running round, and round. I think three, four, five, six times. And, of course, the miracle of it is Geneviève's expression, the way she's going through all this. It was just unbelievable to watch what was going on, looking at her face. I think we did three or four takes. It was very difficult to do, and Geneviève basically held the whole thing together.

GENEVIÈVE BUJOLD: I got caught in the joy of doing that shot. It was just full of joy, and I was so happy to be doing it. The film was so beautifully done by Vilmos and Brian that you forget the revenge story.

CLIFF ROBERTSON: I was able to immerse myself in her face. We were, in effect, oblivious. We were in this wonderful white water of this wave. It was delirious and delicious and delightful as the song says, but we were immersed in this conclusion.

PAUL HIRSCH: I had an idea for an optical effect at the end of that shot, which I never got to work. Since the camera is turning around them, I had wanted the film to slow down gradually and to stop on a specific frame. But there was too much pressure to get Bernard Herrmann to score it precisely and to work with the optical house, and so we just stopped on the frame, without that gradual slow down.

ROMANCE OF A LIFETIME

The studio held back releasing *Obsession* for nearly a year, finally launching it to theaters in August 1976, three months before *Carrie*. The film received mixed reviews: Vincent Canby of the *New York Times* wrote, "To be blunt, *Obsession* is no *Vertigo*, Hitchcock's witty, sardonic study of obsession that did transcend its material, which wasn't all that bad to start with. The Schrader screenplay . . . is most effective when it's most romantic, and transparent when it attempts to be mysterious . . . The plot . . . is such that you'll probably have figured out the mystery very early." But Rex Reed of the *Daily News* commented, "This is an immensely important cinematic work with a throbbing, lusty score by the late Bernard Herrmann that conjures haunting memories of the films of Alfred Hitchcock . . . It's as good as, and often better than, anything Hitchcock has ever done." Ron Pennington's review in *The Hollywood Reporter* was most enthusiastic, "Brian De Palma's *Obsession* is a stylish, finely crafted romantic suspense drama in the classic tradition that fully establishes the director as one of the industry's more

An ad featuring quotes from the best reviews and highlighting screenwriter Paul Schrader's Taxi Driver *credit.*

outstanding young filmmakers," while Pauline Kael in *The New Yorker* wrote (in her review for *Carrie*) that "*Obsession*, though no more than an exercise in style, with the camera swirling around nothingness, was great on-the-job training for *Carrie*." Amusingly, *Obsession* was parodied and featured on the cover of *MAD* magazine, redubbed *Sobsession*.

PAUL HIRSCH: Brian was tagged early in his career as a Hitchcock imitator, largely after *Sisters* and the fact that he had used Bernard Herrmann, and the similarities to *Psycho*. The perception of *Obsession* was, and remains to this day, in many people's eyes, another Brian De Palma knockoff of a Hitchcock film. Every director chooses their influences and is influenced by the art they have absorbed and seen growing up as an artist. In Brian's case, it's a little unfair to say that he simply imitated Hitchcock because, in many ways, Brian is like Hitchcock. From what I know of Hitchcock, they both have a kind of twisted sense of humor and they both have a tinge of gleeful sadism about them. They are both interested in storytelling through visual means and not terribly interested in making filmed records of actors speaking dialogue. That's not their main focus. So, Brian's interests overlap Hitchcock's. As Brian went into this genre, he was able—because of the changing morals in society—to be more risqué, let's say, with some of the sexual issues and the depiction of violence. As time passed, the movies became more explicit, and Brian was interested in pushing the envelope.

GEORGE LITTO: *Obsession* was our first adventure together. And we succeeded. We climbed the mountain together. Also, I got to work in Florence, Italy, which is personal and part of my heritage. The film community was very concerned about making it, but Brian and Paul and I, Geneviève and Cliff, had a great passion for it. To feel so strongly about something and against so many odds, to do it and to succeed is delicious.

VILMOS ZSIGMOND: In those days, every movie was important for us because we were filmmakers. We had people like Steven Spielberg, Brian De Palma, Robert Altman. They were all making individual personal statements about life, and they made their own stories. They did their movie the way they thought it should be made.

PAUL HIRSCH: I have a fondness for *Obsession* because I had been a music student in high school, and I've always loved music. I had a particular special role in bringing De Palma and Herrmann together, and *Obsession* was the last picture we did with him. There's also some beautiful cinematography and I thought it really was the first picture that Brian had done that really looked like a big movie.

GENEVIÈVE BUJOLD: I love the first meeting in the church in Florence. It's like an apparition. I find it very moving. It brings tears to my eyes. It's as simple as that. I love when she puts her face against the tombstone; there's tenderness and vulnerability in that moment. Or when she walks into the house in New Orleans and puts her face on the rail of the staircase and says, "It's beautiful!" And of course, the ending. I'm very proud of the film or I wouldn't be doing this interview. This one can't go down. I'm taking it with me.

CLIFF ROBERTSON: I've never been satisfied with any film I've ever done. I'm less dissatisfied with *Charly*, or a picture I wrote and directed where I had a lot of creative involvement, and even control. And with *Obsession*, I am less dissatisfied. If you're satisfied, then you're getting lazy. But I'll never forget *Obsession*. I loved the movie, loved working on it. And I loved the people I worked with. They were great, and I just hope it happens again.

JOHN LITHGOW: The strongest thing that my experiences with Brian had in common was fantastic people. He had the greatest crews and he really loved fine filmmaking. He didn't like the process. He was Hitchcockian in that way for sure. He loved the preparation. That's when he felt most relaxed, most creative. Once we started shooting, he would get a little bit withdrawn and reserved. He would sit in his director's chair and just wait for the crew to get the shot set up. He was like a big grump. I would tease him about it. I would fish for compliments at the end of a take. And I would say, "Brian, was that okay?" He'd reply a simple, "Yeah." "But was it okay? Brian, was it good? Please, Brian, tell me, hug me, Brian. Hug me." I would just tease him that way in front of everybody. Brian reminds me a lot of George Roy Hill [with whom I did *The World According to Garp* in 1982]. All business. "Let's get this over with. Okay. We've got that. Let's move on."

BRIAN DE PALMA: After you've been thinking about this stuff for three or four or five years, finally, you're on the set and all the elements are there for the first time. I don't have time for chitchat. Don't even say good morning to me. I'm not interested in interacting with anybody. I'm just focusing on what's gonna go on film in that time frame, which, of course, is under an immense amount of pressure. And if I get a different idea, I want to make it work. So, I'm always considered a kind of remote director on the set. Though [I try to be] warm and congenial with the actors, because if they're not happy, your film is going to die. So, you got to figure out how to communicate with them in order to make them relaxed and do the best they can.

JOHN LITHGOW: While Brian didn't lavish me with compliments, he taught me how to act in movies. This whole basic thought of acting better off camera than you do on camera.

Give the other actor everything. I somehow got a sense of that from Brian. And just this feeling that you're in very good hands because everything has been thought out ahead of time. He was the best prepared of any director I ever worked with. [When I started with Brian] you knew you were in a golden age. And time has proved us right. That was when America really did great films, and they all knew each other; the first people whom Brian wanted to see his cuts were Scorsese and Spielberg. His friends. They couldn't wait to share what they were doing with one another.

BRIAN DE PALMA: An artist loves beauty and can create beauty. In *Obsession*, the emotions are so strong, and the locations are so exquisite in the way they're photographed, much like one feels about *Vertigo*. It's just a feast for the eyes, and

Bujold in another emotional, haunting, and heartfelt moment.

that's what I tried to achieve in *Obsession*. I like emotions, characters that care, romance, and tears. That's what got me into the movies: being taken to places you've never seen, being carried away in the emotions of characters that end in some strange ambivalent way—tragedy or comedy. As George Lucas always said, "We make the movies we want to see," which is exactly right. I don't look at my movies too often, but I like *Obsession* for the beauty and the emotions. *Sisters* or *Dressed to Kill*, they're more technical, not as emotional. *Obsession* has a kind of purity about it, and it's so romantic.

MY OBSESSION

As I shared earlier, *Obsession* launched me on my fascination with De Palma's cinema and his visual language. I remember leaving the theater out of breath, as if I had experienced the similar emotional ending as the characters. That speaks to the power that De Palma truly had over me as an audience member. His camera work engaged me, as did Herrmann's music. It's impossible for me not to weep each time I watch the film, especially the scene where Geneviève Bujold retreats to childhood, playing herself as a nine-year-old, as Lithgow tells her that her mother is dead and that her father doesn't want her anymore. She screams, calling for her "Uncle Bob" as she is being dragged to the plane. The score and the success of De Palma's approach to the scene, combined with Bujold's performance as her younger self, is textbook material. The boldness of the filmmaking, the power of the performance, and the trust in the result coming from both sides of the camera represent De Palma at his best and confirm him as an auteur in a league of his own, in addition to showing a yet-unseen aspect of this filmmaker—a romantic side. Sadly, of all the movies discussed here, *Obsession* remains the most obscure; it was never quite discovered or re-discovered. But after making a documentary on it in 2001, I received the following email from De Palma:

Judging by the critical response to my films, I've always been either ahead of my time or hopelessly behind it. Few were embraced when they came out and even those supporters aren't around anymore to guide the viewer. And in recent years, it's gotten worse. But this afternoon, to see all my Obsession collaborators saying such intelligent and strongly felt things about a project we did so many years ago, makes the hell of this business all worthwhile. Obsession was truly a labor of love. We all tried with all our artistic skill to make something heart-wrenching and beautiful. I think we did, and so did you.

Saving the best for last, my favorite moment in Obsession is when Michael returns to the church in Florence where he first met his wife and encounters Sandra. There's a fascinating and beautiful dialogue between them as Sandra is preparing a fresco of the *Madonna and Child*, painted in 1328 by Bernardo Daddi (1280–1348) for the restoration experts. She explains that moisture seeped into the fresco, causing it to peel, and revealed an older one underneath.

"Should they destroy a great painting by Daddi, to uncover what appears to be a crude first draft underneath it, or should they restore the original, but never be sure what lies beneath it?" she questions before asking Michael, "What would you do?"

"Hold on to it. Beauty should be protected," he replies.

"Good. That's what the scholars decided to do."

This of course feeds into the identity of Sandra as Michael's daughter, Amy; she is what lies beneath the original (her mother). Michael's answer reflects his state of mind, trying to re-create his wife through Sandra. And, of course, the clue in plain sight is the name of the artist, Daddi—as in "daddy" or "father." By proxy, Sandra is telling Michael that he is her father. And "daddy" is what she repeats as she embraces her father at the very end of the film.

The film is very much like the painting behind the painting that Sandra is restoring. The question remains: Stick with the surface, or dig deeper, look beyond, and discover what lies beneath? It's up to each of us to decide.

*"Murder has a sound all of its own..." John Travolta as Jack Terry in De Palma's
Blow Out.*

BLOW OUT

—— 1981 ——

Personal Effects was a good title for
what the movie's about but it's not very
commercial. It became Blow Out, which is
a very dynamic title. Unfortunately, it gets
compared to Michelangelo Antonioni's
Blow-Up [1966] all the time, but so what?

—BRIAN DE PALMA
(WRITER / DIRECTOR)

THE STORY: A psycho killer is stalking a girls' college dorm. As he pulls back the curtain on a young woman in a shower, she screams—but it's not right. It's a terrible scream, and we realize we were watching a film within a film. Jack Terry (John Travolta), a sound effects designer for B movies, is sitting at the mixing board with his director who asks him to get a new scream. We then find Jack on a bridge, recording wild sounds, when he suddenly becomes witness to a car accident, seemingly caused by a tire blow out. The car drives into a river. Jack manages to rescue one of the passengers, Sally Bedina (Nancy Allen), but the other passenger, presidential hopeful Governor McRyan, dies. McRyan's associates seek out Jack and beg him not to reveal there was a call girl with the governor in the car. Later, as Jack listens to the tape of the accident, he notices a gunshot before the blow out. Far from an accident, he witnessed an assassination. Jack catches on to the conspiracy behind the governor's "accident"; this is familiar ground for him. He worked undercover, wiring cops to denounce police corruption. He turned to B movies after a cop, wearing a faulty wire Jack had provided, was murdered. But now, through this new case and his bond with Sally, Jack gets a possible chance for redemption. Sally helps him recover film taken by a sleazy photographer named Manny Karp (Dennis Franz) on the scene of the crime. Karp originally intended to take compromising pictures of McRyan for blackmail. With the help of a now-remorseful Sally, Jack uses the images, matching them to his sound recording to prove it was murder. But the triggerman, Burke (John Lithgow), is on the move, killing Sally look-alikes to establish a cover-up for when he gets to the real Sally. Burke also breaks into Jack's workroom and destroys much of Jack's evidence. Posing as television reporter Frank Donahue (Curt May), Burke arranges to meet Sally. Jack has Sally wear a microphone so he can listen to the conversation. Realizing the subterfuge, and in a mad scramble through the streets of Philadelphia during a parade, Jack rushes to rescue Sally, but is, ultimately,

> too late. She's killed by Burke, who Jack stabs to death. All Jack is left with is a recording of Sally's death scream, which he uses to complete the soundtrack of his latest slasher film.

Personal Effects (a play on "personal" as in intimate and "effects" because of sound effects) started off as a modest, low-budget project. De Palma wrote an initial story treatment in 1978 that follows the final film closely, though there are a few differences—including that the opening film within a film only involves a single woman and, more significantly, the killer doesn't get caught in the end. In collaboration with *Take One* (the first professional Canadian film publication), De Palma organized a contest in 1979, inviting readers to write two scenes based on his treatment.

BRIAN DE PALMA: *Take One* published the *Personal Effects* story and people submitted. And then, if it was good enough, they would be paid to write the screenplay. Ultimately, there were three finalists, and somebody won. I gave the prize money to the winner, but one of the other contestants felt they deserved the prize money, too, and he sued me for not giving [it to] him. I had to go to court, and I wound up buying that screenplay and the other ones as well, so I wouldn't have any more lawsuits. And I heard there's some guy who still thinks he had something to do with the final screenplay. But, as I remember, none of the screenplays was anything like the final movie. It was just an idea to encourage young screenwriters. No good deed goes unpunished.

De Palma's first script, dated 1980, reflects the treatment and the final film with one significant difference—the film's biggest action set piece, the fictional Liberty Bell Day Parade, was entirely absent. In this early draft, Sally still gets killed, but her death occurs at the university campus where the film that Jack is working on takes place. It's an ironic touch as Sally's scream becomes part of the film.

BRIAN DE PALMA: While working on *Dressed to Kill*, we were putting [the sound of] wind in a scene. I said to my sound editor, Dan Sable, "I've heard that wind a thousand times. It's been used in movie after movie. You keep on giving me the same sound effects. Get me some new wind." So, Dan went out in his backyard with his mic and got some new wind for me. That was the whole beginning of the idea for the film. Later, John Travolta sent me a script that he thought I'd be interested in directing. I wasn't, but he asked me what else I was working on. I mentioned *Personal Effects*, and he said, "Well why don't you let me read it?" At first, it was like a couple million–dollar movie, a little movie. Then, suddenly, John liked it, and it became a ten-million-dollar movie. Everything started getting bigger because John was in it.

A FAMILY AFFAIR

Blow Out is home as the director returns to Philadelphia where he grew up, and he reunites John Travolta and De Palma's then-wife Nancy Allen, a pairing he owed to *Carrie*. We meet again De Palma familiar figures: Dennis Franz, John Lithgow, and J. Patrick McNamara as well as Vilmos Zsigmond as director of photography, Paul Hirsch editing, and Pino Donaggio scoring. By now, as viewers, we recognize the De Palma world.

There's a sense of a filmmaker shedding his skin as the independent director, best expressed in the opening sequence of

De Palma posing with stars Travolta and Nancy Allen in front of Philadelphia's historic William H. Gray III 30th Street Station.

Blow Out and the film within the film, *Co-Ed Frenzy*. It's De Palma creating almost a parody, and announcing, "This was then, and *Blow Out* is me now." Yet, *Blow Out* is also as sad, intimate, and as tragic as his previous films, perhaps even more so. And with immense talent embracing the scope of a much larger canvas, he still uses his signature shots and visionary devices.

NANCY ALLEN ("SALLY BEDINA"): I always tried to do films with other directors, and then come back to working with Brian. *Blow Out* was not on my radar but I knew he had a very specific vision for it. He wanted the characters to be a bit more cerebral, perhaps, older, and maybe just a little run down, so to speak . . . On the list for the main part were John Heard and Tom Berenger. I was going to Europe to promote *Dressed to Kill*, and Brian called, saying he had spoken to John [Travolta]. Since the role was so clearly for someone else, I said, "What if he likes it? Then, what are you going do?" He replied, "He's going to see that it's not really for him." I knew that if I were reading that script, I'd want to play that part. Sure enough, that's what happened. By then, I was in Italy, and Brian called again to tell me John wanted to do the part. When Brian asked who John saw in the part of Sally, John said it should be me! The idea of working with John again after *Carrie*, knowing the chemistry we had, I was beyond over the moon.

BRIAN DE PALMA: By then, I made three films with Nancy; *Carrie, Home Movies,* and *Dressed to Kill.* We thought it was time to take a little break from each other. I did not necessarily write Sally for Nancy. But John Travolta likes working with her so much that I said, "Well, let's do it with Nancy." She had a fantastic relationship with John, and I just worked that into the movie. They were great together.

NANCY ALLEN: I don't know if you can put into words the kind of relationship I had with John as actors. It's kind of like meeting someone and falling in love . . . It's a match. When I originally tested for *Carrie*, I first read with Michael Talbott [Freddy in the film], but then John came in, we sat down, and we just had that thing. What's different about John is that he is a very supportive actor. He's hardworking, and there is a vulnerability about him. He's just so funny and sweet. And he is so generous. He wants you to be good. Brian does multiple takes and John likes to keep it fresh, so he'll throw in something new, and if you go with it, it becomes magical. There's a scene where John's character tells me about his past. He whispers something in my ear, and I smile and say, "I'll think about it." John loves to eat and he was actually whispering, "If we stick around, we can eat some ice cream and pizza."

Allen in her Sally Bedina wardrobe designed by Ann Roth, with De Palma and Travolta on set.

BRIAN DE PALMA: It was a family situation, including shooting in Philadelphia where I grew up. I knew all the locations.

DENNIS FRANZ ("MANNY KARP"): It was clear that *Dressed to Kill* was going to be successful. They had some screenings of it, and it looked like Brian had a hit on his hand. He was excited and looking forward to his next project. He called to ask if I was available. When I said yes, he started laughing as he went on to explain the character of Manny Karp. I thought it was such a funny, sleazy name. Indeed, it represented a truly sleazy character. Brian gets a kick out of slightly off-center things; I share that with him, and I thought, "Well, that would be a fun character to play."

NANCY ALLEN: Sally was a very independent, confident woman. But when I first read the part, I didn't like her, and it's very hard to play someone you don't like. She's such a victim. Brian and I talked about it, and he said, you need to see Giulietta Masina's performance in Fellini's *La Strada* [1954]. I watched it, and I was also familiar with Judy Holliday in *Born Yesterday* [1950]. I thought between those two characters, it's somewhere in there. I remember waking up one day and going for a walk, which is how I ruminate; I don't really sit down and study. I thought about the women I met who don't want to take responsibility for their life, don't want to grow, and they have almost a little voice saying, "Take care of me." I told Brian and we did some improvisation. I thought maybe she has a dream—and that's how we came up with her wanting to be a makeup artist. Somewhere, she probably knows she can't do it, but that's how she came together for me. That's how I could do it, not dislike her, but fall in love with her a little bit.

A deleted scene in which Sally meets Governor McRyan (John Hoffmeister) at a ballroom party.

Ann Roth created my costumes. Vicky Sanchez did the other actors. But Ann and I had met on *Dressed to Kill*. I have the greatest admiration for her. She's a brilliant, amazing woman. She asked me what I was thinking, and I told her about a rag doll image with curls. She immediately recommended Lyn Quiyou to do my hair. And then, in discussing the character, Ann said, "She's not really a hooker but she kind of is." We talked about wearing boots and incorporating a subtle red, white, and blue color theme. Then, Ann said, "I have a feeling maybe she's superstitious. What if she had a little rabbit's foot on a pink ribbon around her neck?" You barely notice it, but it's there. Ann gets characters; she's incredible.

JOHN LITHGOW ("BURKE"): In *Blow Out*, I was playing a character who was pretending to be a psycho and he was a true believer, a political operative who felt the end completely justified the means. And the means were to pretend he was a psycho killer and to murder several women so nobody would perceive the real motive. I remember referencing to Brian the thriller called *The Sleeping Car Murder* [*Compartiment Tueurs*, a 1965 film by Costa-Gavras]. He said, "That's it!" He was almost worried that people would spot that. On the other hand, Brian loved it when people spotted his references. But it was very ingenious and, for me, the great fun of it was draining this character of any humanity, just making him an operative.

PAUL HIRSCH (EDITOR): I gave John Travolta lessons, more than once. He came to the cutting room, and I showed him how to use the equipment. But, in the opening sequence, you hear the director saying, "You call that a scream?" And he turns to his sound designer, played by John, telling him to get a better

Jack records sounds for a B movie when he captures what turns out to be the assassination of a governor.

scream. There's no picture editor in the scene! Where is the editor? So, as far as enjoying the depiction of my craft in *Blow Out*, it's not there! [*Laughs*]

NIGHT SWIMMING

Blow Out starts in parody, with footage of the B-movie slasher *Co-Ed Frenzy*, followed by Jack arguing with the director of the film about the mediocrity of the acting. We then cut to credits, including the title and cast names, each identified with a specific sound. Under Nancy Allen's name, you can hear the scream from the moment of her death, literally spelling out the story's tragic outcome. We then find Jack in his studio, affectionately called Personal Effects—a relic from the film's original title—while a TV newscast introducing McRyan is shown alternately in split screen or using split diopter, connecting Jack and the unfolding political subplot on the same focal plane. We then go to the bridge, where we find Jack collecting wild sounds. De

Palma displays his cinematic cadence by setting up the geography of the scene clearly through images and sounds. Suspense builds prior to the blow out and crash as Jack hears a zipping sound—later revealed to be the killer's weapon of choice: a thin wire wrapped inside his wristwatch used to strangle his victims. (In 1963 the James Bond film *From Russia with Love*, the killer, Grant, played by Robert Shaw, uses a similar weapon.) Excluding the music for *Co-Ed Frenzy*, the brilliant score by Pino Donaggio kicks in right after Jack stops recording sounds and jumps into the river to rescue Sally. We're nearly twelve minutes into the film as it purposely transitions from the realistic world of sound to dramatic music. Barely noticeable, Manny Karp flees from under the bridge; De Palma has set up the complete tapestry that serves as the basis of *Blow Out*'s world.

A prop from the film— the News Today *magazine featuring images from McRyan's crash.*

BRIAN DE PALMA: The Wissahickon Creek location was huge. It took Vilmos a lot of time to light it. But I had worked it out; I knew it well. I set up the geography for the audience, so they knew where everything was before the car goes into the creek.

PAUL HIRSCH: The images in the film are beautiful. Vilmos was at the top of his game. Brian made these storyboards that I always found indecipherable. But I understand Brian's visual syntax, I know why he shoots something in a particular way, and how he has it in mind to be used. Having developed as a young editor working strictly for him, created a shorthand, I understood what he was going after. In that scene, you have John's character grabbing wild sound. At one point, there's a frog, and I remember Vilmos saying it was the first time he'd ever done an "over-the-shoulder shot" with a frog. [*Laughs*]

NANCY ALLEN: When the day came to shoot the scene where Sally is trapped in the car, Brian suggested we take a look at the set before I got dressed. We walked into the sound stage and walked to the tank [a huge pool that was for the close shots from the car crash] and all I could see was the roof of the car. The car was completely underwater. Protruding from the roof was something that looked like a chimney, which opened into the inside of the car. I had to slither down this tube to get in. Brian was a bit shocked. He had told special effects that I was claustrophobic and needed to have a simple escape. He was angry and the car wasn't constructed in a way that made it easy for me to perform the scene. But we had to shoot.

Once the action was called, the car would begin filling up with water at an alarming speed. There was a crew person on the floor near the front seat with scuba equipment in case I needed it. It was terrifying. I did my best to show my face to

Jack listens as he trails Sally when she meets up with a man she believes is a reporter, but is, in fact, an assassin.

the camera and then find my escape hatch. But I was in full panic. When I got out Brian was there waiting for me, and I couldn't speak.

I was in shock. The crew was in shock, too, because they hadn't tested the car and didn't expect the water to rush in the way it did. One thing was clear—there wouldn't be a second take. Not with me. Everything else was shot with my double. I felt like a failure because I couldn't perform a very important scene. But thanks to excellent editing by Paul Hirsch and my double, the scene is very good. I can tell you one thing, when you see fear and panic on my face, it's real.

The McRyan plot also inevitably recalls the 1969 Chappaquiddick incident in which Senator Ted Kennedy crashed his car off a bridge into a pond, causing the death of Mary Jo

Kopechne, one of his brother Robert Kennedy's campaign work-ers. Meanwhile, Burke wears a watch cap in his introductory scene, reminiscent of the one worn by the Boston Strangler. The world of *Blow Out* is not trustworthy; it's about conspiracy and where all can be erased (like Jack's tapes), covered up, or, better yet, substituted (like the scream in the B movie). The plot relies heavily on interrupted and blocked communication.

PERSONAL EFFECTS

Blow Out is a look behind the curtain at sound effects design, recording, and dubbing techniques as well as a journey to find the perfect scream. As Quentin Tarantino mentions in his book, *Cinema Speculation*, which I also recognized, the character of Jack is very much like Peter Miller in *Dressed to Kill*—a science geek and genius. (Peter is also an amateur sound "peeper"; he has a device that allows him to hear and record Detective Marino's interro-gation of Dr. Elliott at the police precinct.) But, in *Blow Out*, Jack tells Sally, "It all started in school, okay? I mean I was the kind of kid who fixed radios, made my own stereos, won all the science fairs . . . You know the type." De Palma is describing himself.

In this same sequence, the director presents a short version of *Prince of the City*—a project he had been developing for over a year and, to his chagrin, didn't get to make—with a flashback involving Jack wiring a cop in an operation to expose police corruption. *Prince of the City* was based on the 1978 nonfiction book of the same title by Robert Daley, former New York Police Department deputy com-missioner. The story focused on Detective Robert "Bob" Leuci, team leader of the Narcotics Division of the New York Police Department, who joined forces undercover with the federal government by wiretapping mobsters as well as his own partners. De Palma collaborated with Leuci, only to see the project changing course with director Sidney Lumet, screenwriter Jay Presson Allen, and Treat Williams in the lead.

BRIAN DE PALMA: I had worked on *Prince of the City* for a year with David Rabe. I was trying to do it with Bob De Niro, but I couldn't get him to commit. What happened is that Sidney Lumet wanted to do it. And his screenwriter, Jay Presson Allen, conspired with the studio, so when we turned in our screenplay, they rejected it. And, the next thing I knew, Lumet was doing it.

JOHN LITHGOW: During *Blow Out*, everybody would meet in a bar on Friday night, and Brian and I ended up alone together at a table, just the two of us. And he told me his whole Philadelphia history and how his parents had inspired some of the characters in *Dressed to Kill* and *Home Movies*. I remember being

Sally visits Manny Karp (Dennis Franz), the sleazy photographer who took photos of the McRyan crash.

startled by all those connections. I thought, this was nuclear materials. His emotional rocket fuel. He's fearless about his own emotional life. And he almost makes baroque opera out of it.

De Palma also brings a personal touch in the scene where Sally visits Manny Karp in a sleazy hotel room. On the television, De Palma's own *Murder à la Mod* is playing. The film clip prophetically takes place in a cemetery.

De Palma wields his signature 360 trademark again in *Blow Out*, with the most notable use when the camera pans around Jack's room as he discovers that all his tapes have been erased. Much like the climactic airport scene in *Obsession*, there is a slight unintentional yet compelling and appropriate strobing effect that accompanies perfectly the sound emanating from the erased tapes.

BRIAN DE PALMA: Vilmos and I were on ladders looking down into the set, and the camera operator was running around in circles. John had to be in certain spots on cue. I don't know how many times we did it, but we finally got it right with the camera catching him at the right time.

JOHN LITHGOW: My favorite scene in the film was the 360-degree coverage of the phone booth, where I go from one character [pretending to be a killer confessing to the police] to another [talking to a government official about the conspiracy], all done in one scene. But, as Brian frequently does, he recut afterward to tell the story properly, and he split the moment into two separate scenes. I was devastated because I so loved the fact that it all happened at once. Of course, it didn't make any difference to anybody but me.

Reunited on-screen for the first time since Carrie, *Travolta insisted on having Allen as his co-star in* Blow Out.

THE LIBERTY BELL DAY PARADE

Blow Out is a different De Palma, with a much bigger budget and scope, especially in the third act, with helicopter shots of Jack driving through the city and parade crowd, stunts, and all, followed by fireworks that, sadly—combined with the ringing of the Liberty Bell—spell doom for Sally.

Watch the window display as Jack careens his Jeep into it. If you look closely at the display in the window, you spot a re-creation of a revolutionary man with a rope around his neck, ready to be executed. As Jack drives through the window—in slow motion—the mannequin literally hangs, announcing Sally's impending strangulation. Later, Jack rushes up the stairs—also in slow motion—while fireworks go off in the sky, but fails to save her. The contrast of the joyful celebration intercutting with murder is as powerful as Carrie's coronation, with both sequences ending in tragedy.

BRIAN DE PALMA: We created the parade completely. We had a lot of great cooperation from the Philadelphia people. It was freezing cold, that's all I remember. In fact, it snowed, and I thought of a shot of John listening to the playback of his last conversation with Sally, sitting on a bench in the snow. I said, "John, get out there, put the headset on, I'm going to shoot you as you're listening to the playback."

NANCY ALLEN: My death scene was hard. It was a very emotional thing for me to shoot, and John [Lithgow] was so afraid of hurting me. He's very tall, a big guy. But if you just let go there, you can feel the terror. I get emotional when I think about what she goes through. In that moment, it seemed so real. I get upset when people say, "Oh, is that really your scream?" Yes, it's my fucking scream! [*Laughs*] We didn't really rehearse it. We just shot it. We just shot it. I think I did it three times.

BRIAN DE PALMA: I don't remember Nancy screaming for Jack too many times, but we were always fighting the light. The first time we tried it, it took us all night to light the scene. By the time we got it lit, the sun was coming up. We couldn't shoot; we had to go back the next day and work a little faster.

JOHN LITHGOW: That big scene was unbelievable. I'd never been in such a gigantic production number with hundreds of extras and working all night. And fireworks; it was tremendous. Again, with *Blow Out*, you knew you were going on this great trip with Brian. Even a detail like pulling the string from my wristwatch—only later did I realize it was to include the

John Lithgow, as the assassin Burke, rides the Philadelphia subway with Sally.

sound design that John heard before he recorded the blow out.

NANCY ALLEN: John and Brian were very aligned on Sally being killed. I never fought for her to live, but George Litto wanted her to live. Perhaps what was missing was a stronger relationship between Jack and Sally, so you could look at them as Romeo and Juliet, a tragedy, a lost love.

BRIAN DE PALMA: Killing Sally was always the plan. At the time, John Travolta could do anything, and he backed me up with everything I wanted to do, basically.

JOHN LITHGOW: I thought it was very courageous and bold [to kill Sally]. But that's what Brian does; it's classic Brian. It's taking people's longings and upending them. [Filming scenes of murder] you can't help being a little unsettled and have nightmares. Everybody always asks, "Do you take it home at night?" I don't! But particularly the scene in the vacant lot at night, where I use the ice pick to carve a Liberty Bell shape on the torso of one of the victims, that was gruesome stuff. Brian says, "I don't know why I like John Lithgow playing the villain." But of course, I know why. He loves the nice guy to be revealed as diabolical. He's interested in the lurking horror. It's a great De Palma device.

PAUL HIRSCH: I suggested an alternate ending. They're watching the scene with Sally's scream in it, and the director says, "Now, that's a scream." And you cut to Travolta, then pan over and there is Sally sitting next to him with a bandage around her neck. That was my suggestion. I wanted her to survive. I remember the path from first cut to final cut was not a straight line, and it seemed to be particularly torturous. So, my memory of the film is colored by the process of blind alleys we went into and the things we tried.

PAPERBACK MYTHOLOGY

As with *Dressed to Kill* and *Phantom of the Paradise*, a novelization of De Palma's screenplay was written by author Neal Williams, who added fascinating mythology to both the story and the characters. A lot more background information is revealed about Jack (whose last name is Luce; most certainly in reference to Robert Leuci, the real-life inspiration for *Prince of the City*), primarily his time working for the Keen Commission (standing in for the real-life Knapp Commission), as well as Sally's own devastating and dark journey of abuse. Williams offers a deeper exploration of her relationship with Jack as they become a couple. Burke is also much more of a character. Most notably, we learn of his background in the army and how his killing of a captain lands him in jail and, eventually, introduces him to the world of political corruption. Additionally, a foreign sniper—not Burke, pulls the trigger on McRyan's car. Burke doesn't try to create copycat murders of Sally look-alikes as in the film, but he kills a woman he mistakes for Sally, and eventually also murders Manny Karp. The most striking differences are in the climactic ending; among other details involving Burke getting the original film and tape of the McRyan assassination, he kidnaps Sally and has her gagged in the trunk of his car. He brings her to the fireworks site, where they are tracked down by Jack. A struggle ensues and, as in the film, Jack kills Burke. However, Sally seems to have vanished and the book ends with her on a bus, going south, and turning down a sleazy guy trying to pick her up.

LOST FOOTAGE

In the most bizarre twist of life imitating art, original footage from the film was stolen—a complete catastrophe when you consider the cost of each day of filming. The parallels with Burke destroying Jack's footage with this production tragedy are simply uncanny.

BRIAN DE PALMA: When we were mixing the movie in New York, part of the negative was stolen from a shipping truck. It had parts of the scenes at the creek and the parade. We had to go back and reshoot some of that stuff. Vilmos was no longer available, so another director of photography, László Kovács, came in. I went all over Manhattan looking for the negative because I figured some kids had stolen it. I thought, they opened it and said, "Oh, this is nothing." And maybe they dumped it somewhere. I spent hours going through every trash bin in and around where it got stolen, which was on 6th Avenue and 54th Street. It was devastating. Of everything that has happened to

me in the moviemaking business, once you've had your negative stolen, it can't get any worse.

PAUL HIRSCH: By re-photographing the dailies, we saved
some of the shots. We were able to salvage some of it. Meaning:
Reproducing film negative was an essential part of the distribution process because negative can wear out. The camera
negative wasn't used to manufacture the thousands of prints
needed for wide-scale distribution. Duplicate, or dupe, nega-
tives had to be made. The technology was photosensitive, so
a copy of the negative turns out positive. That was the first
step, called an interpositive. From that, internegatives were
made that were then used to make the prints. Because the
original neg was stolen, there wasn't yet an interpositive, but
the lab was able to use our workprint in its place. They made

Jack re-creates the McRyan crash by filming the photos taken by Manny Karp.

replacement negs from it. In some cases, that turned out to be impossible, so Brian was forced to do some reshooting.

FEEDBACK

The reviews for *Blow Out* were, happily, better than usual. The film was called "excellent suspense" by Robert Alan Jones in the *St. Petersburg Times*. Ron Pennington wrote in the *Hollywood Reporter*, "It is an exciting, stylish work in which the tension is relieved by liberal doses of humor, and it is probably one of De Palma's most original, least derivative movies in some time." Gene Siskel gave the film 3.5 stars in the *Chicago Tribune*, praising De Palma as "a master of fluid filmmaking," but wondering if audiences would embrace a throwback "to the political filmmaking of the early seventies." Vincent Canby of the *New York Times* advised not to look for plausibility or else, "you'll miss the enjoyment of the film." Yet, *Variety* predicted *Blow Out* would not be a smash hit (which, sadly, it wasn't). But it's Pauline Kael's glowing review in *The New Yorker* that truly summarizes the impact of the film: "At forty, Brian De Palma has more than twenty years of moviemaking behind him, and he has been growing better and better. Each time a new movie opens, everything he has done before seems to have been preparation for it." Kael also praised the performances as "radiant," noting that Nancy Allen gave the film "its soul" and that Travolta's portrayal is the type of screen acting that made generations of filmgoers revere Brando in *On the Waterfront* (1954).

BRIAN DE PALMA: I was very involved with the marketing, but the studio was so unhappy with the movie . . . They were just in total despair. I'll never forget when I showed it to the executives; they were appalled. That ending killed them. They didn't know what to do.

NANCY ALLEN: I loved the film when I first saw it. I was moved by it. I thought it was visually stunning. But here's the thing; I knew I would. I knew it was a good movie because I felt it on set. When that machine is going, it just goes. It happens and you have a sense of it. I was really thrilled. Of course, I was critical of myself. You know, I should have done this or that. But I was taken by the movie.

JOHN LITHGOW: Brian occasionally got a bad rap for being master of the macabre. But look at Shakespeare, for God's sake. *Titus Andronicus*. And *Richard III*. And even *Macbeth*. These are ghoulish horror stories. And they quicken our emotions and they're very often morality tales, as is the case of Brian.

BRIAN DE PALMA: *Blow Out* is today considered this great masterpiece. When it came out it was considered a disaster. And as I've always said, you're judged against the style of the day. But that style changes. Remember Cecil B. DeMille was the most successful director of all times, and his movies are now like the worst things you've ever seen. [*Laughs*]

Blow Out is, curiously, not dated, even though it relies heavily on obsolete technology, such as a phone ringing busy or Sally mistaking a killer for a famous reporter simply because she doesn't watch the news! This would never happen today, but the characters are so fully realized and so much part of De Palma's world that we embrace it all without questioning it. In that way, there is a very strong nostalgic aspect to simpler times that enhances the suspense and the sense of isolation.

I clearly remember seeing *Blow Out* for the first time in Paris, at the first showing on the day it came out, and realizing it was a transitional film for De Palma. I can't deny that I missed the gloss of *Dressed to Kill*, *The Fury*, and *Obsession*, which was sub-stituted for grit and film grain in *Blow Out*. But what stands out are my tears. The end of *Obsession* had tears of joy, *Blow Out* was pure tragedy, bold and, frankly, a revelation of the true nature of De Palma's beating heart.

A GOOD SCREAM

Blow Out concludes the De Palma decade, which began with *Sisters*, and is really a fantastic summation of the director's the-matic as explored across his previous thrillers and horror films.

Guilt: We've seen Danielle, the surviving conjoined twin of *Sisters*, take on her identical sibling's personality to cope with her loss. We've followed Michael Courtland's *Obsession* to re-create the image of his dead wife with another woman he believes is her look-alike to overcome his grief and sense of

Jack plays back the blowout he recorded on the bridge.

responsibility. In *Carrie*, Sue Snell feels guilty about her partic-
ipation in bullying Carrie White and convinces her boyfriend to
take Carrie to the prom instead of herself. Both Peter Sandza,
in *The Fury*, and Peter Miller, in *Dressed to Kill*, are motivated by
guilt, and avenging the loss of a loved one. Finally, in *Blow Out*,
Jack is purely looking for redemption by solving the assassination of a governor after causing the murder of a cop.

Voyeurism: De Palma explores voyeurism when Winslow is
"peeping" on Swan in bed with Phoenix (unaware that a camera is spying on him as well) in *Phantom of the Paradise*. *Sisters*
bluntly opens with a TV game show, *Peeping Toms*, with a man
watching a blind woman undressing, and later Grace becomes
witness to the man's murder when looking out her window.
Peter Miller listens to conversations and records patients coming in and out of Elliott's office in *Dressed to Kill*, and Liz is being
spied on both by a female cop and Bobbi. In *Blow Out*, the voyeurism is present in the B movie, *Co-Ed Frenzy*, with a killer peeping on a girls' dormitory, and it is also present through sound,
with Jack, literally, called out as a Peeping Tom himself when
he's spotted by an amorous couple while recording wild tracks
on a bridge. Burke is also an auditory voyeur, tapping into Jack's
phone line so he can listen in on his conversations.

The Double: We've been introduced to doubles and split personalities in obvious and literal ways. It is also present in *Blow
Out* via the cover-up of the political assassination of McRyan, as
Burke murders two women who look like Sally. De Palma doubles
up the connection when the second victim is grabbed and gar-
roted from above the bathroom stall, with her feet dangling in the
air, just like the cop whose death was caused by Jack—he was also
suspended in a bathroom stall, strangled with his wiretap device.

In *Blow Out*, life doesn't win (Sally dies), but cinema does
(her scream perfectly fits and works for the slasher film Jack is

working on). Sally has morphed into another body—the fictional on-screen victim.

Pauline Kael points out that *Blow Out* begins with a joke—a slasher film. But as Sally's scream is heard and used in the film within the film, Jack has accomplished the job and the power of filmmaking is very clear; it can turn a bad scream into a convincing one. De Palma's camera travels in half-circle, showing Jack, destroyed by loss, and mumbling to himself, "It's a good scream," and, as he tries to block out the sound, we freeze-frame on him. Yet, the scream itself continues as we fade to black, and the last tragedy of *The De Palma Decade* concludes. Life has lost. Cinema has won.

AFTERWORD

Blow Out coincided with my moving to America. As I started my own modest, yet passionate, journey in cinema in New York, the next De Palma film I saw was *Scarface*. Incidentally, that day watching *Scarface* for the first time, Keith Gordon of *Dressed to Kill* was sitting right in front of me—which I interpreted as a sign of De Palma things to come.

But over the years, through my first book, *The De Palma Cut* (1988), and later with my involvement with the home entertainment revolution, I got to make my own modest contribution to the De Palma oeuvre, directing and producing several retrospective documentaries—the first ever done on his films—released on Laserdisc, DVD, and Blu-ray. It's hard to believe but important to note that when I did those initial interviews, Google or Wikipedia didn't exist; my questions at the time were purely based on very hard and in-depth research that wasn't readily available. And now this new book has allowed me to create a new approach that mixes my past discussions with new ones. And, in the middle of it all, literally as I wrote these words, Piper Laurie passed away, underlining the importance of the oral history captured in this volume. I'm particularly proud of my conversations, not only with Brian himself, but with his collaborators behind and in front of the camera. Unanimously, his colleagues have praised his humanity, his humor, his vision, and all have highlighted how much they've learned from working with him.

Revisiting these films was nothing short of inspiring. I set the goal of discovering new things I had never noticed before, even after so many viewings and, to my delight, I did! And looking beyond the frame, by going as far back as novels, early scripts, and story treatments, I solved riddles I never knew existed in how certain scenes ended up in the final films. This journey confirmed the richness of De Palma's visionary and layered approach and how he transformed and interpreted words into images. It was akin to discovering newfound facts about a best friend, facts that made you appreciate the friend even more. De Palma's desire to challenge the most mundane scene for something visually innovative cannot be taken for granted; here is a director who, despite his critics, has strong beliefs in pure cinema. I hope the book has encouraged a better and fresh examination of one of America's most seminal directors.

ACKNOWLEDGMENTS

It's often said that writing is a very solitary experience. That was not the case with this book, which is the culmination of years of interviewing Brian De Palma, his actors, and his colleagues. As detailed in my introduction, many of the interviews were conducted in connection with my documentary films on *Obsession*, *Carrie*, and *Dressed to Kill*, but just as many new ones were done exclusively for this book.

The De Palma Decade is the result of not only studying the films but also making my own documentaries on them and discussing their values with those who made them. I am forever grateful to Brian himself, who has had to endure my fascination with his work for decades. He may have perceived me first as crazy, but he eventually came to realize I was not a stalker and has most generously contributed to my documentaries and this book.

I also want to thank my other "victims," the incredibly talented actors, visionary colleagues, friends, and appreciators of Brian's—sadly, some are no longer with us—whom I've admired for years and who've chatted casually with me over time about their collaboration or views on the films featured in this volume, and participated in the films or read over their quotes.

In alphabetical order:

Nancy Allen | Betty Buckley | Geneviève Bujold | Lawrence D. Cohen | Angie Dickinson | John and Peter Farris | Jack Fisk | Dennis Franz | Keith Gordon | Jerry Greenberg | Jessica Harper | Paul Hirsch | Amy Irving | William Katt | Piper Laurie | John Lithgow | George Litto | Priscilla Pointer | Cliff Robertson | Jennifer Salt | P.J. Soles | Sissy Spacek | Andrew Stevens | Paul Williams | Vilmos Zsigmond

I've had many engaging discussions and exchange about Brian's films and cinema through the years with these other great people:

Rutanya Alda | Manoah Bowman | Mark Harris | Ben Hasler Sam Irvin | Meredith Kaulfers | Jeffrey Kramer | Laurent Vachaud

A special thanks to Christopher A. Davis, who generously read over the entire manuscript. And finally, I am so grateful for the amazing and generous quotes I received on this book from: Ernest Cline, Guillermo del Toro, Elvis Mitchell, Julie Salamon, and Edgar Wright.

This book began when my literary agent extraordinaire, Mark Falkin, introduced me to Randall Lotowycz, an amazing editor at Running Press. We chatted for months about film and why we love a certain type of cinema. What we immediately shared was a fascination with Brian De Palma. Partnering up with Randall on this book was and always will be one of the most satisfying collaborations I've had in my modest career.

Designing the book was another exciting part of the project, beginning with illustrator Doaly, who truly captured the spirit of *The De Palma Decade*; he made it "pop" and modern. And then there's the entire design, editorial, and publicity and marketing teams, including Amanda Richmond, Melanie Gold, Seta Zink, Frances Soo Ping Chow, Cindy Sipala, Betsy Hulsebosch, and Kristin Kiser.

Big thanks to, as always and forever, my patient and loving husband, Markus Keith. One of the first things we ever talked about was Brian De Palma! My best friend, Laurent Hagège, who helped me in my research. My sisters, Cécile and Géraldine, and my parents, Micheline and Daniel, who first took me to see De Palma's *Obsession* in Paris, unaware of the effect and impact it would have on me.

During the summer of 1984, friend and actor Richard

Bright took me to the New York premiere of a film called *Best Defense*. Coming out of the event, we bumped into Brian De Palma. Richard knew him (his wife Rutanya Alda had starred in several of his films), introduced me, and asked if he could give me his number. De Palma agreed, though I kept asking him to repeat it to the point where Richard had to apologize, "He is French . . ." Nothing came of this first encounter, but I persisted, and when I started directing retrospective documentaries for the exploding home entertainment market, I finally got a chance to dig deep into what I consider to be some of the most important films in cinema history. I am so grateful for the opportunity to write this book, which in a sense represents the culmination of a passion—an obsession—that began for me nearly fifty years ago.

INDEX

Page numbers in **bold** refer to photographs or their captions.

INDEX